A Place to Live, a Means to Work

How Housing Assistance Can Strengthen Welfare Policy

Edited by
Barbara Sard
Center on Budget and Policy Priorities

Amy S. Bogdon
Fannie Mae Foundation

ISBN: 0-9662039-1-7
Library of Congress Cataloging-in-Publication Data available upon
request.

The Fannie Mae Foundation, through its publications and other programs, is committed to the full and fair exposition of issues related to
affordable housing and community development.

The Fannie Mae Foundation supports and encourages the redistribu-
tion of its publications for noncommercial, educational, and informa-
tional purposes. Multiple copies of some publications are available on
request for classes or conferences. Before reproducing Foundation
materials, please request permission by mail, fax, or e-mail, indicating
what material you want to copy, the approximate number of copies you
plan to make, and for what purpose. Send requests for extra copies or
permission to duplicate to:

Fannie Mae Foundation
4000 Wisconsin Avenue, NW
North Tower, Suite One
Washington, DC 20016-2804
Fax: 202-274-8111
E-Mail: fmfpubs@fanniemaefoundation.org

Table of Contents

Preface

The enactment of the Personal Responsibility and Work Opportunity Reconciliation Act (PRWORA) of 1996 represented a major change in U.S. welfare policy. PRWORA introduced time limits for assistance and explicitly focused on moving assistance recipients into employment. Despite many dire predictions about what would happen to former welfare recipients, welfare reform seemed to be a success in many ways— welfare rolls declined in most states and the number of TANF (Temporary Assistance to Needy Families) recipients holding jobs increased. Yet looking deeper at the results, one finds many who have left the welfare rolls but have not found jobs. Even many of those able to find and keep jobs often remain in poverty.

An important issue to be addressed in the welfare arena going forward is how to help assistance recipients become truly self-sufficient. The role of such services as child care, transportation, and health care benefits in helping families transition to self-sufficiency has already been recognized. However, the potential role of housing assistance in providing transitional support has received far less attention. It is clear from theory that receiving in-kind support like housing assistance can provide a disincentive to work. Yet having safe, stable housing that is accessible to employment opportunities can make it possible for parents with young children to obtain and keep jobs. Recent evidence analyzed by Manpower Demonstration Research Corporation and reported in this volume suggests that the stabilizing role of housing may be stronger than the disincentive effect, particularly when combined with assistance program rules that reward employment. More research in this area would improve our understanding of the role of stable housing in promoting self-sufficiency, yet research is hampered by a lack of available data on the housing status of TANF recipients.

Moreover, discussions about welfare reform often focus narrowly on the issues of welfare benefits and employment, ignoring other key structural contributors to wealth creation and financial self-sufficiency. Although this volume examines the role of housing assistance, it is important to keep in mind the larger context in which these issues occur. Like everyone else, welfare recipients need access to a rich set of tools to build long-term financial independence. These tools include access to meaningful employment, quality educational opportunities, and decent affordable housing. They also include efficient financial services and wealth-building opportunities, such as access to affordable mortgage credit and a reliable social safety network, including health insurance and other assistance that helps people return to and maintain viable employment. A serious examination of welfare policy should include conversations about the extent to which financially vulnerable households have the full set of tools necessary for them to achieve sustainable financial self-sufficiency.

James H. Carr
Senior Vice President
Fannie Mae Foundation

Acknowledgments

The editors acknowledge and thank the many people who have provided inspiration, assistance, and support for the publication of this volume. The chapters published in this volume originated as part of a research roundtable, *Managing Affordable Housing Under Welfare Reform: Reconciling Competing Demands*, which was co-sponsored by the Fannie Mae Foundation and the Center on Budget and Policy Priorities. Steven P. Hornburg and Eliza Gleason Kean played an important role in organizing the event and shaping its content, and Carol Bell oversaw the editing and preparation of the conference binder.

We thank the speakers and panelists at the roundtable for their thoughtful presentations and lively discussions of the issues. In particular, we acknowledge the work of David Bryson of the National Housing Law Project, who passed away before he was able to revise the paper he presented at the roundtable. Contributors to the roundtable included (in alphabetical order): Deepak Bhargava, Michael Bodaken, Gordon Cavanaugh, Kari Davidson, Ricardo Diaz, Helen Dunlap, Lou Ann Frederick, Robert Greenstein, John Hiscox, Barbara Huppee, Langley C. Keyes, Jill Khadduri, Ed Lazere, Paul Leonard, Cindy Mann, John K. McIlwain, Jonathan Miller, Kathryn P. Nelson, Clarence Page, James A. Riccio, William M. Rohe, Elaine M. Ryan, Mark Shroder, Rochelle Stanfield, Gary Stangler, Joe Ventrone, and Roy Ziegler. We also acknowledge the contributions of other roundtable participants.

Special thanks go to the authors of the chapters in this volume. We appreciate their patience in the face of the delays in bringing this volume to publication, all their efforts to revise the initial chapters in light of reviewer comments and the constantly changing context, and most important, their intellectual contributions to improving the understanding of the intersection of welfare reform and housing. We also thank the anonymous reviewers for their valuable insights, careful comments, and objective analyses of these issues.

We give our special thanks to our colleagues, Jim Carr of the Fannie Mae Foundation and Bob Greenstein of the Center on Budget and Policy Priorities, for their support of our work on this volume and their commitment to enhancing understanding of policy issues surrounding the intersection of housing and welfare reform. We thank Kathy Litzenberg for her oversight of the copy editing and production of this book. Thanks also to Tia Clark who assisted with the review and preparation of the papers.

In addition, the Center on Budget and Policy Priorities thanks the Rockefeller Foundation, the Butler Family Fund, and their general support funders for sustaining the revision of the conference papers authored by Center staff and for supporting Barbara Sard's time in editing this volume.

Part I—Introduction

Chapter 1

What Has Changed, What Have We Learned, and What Don't We Know?

Barbara Sard
Center on Budget and Policy Priorities

Amy S. Bogdon
Fannie Mae Foundation

Introduction

With the passage of the Personal Responsibility and Work Opportunity Reconciliation Act (PRWORA) in 1996, Congress replaced the primary cash assistance program, Aid to Families with Dependent Children (AFDC), with Temporary Assistance for Needy Families (TANF). The change in title reflects a change in focus as well. Assistance is explicitly intended to be temporary (limited in time) and focused on moving participants into employment. States were given the flexibility to design their own programs within the limits of federal guidelines. Although work requirements and time limits were core elements of welfare reform, discussions related to this dramatic policy transformation recognized that job skills and work readiness alone were not sufficient to move recipients from welfare to work. The need for work supports was acknowledged and included such elements as child care, transportation assistance, and health care.

Housing assistance, however, has been notably absent from most of these discussions of work supports. In part, this reflects the housing assistance system's historic and bureaucratic separation from the welfare system. But it also reflects a lack of information on the role that housing might play in moving recipients from welfare to work and eventual self-sufficiency. Despite numerous studies on welfare-to-work programs, few even collected information on whether a recipient also received housing assistance and, if so, what type. Further, programs that were funded by the Department of Housing and Urban Development (HUD) to help low-income households become self-sufficient (Project Self-Sufficiency, Operation Bootstrap, and Family Self-Sufficiency [FSS]) did not employ an experimental design or other strategy for assessing outcomes and measuring effectiveness. Several recent welfare-to-work studies recorded housing assistance status, providing new information and insight on this issue. These studies suggest that such assistance may have a net positive effect on earnings and employment.

Only recently have a significant number of policy makers begun to recognize the importance of housing assistance in helping families make the transition from welfare to work and eventually to self-sufficiency. Entry-level wages in most parts of the country do not enable a family to secure decent, safe, and affordable housing. On average, it would take an income of more than $30,000 per year for a family to obtain a modest two-bedroom rental unit that costs less than 30 percent of its income.[1] Yet a person working full-time (2,000 hours per year) at the current minimum wage of $5.15 per hour would earn just $10,300 a year, and the median monthly household income of welfare leavers, updated to 2002 dollars, was just $1,261, an annual rate of $15,132.[2]

On the eve of further changes in federal welfare policy, the issues at the intersection of housing and welfare policy discussed herein continue to be of great importance for housing programs. The chapters in this volume are an outgrowth of work that began with a Research Roundtable organized by the Fannie Mae Foundation and the Center on Budget and Policy Priorities in June 1998, titled "Managing Affordable Housing under Welfare Reform: Reconciling Competing Demands." The next section of this introduction summarizes some of the key features of TANF and outlines the potential role of housing assistance in helping (or hindering) families making the transition from welfare to self-sufficiency. Housing programs also changed in the late 1990s; some of these changes are described in the following section. Next, we provide overviews of the individual chapters in this volume. We conclude with a review of some of the larger issues and policy options, along with recommendations for future research.

---

[1] The housing cost used in this calculation ($764 per month) is the estimated median fiscal year 2003 two-bedroom national Fair Market Rent (FMR), calculated in National Low-Income Housing Coalition (2002). It is based on HUD's 2003 FMRs weighted by the number of renter households reported by the 2000 census. The FMR is the estimate issued annually by HUD for the cost of decent, modest housing in each area.

[2] This number is taken from Sard 2002 and is based on 1999 data from the National Survey of America's Families. It includes earnings and benefits for all members of households of welfare leavers with at least one employed person. Because many welfare leavers do not maintain full-time employment across the year, converting the monthly estimate to an annual number may overstate actual income.

New Welfare Block Grant

At the time of the roundtable, state implementation of the new TANF block grant that had replaced the 60-year-old AFDC entitlement program had only just begun. There was great uncertainty about how poor families would fare under welfare reform, as well as many unanswered questions about what effect the new work requirements, sanctions, and time limits imposed by TANF would have on housing agencies and the federal treasury.[3] Efforts to analyze the possible consequences of welfare reform for housing agencies and the federal housing budget were constrained by the limited information available about the demographic characteristics of federally assisted tenants likely to be relevant to their success in making the transition from welfare to stable employment.

Housing programs and policies were not part of the debates that led to the 1996 passage of the PRWORA that enacted the TANF program. Despite the fact that at the time about a quarter of the families receiving AFDC also received federally funded rental assistance, there was virtually no consideration of how housing programs could contribute to—or interfere with—welfare reform efforts. The proportion of families that received monthly TANF cash benefits and also received federal housing assistance was about the same in 2000 as it was in 1996, but declines in the welfare rolls meant that in 2000 only about 13 percent of those receiving housing assistance also received TANF, compared with around 25 percent in 1996 (Khadduri, Shroder, and Steffen 2003).

So far we know nothing definitive about whether housing assistance helps families leave welfare or escape poverty in the short run or in the long run. In general, assistance programs are likely to reduce work incentives, at least in the short run. However, by providing a stable environment and indirect income support, housing assistance may also ease and encourage the transition to self-sufficiency, thus helping families build human capital and manage the additional costs of working. Further, the effect of the location of assisted housing on access to

---

[3] On July 22, 1997, the Fannie Mae Foundation, in collaboration with the Institute for Policy Studies at Johns Hopkins University, hosted a Policy Research Roundtable in Baltimore titled "The Implications of Welfare Reform for Housing." Using models of the various policy options states could choose in their welfare programs, Sandra J. Newman and Joseph Harkness presented research that attempted to predict the financial effects of the new TANF program on the HUD budget as well as on families' ability to afford private market housing. Data from several states' AFDC waiver programs were used to anticipate future consequences. As the authors recognized, their efforts were handicapped by the limited duration of the AFDC waivers and the scope of the available data, as well as by the absence of any objective basis on which to predict whether families with housing assistance would react any differently to welfare reform initiatives than other families. See Newman and Harkness (1999).

economic opportunities and neighborhood safety may encourage (or discourage) work. A small but growing body of research indicates that the positive effects of housing assistance may outweigh the negative effects on employment and earnings (Lubell, Nelson, and Sard 2003; Sard and Waller 2002).

Concurrent Debates on Housing Policy

In the mid-1990s, there was substantial discussion concurrent with the welfare reform debate about the need for changes in the primary federal low-income rental assistance programs, public housing, and Section 8. (Section 8 includes both a tenant-based program, now called the Housing Choice Voucher Program, and a project-based program. Public housing agencies [PHAs] administer the voucher program, while private owners administer the project-based program.) That debate focused primarily on the need for increased devolution and flexibility at the local level. There was some concern, however, about making programs more supportive of work efforts.

The Quality Housing and Work Responsibility Act of 1998

In 1998, after four years of debate, Congress passed and the president signed the Quality Housing and Work Responsibility Act (QHWRA), which devolves authority over many areas of housing policy that affect low-income families and individuals to the approximately 4,000 state and local PHAs that manage public housing or administer tenant-based Section 8 programs. However, this devolution of control over federal low-income housing programs is not as far-reaching as the devolution of authority over the federal welfare system that took place in 1996, when Congress transformed the AFDC program into the TANF block grant. No new housing block grant program was created, and most federal rules regulating low-income housing programs remain in place.

The limited devolution effected by QHWRA creates both new responsibilities for PHA managers and new opportunities for tenants and other interested members of the community to have input into the decision-making process. The focal point is now the "PHA Plan," which summarizes a PHA's key policy decisions. Each PHA is required to submit its plan annually to HUD. As part of the process of developing and revising the plan each year, PHAs are required to hold a public hearing and consult with an advisory board of public housing residents and families participating in the voucher program. (HUD has proposed to reduce some of these planning responsibilities for small PHAs. This change may take effect in 2003.)

Many of the policy decisions PHAs are authorized to make under QHWRA and required to record in their PHA Plan can potentially affect welfare reform efforts. For example, PHAs now have greater discretion to prefer working families for admission to their housing programs, particularly public housing programs, and to determine whether to define "working" broadly to include families enrolled in job training programs or certain other welfare-to-work activities. PHAs also have more authority to set rents in a manner designed to encourage public housing tenants to go to work and working tenants to remain in public housing. But PHAs have little discretion to adjust rents to encourage work among tenants who receive vouchers, despite the fact that nearly twice as many families with children receive assistance from the Housing Choice Voucher Program than from the public housing program.

The following is a brief summary of the policy changes made by QHWRA that are relevant to welfare reform. Sard and Lubell (1998, January 2000 update) provide a complete description of these policy changes.

Eligibility and Targeting Requirements. QHWRA permanently repeals the federal rules that specified which categories of families must receive preference for admission to subsidized housing and increases PHAs' discretion to set admissions preferences. In doing so, however, PHAs must abide by new "income targeting" rules requiring that at least 40 percent of newly available public housing units be provided to families with incomes below 30 percent of the area median income (AMI) and that at least 75 percent of newly available Section 8 vouchers be provided to such families. Private owners of Section 8 housing projects may not skip a lower-income family in favor of a higher-income family and must provide at least 40 percent of newly available units to families with incomes below 30 percent of AMI.

PHAs can use the greater discretion provided by QHWRA to set admissions preferences that may either help or hinder welfare reform efforts. For instance, on the one hand, PHAs can give preference to families trying to move from welfare to work, thereby providing more families with the stability they need to focus on getting and keeping jobs. On the other hand, PHAs can give preference to working families with higher incomes, thereby reducing the share of subsidized housing available to families attempting to make the transition to work.

Rent Rules. QHWRA greatly expands the options for calculating rents for public housing tenants. For example, tenants can now pay a flat rent that does not depend on their income. (Alternatively, they can choose to pay 30 percent of their adjusted income in rent, as federal rules have required since the early 1980s.) PHAs will continue to be able to set maximum or ceiling rents for their units, with greater flexibility in determining the amount. Both flat and ceiling rent policies can be used to offset the potential disincentive to work caused by a structure that ties rent payments to income. To similar effect, QHWRA expands the categories of families eligible to benefit from a mandatory disregard of earned income in calculating rent payments, including families that have received TANF benefits in the six months before getting a job or increasing their earnings. QHWRA also gives PHAs the right (at their option and expense) to adopt other income disregard policies for public housing families. With limited exceptions, these rent policies do not apply to Section 8 tenants (who represent about 70 percent of all subsidized tenants who have children and receive welfare payments).[4]

Although QHWRA permits PHAs to establish a minimum rent of up to $50 for public housing tenants and Section 8 voucher holders and authorizes HUD to set a similar minimum rent for families in project-based Section 8 housing, the act requires that any minimum rent policy contain a number of hardship exemptions. Among the families exempt from minimum rents are those that have lost income because of time limits on welfare or those that would face eviction as a result of the minimum rent policy. However, QHWRA prohibits PHAs from reducing the rent of families that have lost welfare income as a result of fraud or failure to comply with work requirements.

Section 8 Voucher Payment Standards. Before QHWRA, there were two parallel tenant-based Section 8 programs that subsidized the rents of apartments in the private market: the certificate and voucher programs. These programs have now been merged into a single voucher program. Under this new program, PHAs have greater flexibility to set the payment standards that determine the amount of the rental subsidy. In some locations, higher payment standards can help families afford housing with better access to jobs.

---

[4] While QHWRA makes project-based and tenant-based Section 8 families as well as public housing tenants eligible for the mandatory earnings disregard (but not for optional income disregards), approval in an appropriations act is required before the disregard applies to Section 8 families. No such approval has been granted, although HUD has extended the mandatory disregard by regulation to individuals who have disabilities and participate in the voucher program. Under the mandatory disregard, families that are receiving or that have recently received TANF benefits and go to work, as well as certain other families, pay no additional rent for 12 months after their earnings increase. In the second 12-month period, only half of the household's increased earnings are considered in calculating rent (Sard and Sanders 2001). Any other rent policy that determines a family's rent obligation without considering all of the income that HUD rules otherwise require to be counted is an optional disregard, except for flat rents based on the market value of a unit, as determined by the PHA, and minimum rents, both of which are required by QHWRA (Miller and Riccio 2002).

FSS Program. The FSS program promotes work by providing families with case-management services and enabling them to accumulate funds in an escrow account into which the PHA deposits the increased rental charges that each family pays as a result of increased earnings. Families may withdraw funds from their accounts for any purpose after they successfully complete the program, which usually takes five years. Only residents of public housing and families in the Section 8 voucher program are eligible to participate; families living in project-based Section 8 units are not permitted to enroll. Beginning in 1993, PHAs that received HUD funds for additional public housing units or vouchers were required to establish an FSS program for the equivalent number of families. QHWRA continues the preexisting obligation to operate FSS programs but provides PHAs with an opportunity to satisfy and terminate that obligation. The act also authorizes PHAs that are not covered by the mandate because they did not receive additional units during the 1993–98 period to set up optional FSS programs and allows PHAs subject to an FSS mandate to serve additional families. However, such optional expansions must be approved by HUD.[5]

Community Work Requirement. Beginning October 1, 2000, some nonworking residents of public housing were required to perform at least 8 hours of community service per month. Adults enrolled in an economic self-sufficiency program or otherwise complying with work requirements under a state welfare program (including TANF programs and wholly state-funded non-TANF programs) were exempt from this requirement. Failure of a nonexempt person in a household to comply with the community work requirement could result in the eviction of the entire household from public housing. Implementation of this community work requirement was controversial in some cities. An amendment to the fiscal year (FY) 2002 Department of Veterans Affairs (VA)–HUD appropriations act suspended community work for one year. As of this writing, it is not known whether the requirement will again take effect in FY 2003.

Housing/Welfare Agency Collaborations. Despite claims by some that QHWRA would be the housing companion to the 1996 welfare overhaul, only a few rather limited provisions promote collaboration between PHAs and welfare or job-training agencies. Congress exhorts PHAs to make their best effort to enter into cooperation agreements with welfare agencies to share relevant income and rent information and to provide employment-related services to federally assisted tenants but imposes no parallel obligation on welfare agencies. QHWRA also directs HUD to include in its assessment of the quality of public

---

[5] For an explanation of how the FSS program works and an analysis of how it can help promote welfare reform, see Sard 2001a.

housing management the efforts of PHAs to coordinate, promote, or provide effective programs and activities to enhance the economic self-sufficiency of public housing residents. HUD has issued a notice stating that 7 percent of a PHA's overall performance is attributable to its self-sufficiency efforts (HUD 2000). But as of early 2003, HUD has yet to apply this component of the assessment to any PHA.

Housing Agency Discretion and Welfare Reform

The fact that PHAs now have substantial discretion to adopt admissions and rent policies that can promote welfare reform goals does not mean that they will do so. (Private owners administering project-based Section 8 subsidies have far less discretion.)[6] QHWRA did little to create incentives for PHAs to adopt such policies or to undertake programmatic efforts to promote tenant employment, alone or in partnership with other agencies. The one real incentive QHWRA did create—the requirement discussed earlier that HUD include in its assessment of PHAs' performance their efforts to promote residents' economic self-sufficiency—has not been implemented. HUD has, however, recently altered the rules governing public housing operating subsidies to reward PHAs that bring in additional tenant rent payments. These PHAs can now retain half the increased revenue from tenant rent payments and use it to promote tenant self-sufficiency or improve public housing, or for similar purposes. In addition, HUD's voucher rules make it possible for PHAs to increase voucher payment standards in more expensive neighborhoods with better access to jobs without reducing the number of families they serve in the voucher program (Sard 2001b, 2003).

Overview of This Volume

The basic questions examined at our 1998 conference remain relevant today:

* How many recipients of housing assistance also receive welfare assistance and how have these rates changed?

---

[6] HUD's baseline assessments of the uses of new discretionary authority in the public housing and voucher programs indicated that few agencies were using their discretion at all and that even fewer were using their discretion in ways that appear to be linked to promoting employment (Devine, Rubin, and Gray 1999; Devine et al. 2001).

- Are there significant differences among housing programs in the proportion of families receiving TANF benefits and in other features that may affect work?

- Are the answers to these questions different at the state and national levels?

- Do recipients of both welfare and housing assistance differ in important ways from welfare families that do not get housing assistance?

- Should housing agencies play an active role in helping their tenants work, or would such a role conflict with agencies' basic "bricks and mortar" role?

- Would changing the income-based rent structure in assisted housing programs promote work?

- Is any likely gain worth the cost, and should the cost be borne by housing programs?

- Will providing housing assistance to families trying to make the transition from welfare to work help them succeed?

- Should housing agencies design their admissions policies to promote welfare reform objectives?

The chapters in this volume provide critical information to help policy makers and the broad range of other stakeholders in housing, welfare, and employment programs better understand the complex issues raised by these questions. In addition, these chapters are rich in programmatic ideas to help practitioners as well as policy makers implement various policy choices.

Intersection of Housing and Welfare Reform

Chapters 2 and 3 examine the overlap between welfare and housing assistance. In 2000, as in 1996 when PRWORA was enacted, about a quarter of welfare families also received housing assistance. Despite an extensive literature on welfare-to-work programs, only a handful of programs have collected data that allow researchers to examine the effect of housing assistance status (whether or not someone receives a housing voucher or lives in public housing) on the success of these programs.

In chapter 2, Jill Khadduri, Mark Shroder, and Barry Steffen provide an overview of the overlap of welfare and housing assistance. They begin by examining the share of households that receive both types of assistance. Nationwide, the number of families that received housing assistance and also received welfare (TANF or AFDC) declined by nearly 50 percent between 1996 and 2000, from about 1 million to 550,000, although the percentage decline varied from state to state. These authors then assess the theory and empirical literature on the potential benefit of housing assistance in helping families move to self-sufficiency. They find that current evidence is inconclusive: On the one hand, some aspects of housing assistance may deter work effort, while on the other, the stability provided by housing assistance may enable a family to be more productive in the labor market by helping to build human capital.

Extremely low income families (a group that includes most if not all TANF-assisted families) that do not receive housing assistance are likely to experience severe hardship. Also, those receiving project-based housing assistance (public housing or other assistance tied to a specific unit) are more likely than other welfare families to live in neighborhoods with concentrated poverty. This information and the potential importance of housing stability for the development of human capital lead these authors to suggest several ways to encourage progress toward self-sufficiency (such as devoting more attention and resources to programs like FSS). A number of alternative ways to increase the use of housing assistance for those moving from welfare to work are also discussed.

In chapter 3, James A. Riccio and Alan Orenstein examine the experience of recipients and nonrecipients of housing assistance in several large welfare-to-work programs. They find that while public housing residents in Atlanta were more disadvantaged than other program participants were, they actually benefited more from the programs (after accounting for differences in background factors) than the other subgroups studied. In Minnesota and Columbus (OH), the impact of the programs was again stronger for those receiving housing assistance, although this group was not always more disadvantaged. These findings demonstrate the need for further studies of the impact of housing on welfare-to-work efforts and for controlled research that tries to understand why program effects vary by housing status. Despite the positive effects for public housing residents, the results of these (and many other) welfare-to-work programs are still not large enough to move residents to self-sufficiency.

The Role of Housing Providers

Shortly after TANF was enacted, there was concern that housing assistance providers would face funding shortfalls as their welfare-assisted tenants lost income, thereby reducing rental income and raising subsidy obligations. The concentration of many of the lowest-income households in public housing also led to QHWRA's changes in admissions requirements and to an increasing emphasis on the creation of mixed-income communities in public housing. Both of these changes raise the question of what role housing providers should play in promoting the economic well-being of their tenants.

In chapter 4, Barbara Sard argues that housing providers should play an active role in helping tenants move to work and eventual self-sufficiency and that it is in their own self-interest to do so. She begins by outlining several reasons why it is in agencies' interest to promote tenant employment: First, families that lose welfare income and do not work may become destitute, affecting not only their own well-being but also that of their communities. In purely financial terms, PHAs running public housing programs may face revenue losses if tenants lose income. Second, increased tenant employment and earnings may help create mixed-income communities through growth in resident income. Finally, agencies that promote work and increase tenant earning may raise their HUD performance scores and improve the perception of housing assistance generally.

She also argues that housing agencies have a number of inherent advantages in trying to increase tenant employment. These include the ability to concentrate service provision where a number of tenants live (in the case of public housing), the ability to use Section 8 vouchers to provide access to neighborhoods with better job opportunities, incentives to keep encouraging work even after incomes rise to the point where households are no longer eligible for TANF assistance, and the potential to offer employment or encourage contractors to hire public housing and Section 8 residents. She also considers the cost of an active housing agency role in promoting tenant employment and suggests some no-cost or low-cost strategies, among them using advocacy to increase available resources, substituting new means to carry out already funded activities, or creating partnerships with other agencies. She concludes by noting that if housing agencies do not help their tenants in some of these ways, public policy makers may view housing assistance as a trap for poor families rather than as a means to advance other social goals.

In chapter 5, Sunia Zaterman provides another perspective, emphasizing that housing agencies have limited resources but that their current housing mission offers opportunities for partnering with welfare agencies. She contends that the public policy focus should be on reducing poverty rather than on just reducing TANF caseloads. She maintains that it is important to recognize a number of key factors that affect what housing authorities can realistically do. Among these factors are limited resources, regulatory requirements, barriers to tenant self-sufficiency, and competing demands for housing services and resources. In her view, housing authorities need more flexibility to respond to local conditions and needs. The stabilizing role of housing could make providers valuable partners with welfare agencies in moving families from welfare to work.

Rent and Admissions Policies

Under the rent rules for federally subsidized housing, families generally pay 30 percent of their countable income for rent. This creates a sort of tax on additional income, which reduces economic incentives for working. Similar policies apply to TANF payments (although in that case the effective tax rate on additional earnings may be much higher), and many of the welfare-to-work demonstrations disregarded some amount of initial income from work before computing benefit reductions as a way of improving the rewards for working.

In chapter 6, Ed Lazere and Jennifer Daskal consider whether a similar income disregard should be applied in the assisted housing programs. An income disregard for some public housing residents was included in QHWRA, so that eligible families will experience no increase in rent for the first 12 months after their income increases and only half the otherwise expected increase in the following 12 months. This policy is intended to increase work incentives by allowing public housing residents to keep more of their increased earnings. One drawback to this policy is its cost; even small increases in rents free up subsidy dollars that could potentially help additional households. Also, the policy may create some perverse incentives, since it does not apply to those already working unless they received TANF or similar assistance in the previous six months or participate in a training program. Further, the policy provides additional benefits for the lucky few who already receive housing assistance. Despite these drawbacks, a policy of this type may be of greatest help to those whose higher incomes make them ineligible for TANF assistance but who are still not completely self-sufficient. (These authors cite data to show that in most states, eligibility for TANF assistance phases out at income levels below the poverty line.) Further, the employment and cost effects of the income disregards for some public housing residents should be studied before any further policy changes are contemplated.

In chapter 7, Jeffrey M. Lubell, Kathryn P. Nelson, and Barbara Sard consider the role of housing assistance in promoting work and the ways housing programs' admission policies can be targeted to help move residents from welfare to work. Any type of assistance program can create disincentives for participants to work because increases in income from employment can be quickly offset by loss of benefits. These authors contend that such disincentive effects can be overcome and that housing assistance can be used to promote employment because it offers housing stability, frees up some of a family's budget for other uses, and may provide improved accessibility to jobs (when the assistance is in the form of a housing voucher or a well-located subsidized unit).

PHAs now have greater discretion to set admissions policies. The authors argue that to further the aims of welfare reform and promote employment, agencies should give preference for admission to households that are on welfare and enrolled in a welfare-to-work program or have incomes below 30 percent of the area median income and some income from work. This would target the lowest-income workers in the most need of housing subsidies (those whose incomes may still be very low but are nevertheless above the threshold for receiving TANF assistance) and help them move toward self-sufficiency.

Housing and Welfare Reform: Policy Implications and Recommendations for Future Research

In 2002, Congress made some progress in overcoming the isolation in which housing and welfare policy operate. Bills filed in the Senate on both TANF reauthorization and housing program reform contained a number of crosscutting provisions. (In January 2003, the Senate passed a new FY 2003 appropriations bill that also would make the voucher program permanent but does not include funding for new welfare-to-work vouchers.) These proposed changes reflect a recognition on the part of at least some policy makers that affordable, decent-quality housing may promote welfare reform goals and that housing programs can provide additional tools to help families succeed in the workplace.

This recognition is an important first step in designing programs and policies that test whether and how housing might be used to support the transition from welfare to work. Basic steps like recording the housing assistance status of families participating in welfare-to-work studies (and the type of housing assistance they receive) and gathering better data on housing assistance as part of regular federal statistical efforts such as the upcoming American Community Survey would provide important information on the relationship between housing assistance and work outcomes. Similarly, much could be learned about the effect of housing location on welfare receipt and employment if more accurate data were gathered on where current and recent welfare recipients live.

Additionally, the use of income disregards in public housing should be studied as a first step toward considering whether to expand them to the Housing Choice Voucher Program. (Some agencies have redesigned the rent policies that apply to families with vouchers as part of HUD's Moving to Work Demonstration. The impact of these policies should be studied in a controlled manner.) Existing programs, such as FSS and welfare-to-work vouchers, should be rigorously assessed to understand how different incentives interact for participants and how cross-agency cooperation might be encouraged. No controlled research has been done on the effect of the admissions policies of different housing programs on other participants or on eligible families that are not admitted. Since limited resources mean that only about a quarter of eligible households receive federally funded rental assistance, it is important to undertake research that could guide federal policy and local decision making.

In a world in which important housing policies are now decided at the state and local levels despite the continued dominance of the federal role in funding, it is imperative to better understand how to help local agencies make well-considered decisions. This challenge is made more complex by the fact that the costs and benefits of various policy choices may differ from a federal/local or housing/welfare perspective. Innovative ways must be designed to help and encourage program administrators to think "across silos."

Economic theory suggests that housing assistance, like any form of direct or indirect income support, provides a disincentive for people to go to work. Yet several studies that have examined welfare-to-work outcomes by housing status have shown that those receiving housing assistance tend to show greater increases in employment and earnings. It is hypothesized that several aspects of housing assistance may contribute to this result and offset its expected negative effect on work. Housing assistance may help free up money in the family's budget for other expenses, provide greater residential stability, or provide greater access to jobs. Rebecca Blank (2002) suggests that efficiency and equity may be compatible and even complementary in certain circumstances. Two of these cases, transfer programs that impose behavioral requirements and transfers as investments, may apply to some housing programs and help us understand the role housing assistance can play in moving families to self-sufficiency.

Of course, federal, state, and local policy makers and program administrators cannot wait for the results of such research and analysis; they must do the best they can with existing knowledge. While it would be wise to base major program shifts or new investments on greater knowledge, we know enough to conclude that it is important to increase awareness of housing/welfare intersections at all policy and program levels and to encourage better cooperation among housing and welfare (and employment) programs. We hope that this volume will promote these objectives.

This volume will go to press before it is clear whether the TANF program is reauthorized in 2003 (and we do not know yet how federal policy may change). In addition, it is not clear whether changes in housing programs that would promote welfare reform goals will be enacted. Whatever the short-term outcome, however, policy at the intersection of housing programs and welfare reform will continue to evolve in the coming years. Readers interested in up-to-date information on these policy changes may wish to consult our organizations' Web sites at <http://www.knowledgeplex.org> and <http://www.cbpp.org> and to subscribe to the Center's Listserv on Affordable Housing and Welfare Reform. (Individuals may subscribe at <http://www.cbpp.org/pubs/housinginvite.htm>.)

Authors

Barbara Sard is Director of Housing Policy at the Center on Budget and Policy Priorities. Amy S. Bogdon is Director of Housing Research at the Fannie Mae Foundation.

References

Blank, Rebecca. 2002. Can Equity and Efficiency Complement Each Other? NBER Working Paper 8820. Cambridge, MA: National Bureau of Economic Research.

Devine, Deborah J., Barbara A. Haley, Lester Rubin, and Robert W. Gray. 2001. *The Uses of Discretionary Authority in the Tenant-Based Section 8 Housing Program: A Baseline Inventory of Issues, Policy, and Practice.* Washington, DC: U.S. Department of Housing and Urban Development.

Devine, Deborah J., Lester Rubin, and Robert W. Gray. 1999. *The Uses of Discretionary Authority in the Public Housing Program: A Baseline Inventory of Issues, Policy, and Practice.* Washington, DC: U.S. Department of Housing and Urban Development.

Khadduri, Jill, Mark Shroder, and Barry Steffen. 2003. Can Housing Assistance Support Welfare Reform? In *A Place to Live, a Means to Work: How Housing Assistance Can Strengthen Welfare Policy*, ed. Barbara Sard and Amy S. Bogdon, 23–62. Washington, DC: Fannie Mae Foundation.

Lazere, Ed, and Jennifer Daskal. 2003. Will Changing the Rent Formula Encourage Moves from Welfare to Work? In *A Place to Live, a Means to Work: How Housing Assistance Can Strengthen Welfare Policy*, ed. Barbara Sard and Amy S. Bogdon, 181–210. Washington, DC: Fannie Mae Foundation.

Lubell, Jeffrey M., Kathryn P. Nelson, and Barbara Sard. 2003. How Housing Programs' Admissions Policies Can Contribute to Welfare Reform. In *A Place to Live, a Means to Work: How Housing Assistance Can Strengthen Welfare Policy*, ed. Barbara Sard and Amy S. Bogdon, 211–67. Washington, DC: Fannie Mae Foundation.

Miller, Cynthia, and James A. Riccio. 2002. *Making Work Pay for Public Housing Residents: Financial-Incentive Designs at Six Jobs-Plus Demonstration Sites*. New York: Manpower Demonstration Research Corporation.

National Low-Income Housing Coalition. 2002. *Out of Reach*, 2002. Washington, DC.

Newman, Sandra J., and Joseph Harkness. 1999. The Effects of Welfare Reform on Housing: A National Analysis. In *The Home Front: Implications of Welfare Reform for Housing Policy*, ed. Sandra J. Newman, 29–80. Washington, DC: Urban Institute Press.

Riccio, James A., and Alan Orenstein. 2003. Are Welfare Recipients in Public Housing Really Harder to Employ? In *A Place to Live, a Means to Work: How Housing Assistance Can Strengthen Welfare Policy*, ed. Barbara Sard and Amy S. Bogdon, 63–103. Washington, DC: Fannie Mae Foundation.

Sard, Barbara. 2001a. The *Family Self-Sufficiency Program: HUD's Best-Kept Secret for Promoting Employment and Asset Growth*. Washington, DC: Center on Budget and Policy Priorities. Also available at <http://www.cbpp.org/4-12-01hous.htm>.

Sard, Barbara. 2001b. Section 8 Renewal Rule: Use It or Lose It. *Journal of Housing and Community Development* 58(3):27–32.

Sard, Barbara. 2002. *Housing Perspective on TANF Reauthorization and Support for Working Families*. Washington, DC: Center on Budget and Policy Priorities. Also available at <http://www.cbpp.org/3-12-02hous.htm>.

Sard, Barbara. 2003. The Role of Housing Providers in an Era of Welfare Reform. In *A Place to Live, a Means to Work: How Housing Assistance Can Strengthen Welfare Policy*, ed. Barbara Sard and Amy S. Bogdon, 107–65. Washington, DC: Fannie Mae Foundation.

Sard, Barbara, and Jeffrey M. Lubell. 1998. *How the Statutory Changes Made by the Quality Housing and Work Responsibility Act of 1998 May Affect Welfare Reform Efforts*. Washington, DC: Center on Budget and Policy Priorities. Revised in January 2000. The revised version is also available at <http://www.cbpp.org/1-19-00hous.htm>.

Sard, Barbara, and Patricia Sanders. 2001. *Promoting Work among Residents of Public Housing: The Role of Welfare Agencies in Implementing the Earned Income Disregard*. Washington, DC: Center on Budget and Policy Priorities. Also available at <http://www.cbpp.org/10-17-01hous.htm>.

Sard, Barbara, and Shayna Strom. 2002. *Funding New Welfare-to-Work Housing Vouchers Should Be a Priority for FY 2003*. Washington, DC: Center on Budget and Policy Priorities. Also available at <http://www.cbpp.org/8-28-02hous.htm>.

Sard, Barbara, and Margy Waller. 2002. *Housing Strategies to Strengthen Welfare Policy and Support Working Families*. Washington, DC: Brookings Institution, Center on Urban and Metropolitan Policy, and Center on Budget and Policy Priorities. Also available at <http://www.cbpp.org/4-15-02hous.htm>.

U.S. Department of Housing and Urban Development. 2000. Public Housing Assessment System Management Operations Scoring Process for PHAs with Fiscal Years Ending on or after March 31, 2000. *Federal Register* 65:40028. June 28.

Zaterman, Sunia. 2003. An Alternative View of the Role of Housing Providers in an Era of Welfare Reform. In *A Place to Live, a Means to Work: How Housing Assistance Can Strengthen Welfare Policy*, ed. Barbara Sard and Amy S. Bogdon, 167–78. Washington, DC: Fannie Mae Foundation.

Part II—The Intersection of Housing and Welfare Reform

CHAPTER 2

Can Housing Assistance Support Welfare Reform?

Jill Khadduri
Abt Associates, Inc.

Mark Shroder and Barry Steffen
U.S. Department of Housing and Urban Development

Abstract

In 2000 as in 1996, a quarter of welfare families also received housing assistance. So far we know little about whether housing assistance helps families leave welfare or escape from poverty in either the short or the long run. To increase our understanding of this issue, we review the theory and empirical literature about the relationship between housing assistance, work effort, and the development of human capital.

We then show that welfare families that do not receive housing assistance are likely to experience severe hardship, that project-based housing assistance may cause excessive concentration of welfare families in high-poverty neighborhoods, and that no type of housing assistance does much to help welfare families who live in low-poverty neighborhoods. We then discuss policy implications: incentives for work, ways to assist additional families with children, and steps to reduce concentrations of assisted families in higher-poverty areas.

Keywords: Low-income housing; Welfare

Introduction

This chapter is a general introduction to issues raised by the overlap of welfare[1] and housing assistance. At the time the Personal Responsibility

---

[1] Throughout this chapter we use the word "welfare" narrowly, to denote the Aid to Families with Dependent Children (AFDC) program and its successor, Temporary Assistance to Needy Families (TANF). We focus our discussion of housing assistance primarily on the deeply targeted programs—public housing, tenant-based Section 8 housing vouchers, and Section 8 assisted housing projects. These are the programs that served a quarter of AFDC families in 1996 and TANF families in 2000. We also include some discussion of the HOME and Low-Income Housing Tax Credit programs, because these large, growing programs may serve welfare families now and certainly have the potential for doing so in the future.

and Work Opportunity Reconciliation Act (PRWORA) entered the statute books (August 22, 1996), a quarter of families receiving AFDC, the national entitlement for all eligible low-income families with children, also benefited from housing assistance. Four years later, in 2000, a quarter of the families receiving TANF, the block grant program that replaced AFDC, were living in assisted housing. Thus, as the debate over reauthorization of welfare reform begins, whether housing assistance supports welfare reform remains a vital question.

PRWORA changed the system of cash assistance to needy families with children in the following ways:

1. Entitlement to benefits on federal grounds was abolished. States can choose their own criteria for eligibility and pay benefits according to their own formulas.

2. Time limits on lifetime benefits were imposed on at least 80 percent of TANF recipients.

3. States must either place a gradually increasing share of TANF recipients into narrowly defined work activities or incur significant financial penalties. States can reduce or cut off benefits to recipients for noncompliance with various program rules, including participation in work activities.

4. States can use some TANF funds to provide services rather than cash benefits to their welfare families.

Housing assistance to low-income renters underwent significant changes at the same time that TANF was being implemented. The Quality Housing and Work Responsibility Act (QHWRA), enacted in 1998, made changes that, over time, may affect both the number of families that have children and receive housing assistance and the incentives created by the combination of housing assistance and welfare.

1. The federal preferences that governed admission to public and assisted housing from the late 1980s through the mid-1990s were repealed. These preferences ensured that the neediest households were taken from waiting lists ahead of other households.

2. Housing authorities can charge minimum rents up to $50 a month in both public housing and the housing voucher program.

3. Housing authorities must disregard increases in income from earnings for some public housing tenants and have discretionary authority to vary rent charges in other ways.

In this chapter, we first describe the extent to which welfare families also receive housing assistance. We then discuss the theory and the empirical literature on whether receiving housing assistance makes it more or less likely that a family will escape poverty by moving from welfare to work in either the short or long run. The short answer is that we do not know.

We then document what we do know. First, welfare families that do not receive housing assistance are likely to experience extreme financial pressure that may interfere with their ability to develop human capital. Second, project-based housing assistance appears to cause welfare families to live in neighborhoods with a high concentration of poverty to a greater extent than unassisted welfare families do. Furthermore, no type of housing assistance does much to help welfare families live in neighborhoods with low poverty rates. Because the concentration of poverty may be associated with a variety of barriers to long-run self-sufficiency for families, this is disturbing.

We then turn to the policy implications of these findings. What can be done about the short-run disincentives to work created by the current design of housing assistance? If the lack of housing assistance makes it harder for welfare families to develop human capital and escape poverty, how can additional welfare families be served? Finally, what can be done about the concentration in higher-poverty areas of families that have children and receive housing assistance, and how can housing assistance be used to help families with children live in low-poverty areas?

Overlap between Welfare and Housing Assistance Populations

The Department of Housing and Urban Development (HUD) provides rental assistance to 4.4 million households.[2] About 4.1 million have large subsidies that, generally speaking, permit them to pay only 30 percent of their income for rent, regardless of how low that income might be. These subsidies are provided to residents of public housing, to tenants of Section 8 projects, and to holders of Section 8 vouchers.[3]

---

[2] This number does not include Indian housing, which would bring the total to 4.5 million units. Indian housing is excluded throughout this chapter.

[3] For convenience, we usually refer to vouchers and the earlier, similar Section 8 certificate program simply as vouchers.

Some 2 million of these 4.1 million families are families with children.[4] HUD also provides shallow project-based subsidies to about 300,000 tenants,[5] but most of these do not pay income-based rents and very few are welfare families.

In much of this chapter, we use data from the Multifamily Tenant Characteristics System (MTCS) and the Tenant Rental Assistance Certification Systems (TRACS), which collect reports on millions of tenant households from public housing agencies (PHAs) and the owners of subsidized private projects across the country. Data sets of this depth have major advantages over publicly available data sets, which are often surveys of a few thousand households that may or may not be representative of the national or local population from which they were selected. However, housing authorities and owners sometimes fail to make timely and complete reports, which can have negative consequences for the validity of the data. Having worked with both MTCS and TRACS data for some years, we believe that the national averages we report from these systems are reasonably reliable, consistent, and comparable over time. State and local averages, however, may be affected, particularly—in the case of MTCS—when a single very large housing authority is a poor reporter. Appendix 2A provides more detail on the ways in which we have used these data.

Table 2.1 presents a national overview of the number of units in the main programs and their use by families with children and by welfare families.

Table 2.1. **National Totals: Welfare Families in Assisted Housing in 1996 and 2000**

	All Deeply Targeted, HUD-Assisted Housing	Public Housing	Vouchers	Section 8 Projects
Total units	4,100,000	1,200,000	1,500,000	1,400,000
Families with children	2,020,000	550,000	980,000	480,000
AFDC families in 1996	1,010,000	280,000	480,000	250,000
TANF families in 2000	550,000	160,000	280,000	110,000

Sources: Calculated from the February 1997 Multifamily Tenant Characteristics System and the December 1996 Tenant Rental Assistance Certification Systems and from December 2000 MTCS and TRACS. See Appendix 2A for further information.
Note: Numbers are rounded to the nearest ten thousand.

---

[4] For tabulations of income and demographic information on public and assisted housing tenants, see HUD 1998b).

[5] These households live in projects produced under the Section 236 and Section 221(d)(3) below market interest rate programs and, unlike many other households living in such projects, do not also have Section 8 subsidies.

Table 2.1 shows that the number of welfare families in assisted housing dropped by about half between 1996 and 2000. However, during that period the welfare rolls dropped at about the same rate for all families, from 4.4 million to 2.2 million households (U.S. Department of Health and Human Services 2001). The result is that those on welfare in 2000 were as likely to receive housing assistance as those on welfare in 1996. As of 2000, 2.2 million families received TANF, and just about a quarter of those welfare families, 550,000, received housing assistance.

Table 2.2 provides state-by-state estimates of the extent to which welfare families also received housing assistance as of 1996. The first column of table 2.2 shows families receiving AFDC as of August 1996, the month PRWORA was enacted. The second column shows the total number of AFDC families assisted by HUD. The third column expresses the HUD-assisted group as a percentage of all AFDC families.

The fourth column is presented for purposes of comparison. It represents the best official estimate the welfare system had of the proportion stated in column 3, based on Department of Health and Human Services quality control exercises. In most cases, it is a less accurate estimate than the one based on HUD data.[6]

At the beginning of the welfare reform era in 1996, just under one-quarter of AFDC-assisted households were also assisted by HUD; this was also the case four years later. However, there was—and undoubtedly still is—a huge variation in this percentage from state to state, from one in nine households in Michigan to more than one in two in North Dakota. In Alabama, Arkansas, Nebraska, Oklahoma, and South Dakota, more than 40 percent of AFDC households are also assisted by HUD.

In nearly all states, most families on welfare get no help with their housing needs. Since housing assistance is not an entitlement for welfare families, it is natural to ask, first, what the effects of receiving housing assistance are and, second, what the effects of *not* receiving housing assistance are.

---

[6] The quality control estimates are based on samples, and not always large ones, so sampling error may affect the totals. Housing assistance programs are complex and may be poorly understood and identified by both the families receiving them (Shroder and Martin 1996) and by welfare agency staff. In most states, receipt of housing assistance will not affect the level of welfare benefit paid, and those performing the audits on which the estimates are based may not feel the need for precision in measuring this item.

Table 2.2. **Percentage of AFDC Families with HUD Housing Assistance by State in 1996**

	All AFDC Families, August 1996	HUD-Assisted AFDC Households, December 1996	AFDC Recipients Who Were HUD Assisted[a]	Same, per the Health and Human Services 1996 Quality Control Study[b]
U.S. total	4,413,500	1,009,700	23%	21%
Alabama	41,000	16,900	41%	33%
Alaska	12,200	2,500	24%	22%
Arizona	62,400	9,700	19%	14%
Arkansas	22,100	9,100	41%	30%
California	880,400	113,900	13%	10%
Colorado	34,500	13,400	39%	23%
Connecticut	57,300	16,900	30%	37%
Delaware	10,600	2,500	24%	32%
District of Columbia[c]	25,400	5,400	21%	43%
Florida	200,900	43,600	22%	16%
Georgia	123,300	35,200	29%	25%
Hawaii	21,900	6,100	28%	23%
Idaho	8,600	2,200	27%	28%
Illinois[a]	220,300	36,200	16%	18%
Indiana	51,400	17,700	34%	18%
Iowa	31,600	10,400	33%	27%
Kansas	23,800	6,400	27%	21%
Kentucky	71,300	21,800	31%	27%
Louisiana	67,500	19,800	29%	24%
Maine	20,000	5,400	27%	28%
Maryland	70,700	19,100	27%	27%
Massachusetts	84,700	27,200	32%	36%
Michigan	170,000	19,100	11%	11%
Minnesota	57,700	19,600	35%	33%
Mississippi	46,400	13,000	28%	24%
Missouri	80,100	25,300	32%	27%
Montana	10,100	2,900	37%	39%
Nebraska	14,100	6,400	46%	38%
Nevada	13,700	3,000	23%	18%
New Hampshire	9,100	3,100	34%	24%
New Jersey	108,400	24,200	22%	19%
New Mexico	33,400	7,200	24%	28%
New York	418,300	75,700	18%	26%
North Carolina	110,100	35,300	32%	19%
North Dakota	4,800	2,300	55%	54%
Ohio	204,200	61,200	30%	27%
Oklahoma	36,000	16,000	47%	32%
Oregon	29,900	9,500	32%	19%
Pennsylvania	186,300	45,400	24%	16%
Rhode Island	20,700	5,800	28%	31%
South Carolina	44,100	14,600	33%	29%
South Dakota	5,800	1,600	53%	26%
Tennessee	97,200	31,900	33%	30%

Table 2.2. **Percentage of AFDC Families with HUD Housing Assistance by State in 1996** *(continued)*

	All AFDC Families, August 1996	HUD-Assisted AFDC Households, December 1996	AFDC Recipients Who Were HUD Assisted[a]	Same, per the Health and Human Services 1996 Quality Control Study[b]
Texas	243,500	55,300	23%	26%
Utah	14,200	3,800	27%	21%
Vermont	8,800	2,100	24%	24%
Virginia	61,900	21,800	35%	26%
Washington	97,500	18,100	19%	20%
West Virginia	37,000	10,200	28%	24%
Wisconsin	51,900	14,900	29%	15%
Wyoming	4,300	1,200	32%	32%

Source: Calculated from February 1997 MTCS and December 1996 TRACS data.
Note: Puerto Rico and Guam are not displayed separately, but are included in national totals.
[a] In some states the numerator of this percentage includes Indian housing residents not counted in Table 2 or the column immediately to the left.
[b] As a comparison to column 3, the last column shows the percentage of AFDC families that were HUD assisted, based on the 1996 Health and Human Services Quality Control Study (1997). In most cases, this is less accurate than the HUD-based estimates.
[c] The number in the second column and the percentage in the third are known to be too low because of poor reporting by a single large housing authority.

Low-Income Housing Assistance and Self-Sufficiency: Theory and Research to Date

Economists try to evaluate the effects of social programs on work effort by analyzing changes in the "budget constraint" of a typical client, who has certain resources and must pay particular prices for the goods she must buy and sell. One resource that every welfare head of household has is her own time. Her free time is precious to her, as it is to everyone, and she will give it up only in return for goods she values, like food, housing, or clothing. Her willingness to sell her time to an employer may change because a housing program has both *price* effects and *income* effects on the hours she chooses to work.

The price effects are straightforward. If she gets no assistance from HUD, selling an hour of her time will yield her a nominal wage, net of taxes that include the benefit take-away rates in other programs. If she does get assistance from HUD, her net wage will be reduced by another 30 cents on the dollar, because her contribution to rent is supposed to be 30 percent of income. Her participation in HUD programs subjects her to a 30 percent "HUD tax." Obviously, this somewhat reduces her willingness to sell her leisure time to a potential employer.

For those receiving benefits under the old AFDC program, the impact of the HUD tax was almost nil. Most AFDC recipients already faced a 100 percent tax rate on marginal earnings. The net income of the typical HUD program participant would have been essentially unchanged by earnings, and therefore her assisted rent would also have been unchanged.[7]

The effect of the earnings disregards that most states have adopted in their TANF programs has been to increase the HUD tax bite. For example, for a state that moved from a 100 percent AFDC tax rate back to the old (pre-1982) AFDC system in which 33 percent of income is disregarded (i.e., a TANF tax of 67 percent), the effective HUD tax rose from 0 percent to 10 percent.[8]

According to economic theory, housing assistance should also have *income effects*. Historically, admission to one of the deeply targeted programs guaranteed a household the use of a standard-quality housing unit even if the household head had no earnings. Even in the absence of a marginal tax rate on wages, the housing guarantee would make a client somewhat less interested in offering up her free time to the market.

Standard economic analysis therefore predicts that housing assistance programs must depress a welfare head of household's willingness to work *in the short run*. The analysis has two major limits.

First, the prediction might be true but unimportant. We know of four published empirical studies that cast some light on this subject. Murray (1980), using indirect simulation methods, estimated that public housing reduced short-run labor supply by just 4 percent.[9] Studying low-income neighborhoods of Chicago, Reingold (1997) did not detect any effect of public housing on hours worked. Among welfare recipients in four counties in California, Ong (1998) found no effect of public housing on employment and a *positive* effect of tenant-based assistance on employment.

Riccio and Orenstein (2003) report that welfare reform demonstrations in Minnesota, Atlanta, and Columbus (OH) led to large increases in

---

[7] The 100 percent tax rate on earnings is one reason why the combination of AFDC and earnings was not very common.

[8] The calculation is as follows: With a 33 percent disregard, 33 cents of each additional dollar is added to income, and HUD would take 30 percent, or 10 cents on the dollar. This analysis ignores payroll taxes (which reduce net income) and the Earned Income Tax Credit (which increases it).

[9] This number is based on a HUD tax of 25 percent, that is, the pre-1982 rate.

employment and earnings among long-term welfare recipients living in public or assisted housing, but were much less effective among other welfare recipients. The Minnesota program consisted of mandatory employment services (the head of household had to show up or lose some benefits) and generous earnings disregards in the calculation of the welfare benefit. Disregards in the welfare program *raise* the effective HUD tax; other things being equal, theory suggests that HUD-assisted tenants should have been *less* responsive to the program than other welfare recipients.

Second, the *long-term* effects of any program on poverty are more important than the short-run effects. Most heads of welfare families lack what economists call human capital: the skills, attitudes, and other attributes that contribute to productivity on the job. Human capital is the product of upbringing, health, education, experience in the labor market, and other factors; it represents investment by the individual and by society in that individual's productive potential.

Theory is silent about the effects of housing assistance on human capital, and there is very little empirical work. In a national study, Bloom et al. (1993) report that adult Job Training Partnership Act (JTPA) participants who did not live in public housing benefited from JTPA, while those who lived in public housing did not. Moore et al. (1995) report that living in public housing in Atlanta is a risk factor associated with the cognitive and social development of retarded children. However, two articles by Meyers and his collaborators (1993, 1995) find that housing assistance may have significantly improved the health of low-income children in Boston, because they were more likely to have enough to eat. Since people who live in public housing often differ in unobserved ways from those who do not, these findings are all open to legitimate skepticism.

Recent work by Newman and Harkness (2002) shows that living in public housing has a slight positive effect on self-sufficiency outcomes for youth. While those who grow up in public housing have, in their late twenties, worse outcomes on measures such as earnings and educational attainment than others of the same age, controlling for differences in family background reveals that they would have been expected to fare even worse had they not lived in public housing.

HUD is sponsoring several research projects to reduce the uncertainty in this area. The largest of them are the Moving to Opportunity Demonstration, a controlled experiment that will measure the impact of different forms of housing assistance on a variety of measures of self-sufficiency (Goering 1996), and the Welfare-to-Work Voucher Demonstration, a controlled experiment that will measure the impact of tenant-based housing assistance on the self-sufficiency of welfare, ex-welfare, and welfare-eligible families.[10]

Known Effects of *Not* Receiving Housing Assistance

So much for what we do not know. We do know that in the United States, extremely low income families, a category that includes practically all welfare families, are quite likely to experience severe housing deprivation. This deprivation, in turn, is likely to interfere with needed investment in the human capital of both adults and children.

HUD reports periodically on "worst-case needs" for rental housing assistance among those households that do not receive it. Those with acute or worst-case housing needs are very low income renter households (those with incomes below 50 percent of area median income) that live in severely substandard housing or pay over half of their income for rent. Extremely low income families—those with incomes below 30 percent of the median—are the most likely to have worst-case needs. Needs have grown among families with children since the early 1970s, and families with children are particularly likely to have worst-case needs (HUD 1996). By far the most common problem is excess rent burden relative to income.

In 1995, 2.1 million families with children had worst-case needs for housing assistance; of these, 1.7 million had extremely low incomes. Just under a million were on welfare; another 700,000 were extremely low income working families. The worst-case needs of these "working poor" families represent the housing situation of families as they try to leave the welfare rolls. Starting to work at entry-level, minimum-wage jobs will in many cases not provide enough income to raise a family out of worst-case housing needs (Nelson et al. 1998).

The likelihood that a welfare or working poor family with children will have worst-case housing needs varies greatly by location. Figure 2.1 shows that there is a strong negative correlation between the percentage of families receiving housing assistance and the percentage with worst-case needs.

Both figure 2.1 and table 2.3 use the metropolitan files of the American Housing Survey to show the number of families that have children and

---

[10] This program is described in "Notice of Funding Availability" (1999).

Figure 2.1. **Worst-Case Housing Needs of Poor Families with Children Are Highest in Metropolitan Areas Where Housing Assistance Is Lowest**

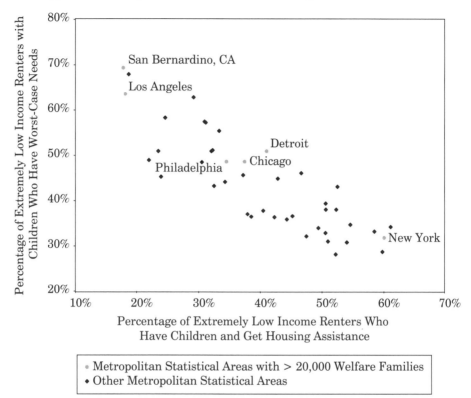

* Metropolitan Statistical Areas with > 20,000 Welfare Families
♦ Other Metropolitan Statistical Areas

are extremely low income renters in 43 metropolitan areas.[11] The third column of table 2.3 shows the percentage of such families that receive housing assistance. It ranges from a high of 60 to 61 percent in New York, Newport News (VA), and Seattle to a low of 18 to 19 percent in Los Angeles, San Bernardino (CA), and Anaheim (CA).[12] The fourth column shows the percentage of extremely low income renters who have children and worst-case needs.

---

[11] The American Housing Survey includes metropolitan areas on a rolling basis, generally at four-year intervals. The metropolitan surveys used here are for various years from 1989 through 1996. Sample sizes in the national American Housing Survey are not large enough to permit similar estimates for states.

[12] These estimates are based on households' answers to American Housing Survey questions and have some of the same problems associated with self-reporting of receipt of housing assistance described in appendix 2A. More than 4.6 million renters claim to be assisted, compared with the estimated 4.4 million households to which HUD has contracted to pay subsidies. Thus, the percentages with housing assistance reported in table 2.3 may be slightly overstated.

Table 2.3. **Number and Percentage of Welfare Families with Worst-Case Housing Needs in Metropolitan Areas**

Metropolitan Area	Year of the Survey	Extremely Low Income* Renters with Children	Percentage of Column 2 with Housing Assistance	Percentage of Column 2 with Worst-Case Needs	Welfare Families with Worst-Case Needs
Anaheim, CA	1994	33,100	19	68	8,700
Atlanta	1996	38,500	47	32	3,300
Baltimore	1991	28,700	43	45	8,500
Birmingham, AL	1992	15,900	52	28	1,300
Boston	1993	59,000	58	33	12,700
Charlotte, NC	1995	14,400	40	38	2,000
Chicago	1995	123,400	37	49	31,300
Cincinnati	1990	18,700	49	34	4,200
Cleveland	1996	28,600	31	48	8,600
Columbus, OH	1995	15,800	51	31	2,300
Dallas	1994	39,200	24	51	2,800
Denver	1995	20,500	38	37	2,200
Detroit	1995	70,600	41	51	22,700
Fort Worth, TX	1994	19,900	33	43	1,900
Hartford, CT	1996	16,700	52	38	2,700
Houston	1991	58,800	24	45	8,600
Indianapolis	1996	11,900	32	51	3,100
Kansas City, KS/MO	1995	18,400	39	36	3,500
Los Angeles	1995	256,800	18	64	83,400
Memphis, TN	1996	16,700	51	33	2,900
Miami	1995	52,900	33	55	10,500
Minneapolis	1993	31,600	51	39	8,600
New Orleans	1995	22,500	51	38	2,500
New York	1995	306,300	60	32	48,400
Newark–Northern NJ	1995	102,800	37	46	19,700
Newport News, VA	1992	22,400	60	29	2,000
Oklahoma City	1996	11,500	44	36	1,300
Philadelphia	1995	79,600	34	49	23,300
Phoenix	1994	28,900	22	49	6,100
Pittsburgh	1995	27,300	55	35	5,300
Portland, OR	1995	14,300	31	57	3,500
Providence, RI	1992	15,600	31	57	7,100
Rochester, NY	1990	12,700	53	43	3,400
Sacramento, CA	1996	22,700	25	58	10,100
Salt Lake City	1992	13,800	34	44	2,900
San Antonio	1995	21,400	54	31	1,700
San Bernardino, CA	1994	51,300	18	69	23,500
San Diego	1994	41,300	29	63	15,300
San Francisco	1993	60,200	32	51	16,600
Seattle	1996	15,400	61	34	3,000
St. Louis	1996	38,600	42	36	8,000
Tampa, FL	1989	14,800	47	46	4,300
Washington, DC	1993	51,200	45	37	3,300
Average		45,691	40	44	10,398

Source: HUD Office of Policy Development and Research tabulations of American Housing Survey metropolitan files.
Note: Worst-case households are very low income renters with rent burdens exceeding 50 percent of income and/or units with severe physical problems.
*Below 30 percent of area median income.

The final column of table 2.3 shows the number of welfare families with worst-case needs in each metropolitan area. In the average metropolitan area shown in this table, the most well-off extremely low income family with excess rent burden would have at most $600 in cash each month to spend on all other needs after paying for shelter.

The high incidence of distress rent levels among unassisted families with children in large U.S. metropolitan areas, especially in metropolitan California, will present special challenges for the continued implementation of welfare reform. It may be difficult for a family to begin working and to stay on the job when it accumulates no savings and is often at risk of eviction.

Known Effects of Receiving Housing Assistance: Concentration of Poverty

If the absence of housing assistance might prove a burden in achieving self-sufficiency, so in some cases might its presence. Many public and assisted housing projects are located in areas of socioeconomic decay, a fact that obstructs the efforts of assisted families to obtain jobs. Connell, Devine, and Rubin (1998) find a spatial mismatch in some metropolitan areas between the locations of jobs and the locations of the public housing projects in which welfare families live. Public housing families face stiff competition for nearby entry-level jobs from other neighborhood residents and will have difficulty commuting to more distant jobs. Coulton, Leete, and Bania (1999) provide extensive documentation for this phenomenon in the Cleveland–Akron (OH) area.

Even where location in a low-income neighborhood does not limit physical access to jobs, other disadvantages associated with that location— low-quality services, limited social networks, absence of positive role models—may decrease the likelihood of a successful transition from welfare to work (Ellen and Turner 1997). The role of neighborhood in the development of human capital is a controversial topic in social science, but there can be little doubt that high-crime, gang-dominated neighborhoods, for example, actively hinder its acquisition by young people. Newman and Schnare (1997) use a variety of descriptors of neighborhood quality at the level of the census tract and find that

> ...project-based assistance programs appear to do little to improve the quality of recipients' neighborhoods relative to those of welfare households and, in the case of public housing, appear to make things significantly worse. (726) ...The one hopeful note in this analysis relates to the certificate and voucher programs, which

appear to reduce the probability that families will live in the most economically and socially distressed areas. (728)

Newman and Schnare's (1997) conclusion is based on the residential location of all housing program participants, regardless of whether they are families with children and regardless of their source of income. To test whether these conclusions hold for the welfare population and for working families with children, we used only one indicator of neighborhood quality, the percentage of persons in the census tract with income below the poverty level.[13] Table 2.4 shows the percentage of families that have children, receive one of three types of housing assistance, and live in census tracts more than 40 percent poor and more than 30 percent poor.[14]

Public housing concentrates welfare families in high-poverty areas to an even greater extent than it does all households. Over half of public housing families that have welfare as their major source of income live in neighborhoods with extreme concentrations of poverty, compared with 40 percent of all households in public housing.

Looking just at the welfare population produces startling results for the project-based assisted housing programs. When all assisted households are considered, Section 8 projects are only slightly more likely than tenant-based vouchers to concentrate households in high-poverty census tracts. *The contrast is much greater for the welfare population.* More than a quarter of welfare families in Section 8 projects, versus only 11 percent of welfare families using vouchers, are located in census tracts with extremely high poverty rates.

Even vouchers, while much less likely to concentrate welfare families in high-poverty areas than either public housing or Section 8 projects, do not appear to help welfare families escape from high concentrations of poverty. Welfare families using vouchers and the welfare population in general live in neighborhoods of highly concentrated poverty at virtually identical rates. Newman and Schnare's (1997) "hopeful note" disappears.

---

[13] This indicator appears to be highly correlated with Newman and Schnare's other indicators (1997), and other analysts have found it to be a good indicator of neighborhood distress (Jargowsky 1997).

[14] Welfare households are defined as those for whom welfare is the major source of income.

Table 2.4. **Percentage of Families with Children in Census Tracts with High Concentrations of the Poor**

Neighborhood Poverty Rate	HUD-Assisted Households			Comparison Groups	
	Public Housing	Section 8 Projects[a]	Vouchers	Welfare Population in General	Unassisted Renters with Incomes below the Poverty Level
Welfare families (majority of income is from welfare)					
More than 40% poor	52%	26%	11%	12%	NA
More than 30% poor	68%	45%	25%	24%	NA
Working families with children (majority of income is from work)					
More than 40% poor	39%	16%[b]	8%	NA	NA
More than 30% poor	57%	30%[b]	20%	NA	NA
All HUD-assisted households					
More than 40% poor	40%	15%	9%	NA	15%
More than 30% poor	57%	29%	21%	NA	26%

Source: Tabulations from *A Picture of Subsidized Households in 1998* (HUD 1998a) (Section 8 projects except for Moderate Rehabilitation), May 1998 MTCS (public housing, tenant-based certificates and vouchers, and Moderate Rehabilitation), and census data. Figures on the welfare population in general are from Newman and Schnare (1997).
Note: NA = not available.
[a] For this table, Section 8 projects include the Section 8 Moderate Rehabilitation program.
[b] All working families, including those without children.

The hopeful note returns, however, for families with children and a majority of income from work. When these families use vouchers, they are less likely to live in high-poverty census tracts than unassisted renter households with incomes below the poverty level (8 percent versus 15 percent). However, when working families with children live in Section 8 projects, they are about as likely to live in high-poverty census tracts as poor families in general, while public housing concentrates working families as well as welfare families in high-poverty locations.

Table 2.5 shows the wide variation among states in the percentage of welfare families living in assisted housing and in high-poverty census tracts. States with large cities identified by previous research as having numerous "underclass" census tracts (Jargowsky and Bane 1990) are likely to have high percentages of public housing welfare families living in concentrated poverty, as are certain southern states with large poor populations. The contrast among the types of housing assistance is more marked in some states than in others. For example, in California, 43 percent of public housing welfare families, but only 4 percent of voucher families and 10 percent of families in Section 8 projects, live in census tracts that are over 40 percent poor.

Table 2.5. **Concentration of Welfare Families in High-Poverty Census Tracts by State and Program**

Tract Poverty Rate	Public Housing		Section 8 Projects		Vouchers	
	30%+	40%+	30%+	40%+	30%+	40%+
U.S. Total	68%	52%	46%	26%	25%	11%
Alabama	83%	72%	53%	27%	43%	27%
Alaska	0%	0%	0%	0%	0%	0%
Arizona	84%	64%	42%	18%	26%	7%
Arkansas	75%	60%	62%	39%	39%	22%
California	65%	43%	27%	10%	15%	4%
Colorado	65%	40%	27%	13%	17%	4%
Connecticut	59%	36%	36%	16%	13%	5%
Delaware	67%	60%	17%	0%	7%	3%
District of Columbia	84%	41%	54%	18%	30%	5%
Florida	71%	52%	57%	26%	21%	9%
Georgia	67%	51%	50%	31%	24%	11%
Hawaii	52%	52%	0%	0%	3%	0%
Idaho	0%	0%	1%	1%	5%	0%
Illinois	86%	80%	68%*	52%*	28%	13%
Indiana	57%	27%	35%	20%	20%	6%
Iowa	0%	0%	20%	15%	10%	6%
Kansas	54%	34%	19%	1%	11%	5%
Kentucky	77%	61%	39%	13%	42%	12%
Louisiana	90%	82%	70%	50%	54%	32%
Maine	8%	8%	25%	0%	6%	2%
Maryland	79%	74%	37%	17%	5%	0%
Massachusetts	58%	34%	52%	10%	14%	6%
Michigan	72%	57%	50%	36%	34%	18%
Minnesota	51%	45%	34%	23%	20%	10%
Mississippi	72%	48%	62%	35%	57%	37%
Missouri	55%	40%	50%	20%	25%	8%
Montana	49%	11%	5%	4%	15%	3%
Nebraska	84%	84%	37%	9%	28%	7%
Nevada	32%	21%	34%	26%	18%	4%
New Hampshire	0%	0%	0%	0%	1%	0%
New Jersey	64%	32%	50%	31%	18%	5%
New Mexico	43%	10%	37%	6%	37%	9%
New York	61%*	44%*	73%	44%	45%	25%
North Carolina	54%	35%	26%	13%	16%	6%
North Dakota	0%	0%	0%	0%	8%	5%
Ohio	71%	52%	56%	42%	36%	15%
Oklahoma	78%	68%	36%	23%	18%	8%
Oregon	22%	4%	7%	6%	9%	4%
Pennsylvania	61%*	49%*	36%	25%	20%	7%

Table 2.5. **Concentration of Welfare Families in High-Poverty Census Tracts by State and Program** *(continued)*

Tract Poverty Rate	Public Housing		Section 8 Projects		Vouchers	
	30%+	40%+	30%+	40%+	30%+	40%+
Rhode Island	17%	2%	20%	13%	14%	3%
South Carolina	47%	28%	34%	13%	25%	7%
South Dakota	0%	0%	2%	1%	5%	0%
Tennessee	81%	70%	33%	19%	24%	12%
Texas	79%	64%	62%	38%	31%	14%
Utah	35%	14%	15%	4%	5%	1%
Vermont	0%	0%	6%	0%	5%	0%
Virginia	76%	67%	37%	11%	10%	3%
Washington	52%	24%	20%	10%	10%	2%
West Virginia	51%	17%	16%	0%	22%	4%
Wisconsin	69%	40%	26%	21%	28%	18%
Wyoming	33%	0%	6%	0%	0%	0%

Source: Tabulations are from *A Picture of Subsidized Households in 1998* (HUD 1998a) (Section 8 projects) and 1998 MTCS data (public housing and tenant-based certificates and vouchers).
*Estimates are known to be biased by poor reporting.

We now consider whether some assisted housing might *deconcentrate* welfare families by helping them afford units in middle-class neighborhoods. In principle, housing programs can make it possible for extremely low income families to afford to live in neighborhoods with small numbers of poor people and, presumably, better access to jobs and services. Table 2.6 shows the percentage of welfare families and working families with children that are living in more affluent census tracts, with less than 10 percent or 20 percent poverty.

No program—not even the tenant-based voucher program—appears to do much to enable welfare families to live in low-poverty neighborhoods. Twenty percent of voucher welfare families live in census tracts less than 10 percent poor, but so do 25 percent of welfare families in general. Fifty-three percent of welfare families using vouchers live in census tracts less than 20 percent poor, but so do 51 percent of all unassisted families with incomes below the poverty level.

These figures may understate the extent to which vouchers enable welfare families to live in low-poverty neighborhoods. Welfare families using housing assistance may differ from welfare or poor families in general: They may be more likely to be poor for long periods of time than the overall welfare population. Families often have been on waiting lists for several years before they receive assistance.

Table 2.6. **Percentage of Families with Children in Census Tracts with Low Concentrations of the Poor**

Tract Poverty Rate	HUD-Assisted Households			Comparison Groups	
	Public Housing	Section 8 Projects[a]	Vouchers	Welfare Population in General	Unassisted Renters with Incomes below the Poverty Level
Welfare families (majority of income is from welfare)					
Less than 10% poor	5%	9%	20%	25%	NA
Less than 20% poor	17%	32%	53%	NA	NA
Working families with children (majority of income is from work)					
Less than 10% poor	7%	19%[b]	26%	NA	NA
Less than 20% poor	24%	50%[b]	60%	NA	NA
All HUD-assisted households					
Less than 10% poor	8%	22%	24%	NA	36%
Less than 20% poor	24%	41%	58%	NA	51%

Source: Tabulations from *A Picture of Subsidized Households in 1998* (HUD 1998a) (Section 8 projects), May 1998 MTCS (public housing, tenant-based certificates and vouchers, and Moderate Rehabilitation), and census data. Figures on the welfare population in general are from Newman and Schnare (1997).
Note: NA = not available.
[a] For this table, Section 8 projects include the Section 8 Moderate Rehabilitation program.
[b] All working families, including those without children.

New Approaches to Subsidized Housing: HOME and the Low-Income Housing Tax Credit

Our knowledge of the extent to which the Low-Income Housing Tax Credit (LIHTC) and HOME are being used *by families with children* in low-poverty neighborhoods is limited by the absence of detailed administrative data at the household level for these programs.[15] However, we do know something about the location of the units produced by these programs.

Table 2.7 shows the distribution of all LIHTC units placed in service between 1995 and 1999 in the nation as a whole by the percentage of poor people in the census tract. Nationally, the percentages in census tracts with 10 percent poverty or less and with 20 percent poverty or

---

[15] Both programs represent a trend toward increasing devolution in authority from federal to state or local governments. Federal income tax credits to individuals who invest in affordable rental housing developments are allocated by the states (U.S. General Accounting Office 1997); HOME is a block grant allocated to state and large city and county governments and can assist homeowners, rental developments, or individual renters (Walker et al. 1999).

Table 2.7. **Distribution of LIHTC Units by the Poverty Rate
of the Census Tract**

Persons in the Census Tract below Poverty Line	Percentage of LIHTC Units Placed in Service 1995–1999
0–10%	39
11–20%	28
21–30%	13
31–40%	10
41% or more	10

Source: Nolden et al. (2002).

less (39 percent and 67 percent) are much greater than the figures for the HUD-assisted multifamily stock (22 percent and 41 percent). Thus, LIHTC units could be an important potential resource for helping welfare and working poor families with children gain access to better neighborhoods.

Walker et al. (1999) report that local officials managing HOME programs have not made any special effort to locate projects in low-poverty areas. Table 2.8 is taken from Walker et al. (1999) and compares the extent to which the poverty population lives in low-poverty census tracts with the extent to which HOME rental projects are located in low-poverty census tracts. For HOME programs in cities, rental projects are located in census tracts with less than 10 or 20 percent persons in poverty to a *smaller* extent than the poverty population living in such tracts. In striking contrast, suburban HOME programs appear to be locating rental projects in low-poverty census tracts to a *greater* extent than the percentage of the suburban poor that live in such tracts. If HOME rents in those areas are low enough to be affordable to poor families with children[16] or if such families can gain access to tenant-based vouchers, HOME projects might enable them to live in low-poverty neighborhoods in the suburbs.

More recent analysis of HOME administrative data shows that 58 percent of HOME rental units placed in service through 1999 are in census tracts with a poverty rate of 20 percent or less (Khadduri, Martin, and Buron 2001).

---

[16] The *maximum* HOME rents are set at the lower of the fair market rent or 30 percent of 65 percent of area median income for the size household likely to occupy the unit. In most cases, a poor family could not afford this rent. However, HOME project sponsors can and often do set rents below the maximum.

Table 2.8. **HOME Rental Projects in Low-Poverty Census Tracts**

Type of Jurisdiction	Census Tracts Less Than 10% Poor	Census Tracts Less Than 20% Poor
City poverty population	12%	34%
City HOME projects	8%	25%
Consortia poverty population	26%	56%
Consortia HOME projects	44%	71%
Urban county poverty population	21%	46%
Urban county HOME projects	54%	80%

Source: HOME/Cash Management Information and census data compiled by Walker et al. (1999).

Implications for Policy and Practice

We turn now to the implications of the findings we have presented for the policy and practice of housing assistance. We consider first measures aimed at reducing work disincentives; second, measures aimed at finding additional resources to help low-income families with children meet their housing needs; and third, measures to improve the locations offered by housing assistance.

Reducing Work Disincentives: Conservative Measures

Earlier in this chapter, we argued that long-term, rather than short-term, effects of housing assistance should be the focus for policy makers. The short-term disincentives, however, appear to loom largest for both conservative and liberal policy makers. In general, conservatives try to target the income effect, making the housing guarantee less valuable and more conditional; liberals try to target the price effect, reducing the HUD tax and raising the net wage.

Wiping out housing assistance altogether, of course, would eliminate both income and substitution effects. The imposition of minimum rents[17] takes one step in that direction. A minimum rent of $50 per month ensures that the maximum possible housing subsidy is worth

---

[17] In programs administered by housing authorities (i.e., public housing and vouchers), minimum rents can be set anywhere between $0 and $50 per month in cases determined by the authority to present no hardship. For Section 8 projects, the minimum rent is set at $25.

$50 less. This should, theoretically, raise a head of household's willingness to sell her time to the market. The minimum rent has a (possibly unintentional) price effect as well: For a family with two children, it eliminates the HUD tax for income up to $247 per month.[18] Higher minimum rents would have a more powerful effect on both the income effect and the price effect of housing assistance.

Similarly, a QHWRA requirement that selected public housing recipients provide 8 hours of uncompensated community service in return for their housing subsidy reduces the value of the income guarantee.[19]

Welfare reform also reduces the income effect of the combined receipt of welfare and housing assistance. Time limits and sanctions for program noncompliance reduce the number of families with guaranteed incomes in the absence of work and also in effect remove the marginal tax rate on earnings created by the receipt of welfare.[20] Time limits in housing assistance have been proposed in the past and no doubt will be proposed in the future. A phased-in, time-limited housing assistance program is perfectly feasible in concept.[21]

Reducing Work Disincentives: Liberal Measures

Many proposals to reduce work disincentives increase the generosity of the program in one form or another by cutting the HUD tax rate. One

---

[18] The calculation is as follows: There would be no tax on the first $167 ($50/0.3=$167) of wages, because $50 would have to be paid in rent in any case. There is a $40 per month adjustment to income for each child, so the next $80 is also tax free.

[19] As enacted, the following adults are excluded from the 8-hour requirement: workers, elderly people, most people with disabilities, and TANF recipients (who are subject to work requirements under their state TANF plans). Among the groups apparently not exempt are full-time homemakers supported by the labor of their spouses. The HUD appropriations act for 2002 suspended implementation of this provision.

[20] Another provision of QHWRA prohibits reductions in rent when a family is sanctioned for noncompliance with a TANF work plan, but not when a family reaches the time limit.

[21] We present, without endorsing, a model for implementing a three-year limit. Suppose that the initial family adjusted income is $400, the maximum housing benefit is $500, and there is no inflation. Tenant contribution or rent would be set at $120 in the first 12 months (subsidy of $380). In months 13 through 24, the contribution would be set at $247 (subsidy of $253) and at $385 in months 25 through 36 (subsidy of $115), with no subsidy from month 37 onward, *regardless of actual household income in any particular month or year*. The phased reduction in benefits regardless of income would mean a marginal HUD tax on wages of 0 percent and a progressive reduction in income effects as the value of the subsidy goes down.

approach is the flat rent—a rent that does not vary with income, like rents paid by unassisted tenants. Some PHAs are experimenting with flat rents in the current Moving to Work demonstration; but if these rents are set on average at less than the 30 percent of income the tenant would otherwise pay, they will at least in the short term increase the funding needed for assisted housing.

Cutting the HUD tax by disregarding part or all of earnings also requires higher appropriations from Congress or, alternatively, reductions in the number of households served or the housing and other services provided to assisted tenants. This is the case because of the size of the earnings increases that would have to be induced by the measure for it to pay for itself.[22]

Most proposed reforms run up against one of two barriers:

1. If they yield additional subsidies to the more than 1 million assisted households[23] that already have some earned income, they cost more than policy makers are willing to spend. For example, excluding the first $800 of earnings from the HUD tax (which would lower the assisted family's rent by $20 per month) would have cost $243 million in 1996.

2. If they give benefits only to those who are not already working, they are difficult to administer (agencies must keep track of who was working last year or last month), offer perverse incentives to game the system, and raise troubling questions of equity. A housing assistance recipient already receives benefits that three out of four similar welfare mothers do not; it is not obvious that she should also receive incentives that her neighbor with housing assistance does not, simply because her neighbor has been working all along and she has not.

---

[22] Suppose that an assisted family has an adjusted income of $500 and pays $150 a month for rent. Now reduce the HUD tax rate from 30 percent of adjusted income to 25 percent of adjusted income. Family income would have to rise from $500 to $600 per month—20 percent—to offset the loss of rental income resulting from the 16.7 percent reduction in the HUD tax ($0.3 \times \$500 = 0.25 \times \$600$). Nobody seriously believes this will happen in the assisted population as a whole. The elasticity (responsiveness) of income to changes in the tax rate (20 percent divided by 16.7 percent) would have to be at least 1.2. Most labor economists think the elasticity of labor income with regard to tax changes is not much above zero among married men; among single female parents, the elasticity is higher, but it is still much less than 1. The classic source on elasticity of labor income with regard to tax changes is the Seattle-Denver Income Maintenance Experiment (U.S. Department of Health and Human Services 1983), although there are many other sources.

[23] Some 750,000 are families with children. Another 250,000 families without children also have earnings.

A measure enacted as part of QHWRA requires that increases in the earned income of a public housing tenant should be disregarded for purposes of determining her rent for 12 months if she has been (1) unemployed for the previous 12 months, (2) enrolled in a self-sufficiency or job training program, or (3) receiving welfare in the past 6 months. Eligibility has been limited in this way to reduce the cost, but with the following consequences:

1. Housing authorities must now track two types of past behavior and determine the validity of a "self-sufficiency or job training program," which is not always obvious. Several years after the enactment of QHWRA, those providing technical assistance to housing authorities report that this disregard is rarely calculated correctly.

2. Tenants are offered three new and different ways to game the system: They can time their unemployment spells, time their welfare spells, and/or manipulate training programs.

3. Two tenants who have the same amount of earned income and the same number of children, and live in units with the same number of bedrooms in the same project, will have quite different rents.[24]

By contrast, we believe that the Family Self-Sufficiency (FSS) program, with its individual self-sufficiency plan and an escrow account that does not require new rent calculations, deserves particular attention. In FSS, rent increases resulting from increases in earnings are paid into an account from which the funds will be released to the family only for purposes in the self-sufficiency plan (paying tuition, buying a car to get to work) or upon completion of the plan. As of February 2001, some 55,000 families using vouchers or living in public housing were participating in the FSS program, and 18,000 of them had escrow accounts.

FSS rewards only planned, sustained, and gradual progress. Relief from the HUD tax is not immediate and it is not guaranteed; only continued future earnings and schooling or training can ensure that the family will eventually benefit from it. The escrow builds up as part of a plan for the acquisition of human capital; this implicitly embodies a theory of behavior that is more dynamic, more complex, and more long term than either the conservative or the liberal reforms we have described here.

---

[24] QHWRA allows PHAs to choose an alternative option: Rather than disregard the earnings, they can establish a savings account into which the rents resulting from increased earnings are paid.

Making More Units Available to Families with Children

Appendix 2B provides detail on the portion of each of the major housing assistance programs that served welfare families as of 1996 and gives separate estimates for each state for public housing, project-based Section 8 vouchers, and tenant-based vouchers.

At the start of the new welfare era, at least one out of four HUD-assisted families received AFDC or TANF. By 2000, following the reduction of the welfare rolls for families both with and without housing assistance, less than 14 percent of all assisted housing units served families on welfare.

This decline in welfare receipt among HUD-assisted families may have resulted to a modest extent from new policies under QHWRA that no longer take the neediest households from waiting lists, that may include preferences for households unlikely to have children, and that may include explicit preference for working families over those with welfare income.[25] However, the fairly low rates of turnover in public and assisted housing (well under 15 percent a year) suggest that a decline of this magnitude has resulted largely from families making the transition from welfare to work while continuing to receive housing assistance. This is supported by analysis that matches household-level administrative data across time periods for public housing families and provides an annualized rate at which particular public housing families change their primary source of income from welfare to earnings (table 2.9). The estimates show public housing families leaving welfare at high rates in the late 1990s.

We assume that despite the absence of systematic knowledge on this topic, many readers believe that housing assistance helps fight long-term poverty by making it possible for families—both those on welfare and those who have begun the transition to work—to improve their human capital. There are several potential sources of housing subsidies for poor families with children.

Incremental housing vouchers. The use of tenant-based vouchers by families with children is much higher than the use of other programs. As of 1996, more than 900,000 families with children used vouchers, compared with the 550,000 families with children that lived in public housing and the 600,000 families with children that lived in privately

---

[25] Data incompatibilities make it impossible for us to determine whether these programs were serving a smaller proportion of families with children in 2000 or whether the decline was entirely the result of fewer families with children having welfare income.

Table 2.9. **Annual Rate of Transition from Welfare to Work in Public and Assisted Housing**

	Percentage of Welfare Households Moving to Work Annually				
	1997	1998	1999	2000	2001
Public housing	6.5	NA	23.8	NA	19.9
Vouchers	11.5	NA	27.5	NA	26.0
Section 8 projects			15.3	NA	NA	21.8

Source: Estimates are derived from tabulations of individual households that moved from welfare to earnings as their primary source of income during various periods of continuous housing assistance. The original tabulations were performed by HUD's Office of Policy Development and Research, Division of Research Evaluation and Monitoring. See appendix 2A for more detail.
Note: NA= not available.

owned HUD-assisted housing. In large part, this difference is structural. The voucher program can serve households of any size, while efficiency apartments are not recommended for parents with children and one-bedroom apartments are generally inappropriate when there is more than one child. Many units in public housing and Section 8 projects are efficiencies and one-bedrooms, and the projects in which they are located were designed with the elderly in mind (for example, they have no playgrounds).

In 1999, following a four-year period in which there had been no appropriation of additional housing vouchers, Congress funded 50,000 units explicitly targeted to families that had children and were making the transition from welfare to work. The average annual appropriation for 2000–02 was slightly more than 50,000 incremental vouchers, with no special targeting to families with children. However, past experience indicates that it is likely that families with children will use about two-thirds of all new vouchers.

HOME and LIHTC. As noted earlier, little systematic information has been available about those whom HOME and LIHTC developments actually house. Both programs have flat rents that do not vary with actual household income; the maximum flat rents set by law are high enough that they cannot be paid by welfare families or the working poor at any reasonable percentage of their income (Nelson and Khadduri 1992). However, the perception that these programs are not relevant to the welfare-to-work population is wrong.

HOME rental projects often house extremely low income households (those with incomes below 30 percent of area median income, which is approximately the poverty level). A recent survey of the occupants of HOME rental units suggests that almost half (47 percent) have extremely low incomes (Herbert et al. 2001). A 1997 U.S. General Accounting Office study of the LIHTC showed that extremely low income households occupied 29 percent of such units.

The housing already developed by these programs could probably be used to a greater extent for welfare-to-work families. It is suggestive that 54 percent of HOME units have two or more bedrooms, but only 43 percent of HOME units are occupied by families with children. Sixty-seven percent of units produced with the LIHTC have two or more bedrooms (Nolden et al. 2002), and it is not known how many of these units are occupied by families with children.

Housing to be developed in the future could be more explicitly planned with the needs of the welfare-to-work population in mind: through the state Qualified Allocation Plans that govern the use of the LIHTC program and through the Comprehensive Housing Assistance Plans that govern the use of HOME funds, for example.

Turnover of Section 8 tenant-based subsidies. Table 2.10 shows how the percentage of tenant-based subsidies used by families with children has grown over time and the percentage used by households with an elderly head has dropped.

Table 2.10. **Increasing Share of Tenant-Based Vouchers Used by Families with Children**

Study/Year of Data	Households with Children (Regardless of Age of Head)	Households with an Elderly Head (62 or Older) and No Children	Households with No Elderly Head and No Children
Drury et al./1976	NA	33%	NA
Wallace et al./1979*	NA	26% urban only	NA
Burke/1979	53%	33%	14%
Leger and Kennedy/1987*	65%	19% large housing authorities only	16%
Casey/1989	61%	23% 65 or older	16% under 65
Casey/1991	56%	14% 65 or older	30% under 65
McGough/1993	60%	13% 65 or older	27% under 65
MTCS/1995	68%	16%	16%
MTCS/1997	65%	16%	19%

Sources: Drury et al. 1978; Wallace et al. 1981; Burke 1984; Leger and Kennedy 1990; Casey 1992; Casey 1997; McGough 1997; HUD Office of Policy Development and Research analysis of 1995 and 1997 MTCS data.
Note: NA = not available.
*These studies may have included elderly-headed households with children among elderly and not among households with children.

About 11 percent of tenant-based units, or 150,000 of the 1.4 million subsidy slots, turn over every year. It is hard to predict whether the use of turnover slots by families with children will increase further[26]; that will depend on the rate at which families with children versus other types of households get on waiting lists. It may also depend on the policies of housing authorities.

QHWRA repealed federal preferences ensuring that households with severe rent burden or substandard housing were placed before others on waiting lists. Instead, housing authorities now can choose their own local preferences as long as illegal discrimination does not result. Federal preferences were replaced by a minimum number of households with incomes below 30 percent of the median that must be admitted to the program. In the case of tenant-based vouchers, this minimum is 75 percent. It applies to each housing authority and in some places may increase the extent to which the tenant-based program is used by welfare or other poor families with children.

Some housing authorities may choose preferences that target assistance explicitly to the welfare-to-work population. Others may choose to favor the elderly or other households without children, although the latter might be subject to challenge on fair housing grounds.

Tenant-based assistance funded by HOME. Tenant-based rental assistance is one of the eligible uses of HOME funds. It is a very small use so far—averaging 8,500 units per year (HUD 2002). This program is similar to the federal tenant-based Section 8 program in most respects. Participating jurisdictions can commit only two years' worth of funds for each unit of assistance from any year's allocation of HOME funds, but the assistance can be renewed from future HOME allocations.

This small program is even more heavily targeted to extremely low income households than the federal tenant-based program (82 percent versus 75 percent) and serves about the same proportion of families with children (65 percent).[27] If the local and state governments administering HOME were to spend more of their allocations on tenant-based

---

[26] Since 1994, HUD regulations have required housing authorities to keep a single waiting list without regard to the size of the unit a household needs. The effect was that housing authorities could no longer reserve a portion of the program for the elderly. This may have reinforced the pattern the table already shows for earlier years: a program increasingly serving families with children and also younger childless households (probably often with disabilities), rather than the elderly.

[27] These are tabulations of data from the HOME program's Cash Management Information (CMI) system as of May 1997, by Marge Martin, Office of Policy Development and Research, HUD.

rental assistance, this could be an important resource for families making the transition from welfare to work.

Turnover in public housing and project-based assisted housing. Many more units in public housing and privately owned assisted projects could house families with children. Table 2.11 provides cautious counts of the number of units that could be occupied by families and are not at present.[28] The first count is the difference between the number of two-bedroom units and the number of families with children: 128,000 public housing units and more than 100,000 units in Section 8 projects. Families without children may legitimately occupy some of those units—for example, related adults who are not husband and wife or unrelated individuals sharing housing under the HUD regulations that permit this. Therefore, the second count is units that have less than one person per bedroom—a clear-cut measure of "underoccupancy" under HUD rules. There are 86,200 public housing units and 65,000 units in privately owned assisted projects with more bedrooms than occupants.[29]

Much of the underoccupancy of assisted housing comes about because of decreases in household size—for example, when children grow up and move out of the parent's apartment. Housing authorities and owners of Section 8 projects are supposed to move such households to the next available unit that has the number of bedrooms now needed.

It is unrealistic to expect additional units in public housing and Section 8 projects to be made available for families with children other than through turnover—turnover in the underoccupied units themselves and turnover in smaller units to which the "underoccupier" would be asked to move. Our best estimate of the turnover rate in both programs is 13 percent per year. The third row of table 2.11 applies this turnover rate to the numbers in the first two rows to produce a range of additional units that could be made available for families with children each year: 20,000 to 30,000 for both programs combined—not a huge number, but not a trivial one either.

---

[28] We have applied a working definition of elderly housing to HUD program data to exclude projects designed for the elderly or persons with disabilities from these estimates.

[29] In the early 1990s, about 9 percent of public housing tenants were occupying units with too many bedrooms, as were 4.3 percent of tenants in Section 8 and Section 236 projects (Loux, Sistek, and Wann 1996). Applying these percentages to program totals yields 108,000 underoccupied public housing units and 73,000 underoccupied units of project-based assisted housing.

Table 2.11. **Additional Units That Could Be Occupied
by Families with Children**

	Public Housing	Section 8 Projects	Both Programs
Number by which 2+ bedroom units exceed families with children	128,000	100,600	228,600
Number of units with more bedrooms than occupants	86,200	65,000	151,200
Potential additional units each year for families with children	11,200–16,600	8,400–13,000	19,600–29,600

Source: Tabulations are from *A Picture of Subsidized Households in 1996* (HUD 1996).
Note: Only units in "family" projects (with fewer than 80 percent elderly or disabled heads) were counted.

Deconcentration of Housing Assistance

What can be done to reduce the extent to which housing assistance concentrates welfare families in high-poverty neighborhoods and to increase the extent to which housing assistance helps them move to low-poverty neighborhoods? The answer is different for the three types of deeply targeted housing assistance: public housing, Section 8 projects, and tenant-based Section 8 vouchers.

Public housing. A transformation that is now under way will remove about 100,000 units from the public housing stock (HUD 2002). The rules that require housing authorities to demolish certain developments say nothing about the poverty rate of the project's location. However, projects likely to fail the mandatory conversion test required by law—those with over 300 units, those with over 15 percent of those units vacant, and those whose costs (including needed rehabilitation) are greater than providing the same households with vouchers—are highly likely to be in locations characterized by extreme poverty. At the same time, a very large number of the households living in these public housing projects are families with welfare income.

Whether the demolition of public housing units reduces the concentration of welfare families in high-poverty locations depends on the housing assistance that replaces those projects. Sometimes replacement housing is built on the same site. This site may have some potential for attracting tenants who are not poor—which in turn often means that the project is not in a high-poverty location or is in an area of the city that has some advantages such as proximity to jobs or transportation. Developments in the highest-poverty locations are the most likely to be replaced—or substantially replaced—by vouchers.

Analysis of the locations to which families moved from projects redeveloped during the 1990s by the HOPE VI program—an important subset of the demolished public housing—shows that, on average, families that used housing vouchers as their relocation mode moved to neighborhoods with substantially lower concentrations of poverty than their former public housing locations (Kingsley, Johnson, and Pettit 2001). Many relocating households move to other public housing rather than using vouchers, although in this case they may be able to choose public housing developments in lower-poverty neighborhoods than those from which they moved (Buron et al. 2002).

Analysis of Relocation Patterns

Section 8 projects. One of the changes to the system since the mid-1990s is that some Section 8 projects are being withdrawn from the assisted housing stock and replaced with tenant-based housing vouchers. The transformation of the project-based assisted housing stock is more complex than the transformation of public housing. Some distressed projects fail financially and are withdrawn from the assisted housing stock; further, HUD has announced that it will no longer renew assistance contracts for projects that are in substandard physical condition.

These processes should reduce somewhat the number of welfare families and other poor families with children living in areas of concentrated poverty. Varady and Walker (1998) studied the relocation of households from four highly distressed privately owned projects and concluded that while most did not move far from their original neighborhood, the new neighborhoods had higher average income levels and reduced concerns about crime.

At the same time, the privately owned assisted stock is being transformed in a second way. The owners of some Section 8 projects are choosing not to renew their assistance contracts with HUD when those contracts expire. "Opting out" of Section 8 assistance is particularly likely to occur when the project is in a low-poverty neighborhood (HUD 1999). There is, therefore, a danger that the opportunities provided by *some* privately owned projects for welfare families to live in low-poverty neighborhoods will be lost. Policies designed to respond to the potential loss of units from the assisted housing stock should concentrate resources on these projects rather than on projects in high-poverty locations.

Tenant-based vouchers. How can housing vouchers better realize their potential for helping welfare families and other poor families with children live in low-poverty neighborhoods? Demonstrations now under way, including the Moving to Opportunity Demonstration (Feins, Popkin, and McGinnis 1997) and the Regional Opportunity Counseling Program, will provide additional knowledge about the extent to which counseling and search assistance can help and what *kind* of assistance has the most effect and is the most cost-effective. Some effort has been made to assemble information on best practices (Turner and Williams 1998), but so far there is too little systematic evaluation.

Meanwhile, other measures may also increase the extent to which families using vouchers move to areas in which less than 10 or 20 percent of the population is poor.

1. *Setting goals for housing authority performance.* The new system used to evaluate the administration of tenant-based vouchers includes "points" for housing authorities that have policies in place to help families move to lower poverty areas and additional points for housing authorities that show results.[30]

2. *Higher maximum benefit levels for higher-rent portions of a metropolitan area.* A recent administrative change has made it easier for housing authorities to appeal to HUD for exception to fair market rents—benefit standards that are up to 20 percent higher than the metropolitan-area standard. Under a provision of QHWRA, housing authorities no longer need HUD approval for benefit standards up to 10 percent higher than the metro-wide standard published by HUD each year.

3. *Changes in housing authority practice that make the program more attractive to owners of rental housing in low-poverty areas.* For example, faster implementation of the administrative processes needed to bring a unit into the voucher program might make owners more willing to rent to subsidized families, especially in locations where it is easy to rent to unsubsidized households.

Conclusion

Several years after the enactment of fundamental changes to the welfare system, the effect of housing assistance on helping poor families with children become self-reliant and escape poverty remains unclear. Despite the theory that housing assistance reduces work effort, empirical research is beginning to show that housing assistance instead helps

---

[30] The Section 8 Management Assessment Program is set forth at 24 Code of Federal Regulations, Section 985.

families build human capital and has a positive effect on work effort and well-being in the long run. Our policy recommendation is for increased attention to and resources for programs such as FSS that focus on steady progress over time and use resources selectively to reward achievement. This is in contrast to earnings disregards that are either very expensive or administratively unworkable. A phased-in, time-limited housing assistance program is feasible in concept, but would need to be tested through careful experimentation.

The decline in the welfare rolls since the enactment of PRWORA has left the same percentage of welfare families receiving housing assistance as was the case in 1996 (about a quarter). At the same time, housing assistance programs are serving fewer welfare families, and the drop has been consistent with the overall drop in the number of welfare families. It is hard to draw any firm conclusion from these patterns, other than that a very large number of HUD-assisted welfare families have adjusted to life after AFDC without notable new suffering.

Poor families with children, whether on welfare or working for low wages, are likely to experience severe housing deprivation if they do not have housing assistance and this, in turn, may interfere with the development of human capital. We have outlined several ways in which levels of housing assistance could be increased for families with children. At the same time, policy makers should renew efforts to use housing assistance to help families with children live in neighborhoods with access to jobs, good-quality services, expanded social networks, and positive role models.

Appendix 2A

Technical Notes on the Use of HUD Administrative Data for Estimates of Households Receiving Housing Assistance and Welfare

MTCS receives tenant data from public and Indian housing authorities for the public housing, Indian housing, certificate, voucher, and moderate rehabilitation programs. TRACS receives tenant data from the owners of privately owned developments assisted by project-based programs, including Section 8. If a housing authority underreports, we assume that the tenants whose records are missing resemble those whose records are in the system, and we adjust their figures accordingly; but if a housing authority does not report at all, we make no assumptions about its families. Poor reporting to TRACS was less common in 1996, but nonreporting has increased since that time. Also, we make no attempt to adjust to control totals for TRACS projects that report partial figures.

Tables 2.1 through 2.3 include the Section 8 Moderate Rehabilitation program with tenant-based certificates and vouchers. Section 8 Moderate Rehabilitation is a hybrid program: It is administered by housing authorities and in many cases takes families from the waiting lists for tenant-based Section 8, but it is a project-based program. In other parts of this chapter, Section 8 Moderate Rehabilitation is treated as project-based assisted housing or omitted because of data limitations. The program has 108,000 units.

The numbers and percentages reported in tables 2.1 through 2.3 should be regarded as lower bounds. The number of HUD-assisted welfare families at the end of 1996 may well be higher in any state and should never be lower than the number presented. In some cases, nonreporting by a single large agency has been known to give a distorted downward bias to the state total. These cases are identified by a note. The true national number of HUD-assisted households receiving AFDC (or the new TANF program) at the end of 1996 was probably about 1.1 million.

For table 2.9, the rates of transition observed during the various periods were standardized for a 12-month period. Public housing and Section 8 voucher estimates are derived from three matched extracts of MTCS data: 1995–97 (the specific months used are unknown but assumed to be 24 months apart); May 1998–July 1999; and September 2000–May 2001. Section 8 project-based housing estimates are derived from matched extracts of TRACS data: December 1995–January 1998 and September 2000–September 2001.

In table 2.11, Section 8 projects exclude Section 202 (elderly) and Section 811 (disabled) developments, but include projects insured and subsidized under the Section 236 and Section 221(d)(3) below market interest rate programs even when those projects do not have any units with Section 8 subsidies. The table does not include Section 8 Moderate Rehabilitation units because the data set on which they are based aggregates that program to the housing authority level and cannot be used for individual projects.

The estimates in table 2.11 should be regarded as lower bounds because no attempt was made to weight for developments that failed to report household data and are thus unrepresented in the Picture of Subsidized Households in 1996 data file. Some 10 percent of public housing developments had no household records (accounting for 7 percent of units), and neither did 20 percent of private project-based developments (18 percent of units).

Appendix 2B

AFDC Households in Public Housing and Section 8 by State in 1996

	Total HUD-Assisted Tenants		Project-Based Section 8		Public Housing		Certificates, Vouchers, Moderate Rehabilitation	
	Families on AFDC	As a Percentage of the Total	Families on AFDC	As a Percentage of the Total	Families on AFDC	As a Percentage of the Total	Families on AFDC	As a Percentage of the Total
U.S. Total	1,009,700	26%	249,300	21%	278,000	23%	482,400	34%
Alabama	16,900	19%	2,000	12%	9,400	19%	5,500	23%
Alaska	2,500	42%	500	49%	700	34%	1,300	44%
Arizona	9,700	28%	2,200	21%	2,100	34%	5,400	33%
Arkansas	9,100	18%	1,300	12%	3,200	19%	4,600	20%
California	113,900	34%	21,400	22%	18,800	44%	73,600	37%
Colorado	13,400	30%	6,100	32%	1,900	25%	5,400	32%
Connecticut	16,900	34%	3,600	23%	6,000	39%	7,200	39%
Delaware	2,500	29%	900	21%	600	46%	1,000	32%
District of Columbia	5,400	31%	2,000	27%	3,400	35%	0*	—
Florida	43,600	31%	10,500	25%	12,600	33%	20,400	33%
Georgia	35,200	34%	6,600	26%	19,100	36%	9,600	40%
Hawaii	6,100	36%	500	17%	1,800	35%	3,800	44%
Idaho	2,200	24%	500	21%	100	12%	1,600	29%
Illinois*	36,200	25%	6,700	17%	10,700	16%	18,800	42%
Indiana	17,700	23%	5,000	19%	4,700	25%	8,000	29%
Iowa	10,400	27%	2,700	19%	800	17%	6,800	34%
Kansas	6,400	22%	1,800	16%	1,600	18%	2,900	34%
Kentucky	21,800	29%	5,200	22%	8,500	30%	8,100	34%
Louisiana	19,800	29%	4,200	25%	8,900	34%	6,700	26%
Maine	5,400	27%	500	13%	1,200	25%	3,800	32%
Maryland	19,100	27%	4,800	20%	6,500	29%	7,900	33%
Massachusetts	27,200	25%	4,400	16%	6,300	21%	16,500	33%

AFDC Households in Public Housing and Section 8 by State in 1996 *(continued)*

	Total HUD-Assisted Tenants		Project-Based Section 8		Public Housing		Certificates, Vouchers, Moderate Rehabilitation	
	Families on AFDC	As a Percentage of the Total	Families on AFDC	As a Percentage of the Total	Families on AFDC	As a Percentage of the Total	Families on AFDC	As a Percentage of the Total
Michigan	19,100	22%	8,900	17%	4,700	21%	5,600	42%
Minnesota	19,600	28%	4,400	26%	3,900	16%	11,300	40%
Mississippi	13,000	27%	3,400	22%	4,600	26%	5,000	36%
Missouri	25,300	29%	5,100	19%	5,600	26%	14,600	39%
Montana	2,900	23%	800	15%	700	30%	1,400	27%
Nebraska	6,400	23%	1,400	18%	1,000	13%	4,100	33%
Nevada	3,000	20%	700	18%	900	24%	1,400	22%
New Hampshire	3,100	17%	800	15%	600	14%	1,600	20%
New Jersey	24,200	22%	5,000	16%	6,600	19%	12,600	29%
New Mexico	7,200	30%	1,500	25%	1,200	31%	4,400	41%
New York	75,700	18%	17,900	21%	6,500	3%	51,300	35%
North Carolina	35,300	32%	6,000	25%	15,100	35%	14,200	33%
North Dakota	2,300	18%	800	16%	300	15%	1,200	18%
Ohio	61,200	34%	21,700	29%	17,900	34%	21,600	41%
Oklahoma	16,000	27%	5,100	37%	3,100	22%	7,700	32%
Oregon	9,500	23%	1,500	13%	1,400	22%	6,700	28%
Pennsylvania	45,400	24%	13,200	20%	14,200	22%	18,100	31%
Rhode Island	5,800	21%	1,400	13%	1,600	16%	2,800	41%
South Carolina	14,600	28%	4,500	25%	4,800	27%	5,400	30%
South Dakota	1,600	16%	600	9%	100	6%	900	15%
Tennessee	31,900	31%	8,000	24%	15,200	33%	8,600	39%
Texas	55,300	28%	13,600	25%	15,700	27%	26,000	31%
Utah	3,800	26%	900	18%	500	23%	2,400	32%
Vermont	2,100	21%	600	17%	200	12%	1,200	29%
Virginia	21,800	27%	6,900	23%	7,400	34%	7,400	27%

AFDC Households in Public Housing and Section 8 by State in 1996 *(continued)*

	Total HUD-Assisted Tenants		Project-Based Section 8		Public Housing		Certificates, Vouchers, Moderate Rehabilitation	
	Families on AFDC	As a Percentage of the Total	Families on AFDC	As a Percentage of the Total	Families on AFDC	As a Percentage of the Total	Families on AFDC	As a Percentage of the Total
Washington	18,100	32%	3,200	19%	5,300	34%	9,600	40%
West Virginia	10,200	28%	2,700	20%	1,800	24%	5,700	38%
Wisconsin	14,900	25%	3,300	17%	2,700	19%	8,900	37%
Wyoming	1,200	21%	600	17%	100	17%	500	25%

Source: Calculated from the February 1997 MTCS and the December 1996 TRACS.
Notes: Puerto Rico and Guam are not displayed separately, but are included in national totals. Public housing does not include Indian housing.
All estimates, both numbers of families and percentages, are lower bounds.
*Known to be too low because of poor reporting by one large housing authority.

Authors

Jill Khadduri is a Principal Associate at Abt Associates, Inc. Mark Shroder is an Economist and Barry Steffen is an Analyst in the Office of Policy Development and Research at the U.S. Department of Housing and Urban Development.

Comments by Barbara Sard, Eliza Kean, Amy S. Bogdon, and two anonymous referees have strengthened this chapter. The views expressed are those of the authors and do not necessarily reflect the positions of the Department of Housing and Urban Development.

References

Bloom, Howard S., Larry L. Orr, George Cage, Stephen H. Bell, and Fred Doolittle. 1993. *The National JTPA Study: Title II-A Impacts on Earnings and Employment at 18 Months*. Research and Evaluation Report Series 93–C. Washington, DC: U.S. Department of Labor, Employment and Training Administration.

Burke, Paul. 1984. *Trends in Subsidized Housing, 1974–1981*. Washington, DC: U.S. Department of Housing and Urban Development.

Buron, Larry, Susan Popkin, Diane Levy, Laura Harris, and Jill Khadduri. 2002. The *HOPE VI Resident Tracking Study: A Snapshot of the Current Living Situation of Original Residents from Eight Sites*. Cambridge, MA: Abt Associates, Inc.; and Washington, DC: Urban Institute.

Casey, Connie H. 1992. *Characteristics of HUD-Assisted Renters and Their Units in 1989*. Washington, DC: U.S. Department of Housing and Urban Development.

Casey, Connie H. 1997. *Characteristics of HUD-Assisted Renters and Their Units in 1991*. Washington, DC: U.S. Department of Housing and Urban Development.

Connell, Terrence L., Deborah Devine, and Lester Rubin. 1998. *Welfare Reform Impacts on the Public Housing Program: A Preliminary Forecast*. Washington, DC: U.S. Department of Housing and Urban Development.

Coulton, Claudia, Laura Leete, and Neil Bania. 1999. Housing, Transportation, and Access to Suburban Jobs by Welfare Recipients in the Cleveland Area. In *The Home Front: Implications of Welfare Reform for Housing Policy*, ed. Sandra J. Newman, 123–48. Washington, DC: Urban Institute Press.

Drury, Margaret, Olson Lee, Michael Springer, and Lorene Yap. 1978. *Lower-Income Housing Assistance Program (Section 8): Nationwide Evaluation of the Existing Housing Program. Technical Appendix*. Washington, DC: U.S. Department of Housing and Urban Development.

Ellen, Ingrid Gould, and Margery Austin Turner. 1997. Does Neighborhood Matter? Assessing Recent Evidence. *Housing Policy Debate* 8(4):833–66.

Feins, Judith D., Susan Popkin, and Debra McGinnis. 1997. *Counseling in the Moving to Opportunity Demonstration Program*. Washington, DC: U.S. Department of Housing and Urban Development.

Goering, John. 1996. *Expanding Housing Choices for HUD-Assisted Families: First Biennial Report to Congress, Moving to Opportunity for Fair Housing Demonstration.* Washington, DC: U.S. Department of Housing and Urban Development, Office of Policy Development and Research.

Herbert, Christopher E., Jessica Bonjorni, Meryl Finkel, Naomi Michlin, Sandra Nolden, Karen Rich, and K.P. Srinath. 2001. *Study of the Ongoing Affordability of HOME Rents.* Cambridge, MA: Abt Associates, Inc.

Jargowsky, Paul A. 1997. *Poverty and Place: Ghettos, Barrios, and the American City.* New York: Russell Sage Foundation.

Jargowsky, Paul A., and Mary Jo Bane. 1990. Ghetto Poverty: Basic Questions. In *Inner City Poverty in the United States*, ed. Laurence E. Lynn Jr. and Michael G.H. McGeary, 16–67. Washington, DC: National Academy Press.

Khadduri, Jill, Marge Martin, and Larry Buron. 2001. Split Subsidy: The Future of Rental Housing Policy. Unpublished paper. Abt Associates, Inc.

Kingsley, G. Thomas, Jennifer Johnson, and Kathryn L.S. Pettit. 2001. *Hope VI and Section 8: Spatial Patterns of Relocation.* Washington, DC: Urban Institute.

Leger, Mireille L., and Stephen D. Kennedy. 1990. *Final Comprehensive Report of the Freestanding Housing Voucher Demonstration.* Cambridge, MA: Abt Associates, Inc.

Loux, Suzanne B., Mary K. Sistek, and Frank Wann. 1996. *Assisted Housing Quality Control.* Prepared for the U.S. Department of Housing and Urban Development by KRA Corporation. Washington, DC: U.S. Department of Housing and Urban Development.

McGough, Duane T. 1997. *Characteristics of HUD-Assisted Renters and Their Units in 1993.* Washington, DC: U.S. Department of Housing and Urban Development.

Meyers, Alan, Deborah Frank, Nicole Roos, Karen Peterson, Virginia Casey, Adrienne Cupples, and Suzette Levenson. 1995. Housing Subsidies and Pediatric Undernutrition. *Archives of Pediatric and Adolescent Medicine* 149:1079–84.

Meyers, Alan, Dana Rubin, Maria Napoleone, and Kevin Nichols. 1993. Public Housing Subsidies May Improve Poor Children's Nutrition. *American Journal of Public Health* 83(1):115.

Moore, Kristen, Martha Zaslow, Mary Jo Coiro, Suzanne Miller, and Ellen Magenheim. 1995. *How Well Are They Faring? AFDC Families with Preschool Children in Atlanta at the Outset of the JOBS Program.* Washington, DC: U.S. Department of Health and Human Services, Office of the Assistant Secretary for Planning and Evaluation. Available from the National Technical Information Service as PB96–172051 or at World Wide Web page <http://www.aspe.os.dhhs.gov/hsp/cyp/jobchdxs.htm> (accessed July 17, 2002).

Murray, Michael P. 1980. A Reinterpretation of the Traditional Income-Leisure Model, with Application to In-Kind Subsidy Programs. *Journal of Public Economics* 14.

Nelson, Kathryn P., and Jill Khadduri. 1992. To Whom Should Limited Housing Resources Be Directed? *Housing Policy Debate* 3(1):1–55.

Nelson, Kathryn P., Jill Khadduri, Marge Martin, Mark Shroder, and Barry Steffen. 1998. *Rental Housing Assistance—The Crisis Continues: The 1997 Report to Congress on Worst-Case Housing Needs.* Washington, DC: U.S. Department of Housing and Urban Development.

Newman, Sandra J., and Joseph M. Harkness. 2002. The Long-Term Effects of Public Housing on Self-Sufficiency. *Journal of Policy Analysis and Management* 21:1, 21–35.

Newman, Sandra J., and Ann B. Schnare. 1997. "…And a Suitable Living Environment": The Failure of Housing Programs to Deliver on Neighborhood Quality. *Housing Policy Debate* 8(4):703–41.

Nolden, Sandra, Jessica Bonjorni, Carissa Climaco, Naomi Michlin, and Karen Rich. 2002. *Updating the Low Income Housing Tax Credit (LIHTC) Database.* Cambridge, MA: Abt Associates, Inc.

Notice of Funding Availability for the Welfare to Work Section 8 Tenant-Based Assistance Program for Fiscal Year 1999. *Federal Register*, January 28, 1999, 4496–5503.

Ong, Paul. 1998. Subsidized Housing and Work among Welfare Recipients. *Housing Policy Debate* 9(4):775–94.

Reingold, David A. 1997. Does Inner-City Public Housing Exacerbate the Employment Problems of Its Tenants? *Journal of Urban Affairs* 19(4):469–86.

Riccio, James A., and Alan Orenstein. 2003. Are Welfare Recipients in Public Housing Really Harder to Employ? In *A Place to Live, a Means to Work: How Housing Assistance Can Strengthen Welfare Policy*, ed. Barbara Sard and Amy S. Bogdon, 63–103. Washington, DC: Fannie Mae Foundation.

Shroder, Mark, and Marge Martin. 1996. New Results from Administrative Data: Housing the Poor, or, What They Don't Know Might Hurt Somebody. Paper presented at the midyear meeting of the American Real Estate and Urban Economics Association, Washington, DC, May 29.

Turner, Margery Austin, and Kale Williams. 1998. *Housing Mobility: Realizing the Promise. Report from the Second National Conference on Assisted Housing Mobility.* Washington, DC: Urban Institute.

U.S. Department of Health and Human Services, Administration for Children and Families. 1997. *Characteristics and Financial Circumstances of AFDC Recipients, FY 1996.* Washington, DC.

U.S. Department of Health and Human Services, Administration for Children and Families. 2001. *Cash Assistance for Needy Families: Average Monthly Families and Recipients for Calendar Years 1936–2001.* World Wide Web page <http://www.acf.dhhs.gov/news/stats/3697.htm> (accessed July 16, 2002).

U.S. Department of Health and Human Services, Assistant Secretary for Planning and Evaluation, Office of Income Security Policy. 1983. *Overview of the Seattle-Denver Income Maintenance Experiment Final Report.* Washington, DC.

U.S. Department of Housing and Urban Development. 1996. *Rental Housing Assistance at a Crossroads: A Report to Congress on Worst-Case Housing Needs.* Washington, DC.

U.S. Department of Housing and Urban Development. 1999. *Opting In: Renewing America's Commitment to Affordable Housing.* Washington, DC.

U.S. Department of Housing and Urban Development. 2002. *Annual Performance Plan, FY 2003.* Washington, DC.

U.S. Department of Housing and Urban Development, Office of Policy Development and Research. 1989–1996. *American Housing Survey.* World Wide Web page <http://www.huduser.org/datasets/ahs/html> (accessed July 16, 2002).

U.S. Department of Housing and Urban Development, Office of Policy Development and Research. 1996. *A Picture of Subsidized Households in 1996.* The public version is available at <http://www.huduser.org/datasets/addthsg.html> (accessed July 17, 2002). The authors used the unpublished version of this data set in which records were not suppressed for confidentiality.

U.S. Department of Housing and Urban Development, Office of Policy Development and Research. 1998a. *A Picture of Subsidized Households in 1998.* The public version is available at <http://www.huduser.org/datasets/addthsg.html> (accessed July 17, 2002). The authors used the unpublished version of this data set in which records were not suppressed for confidentiality.

U.S. Department of Housing and Urban Development, Office of Policy Development and Research. 1998b. Characteristics of Households in Public and Assisted Housing. Recent Research Results, March. World Wide Web page <http://www.huduser.org/publications/periodicals/rrr/rrrhome.html (accessed July 16, 2002).

U.S. General Accounting Office. 1997. *Tax Credits: Opportunities to Improve Oversight of the Low-Income Housing Program.* Report No. 97–55. Washington, DC.

Varady, David, and Carole C. Walker. 1998. *Case Studies of Vouchered-Out Assisted Properties.* Washington, DC: U.S. Department of Housing and Urban Development, Office of Policy Development and Research.

Walker, Christopher, Sheila O'Leary, Patrick Boxall, Peter Tatian, Harold Katsura, G. Thomas Kingsley, and Kenneth Temkin. 1999. *Expanding the Nation's Supply of Affordable Housing: An Evaluation of the HOME Investment Partnership Program.* Washington, DC: U.S. Department of Housing and Urban Development, Office of Policy Development and Research.

Wallace, James E., Susan Philipson Bloom, William L. Holshouseer, Shirley Mansfield, and Daniel H. Weinberg. 1981. *Participation and Benefits in the Urban Section 8 Program: New Construction and Existing Housing.* Cambridge, MA: Abt Associates, Inc.

CHAPTER 3

Are Welfare Recipients in Public Housing Really Harder to Employ?

James A. Riccio
Manpower Demonstration Research Corporation

Alan Orenstein
Consultant

Abstract

Using data from a large, random-assignment evaluation of a welfare-to-work program in Atlanta (Fulton County), this study finds that welfare recipients living in public housing are substantially more disadvantaged than those living in unsubsidized private housing. Over a three-year follow-up period, they also fare worse in the labor market and rely more on welfare. Section 8 recipients fall in between these two groups. Some evidence suggests that these differences may be due more to differences in the characteristics of the people in each housing group than to the advantages or disadvantages imposed by their housing status.

The effectiveness of the welfare-to-work program followed a different pattern, with the largest employment, earnings, and welfare effects in the public housing group. This finding and similar results from two other states suggest the importance of considering housing type in future evaluations and in devising employment strategies to help harder-to-employ welfare recipients.

Keywords: Employment issues; Subsidized housing; Welfare

Introduction

People who live in public housing are widely believed to be among the most difficult recipients of Aid to Families with Dependent Children (AFDC) or its replacement, Temporary Assistance for Needy Families or TANF, to employ. Not only are they thought to have more serious skill deficits, but public housing itself is also seen as worsening their employment problems—for example, by having a rent structure that financially penalizes work, by being physically distant from good job opportunities, and by fostering a social environment that discourages work.

Concern about the low achievement of welfare recipients in public housing has increased for a number of reasons. Some observers fear that, because many recipients in public housing are difficult to employ, they are especially vulnerable to increased poverty under federal and state time limits on welfare benefits. If they cannot make up their loss of welfare payments with earnings, they might have less income to pay their rent, which would require an increase in the subsidies that the federal government pays to local housing authorities when revenues from rent do not cover operating costs (Newman and Harkness 1999). Some observers fear that without increased subsidies to cover a short-fall in revenues from rent, the quality of the housing stock and housing services will suffer (Naparstek, Dooley, and Smith 1997).

Despite the widespread belief that welfare recipients who live in public housing are especially hard to employ, there is only a sparse body of evidence on this topic and on the related question of whether housing status per se contributes to poor employment outcomes. Evidence is also lacking on whether mainstream welfare-to-work programs established for a cross-section of welfare recipients are effective for those who live in public housing.

This chapter examines the experiences of a sample of welfare recipients living in different types of housing in Atlanta and reports on new evidence emerging from studies in Columbus (OH) and Minnesota.

Previous Research

Subsidized Housing and Concentrated Joblessness and Poverty

Nationally, people who live in government-assisted housing have become poorer in recent decades. Newman (1999) points out that among households with subsidies provided by the U.S. Department of Housing and Urban Development (HUD), the percentage of those who also receive public cash assistance (from AFDC/TANF, supplemental security income, or general assistance) has more than doubled since 1966. By the mid-1990s, 26 percent of HUD-assisted households were receiving AFDC, and 23 percent of AFDC families were receiving HUD housing assistance (Khadduri, Shroder, and Steffen 2003). Among all households that had children and lived in public housing developments, only 36 percent had wages as their main source of income (HUD 1998),[1] and almost 50 percent were receiving AFDC (Newman 1999).

---

[1] In project-based Section 8 housing (where the government subsidizes private landlords to rent apartments to low-income people at below market rates), wages were the main source of income for 40 percent of families with children, and in tenant-based Section 8 housing (where tenants receive vouchers or certificates that they can take with them and offer to any qualifying private landlord), wages were the main source of income for 36 percent of the families with children.

Tenants with government housing subsidies not only have low incomes, but they also live in areas with many other low-income people. In the mid-1990s, almost 54 percent of public housing development units were located in high-poverty census tracts (where over 30 percent of the population had incomes below the poverty line) (Newman and Schnare 1997). Among AFDC families living in public housing, 67 percent were in high-poverty tracts (Khadduri, Shroder, and Steffen 2003).[2]

The increasing concentration of the poor in public housing is part of a broader pattern that finds poor people increasingly being concentrated and isolated in inner-city neighborhoods (Abramson, Tobin, and VanderGoot 1995; Jargowsky 1997; Massey and Denton 1993). This concentration is said to make it more difficult for the poor to find jobs and to live without welfare. Studies have found that living in neighborhoods with concentrated joblessness and poverty is associated with other social problems, including higher rates of teenage pregnancy, single parenthood, and family break-up; lower rates of high school completion; higher rates of reliance on welfare; and higher rates of drug use, violence, and other crimes (Briggs 1998; Brooks-Gunn, Duncan, and Aber 1997; Galster and Killen 1995; Turner 1998).

One problem the poor in inner-city areas—including those in public housing developments—face is suggested by the so-called spatial mismatch hypothesis, which holds that inner-city residents are disadvantaged by the lack of entry-level jobs in the areas where they can afford to live and by the transportation costs and difficulties of commuting to the suburbs, where job growth is higher. There has been considerable debate about the size of this effect (Dickens 1999; Ihlanfeldt and Sjoquist 1998; Jargowsky 1997; Kain 1992).

Various studies also suggest that the service environment and the structure of social relationships in high-poverty neighborhoods impede residents' opportunities. For example, in many high-poverty neighborhoods, residents have less access to social networks that can help them advance in the job market (Briggs 1998); there is a less well developed infrastructure of services and supports (schools and transportation) (Kingsley, McNeely, and Gibson 1997; Vidal 1995)[3]; and "collective efficacy" (social cohesion among neighbors combined with a willingness to

---

[2] In project-based Section 8 housing, this figure was 42 percent; in tenant-based Section 8 housing, it was 23 percent.

[3] For example, Vidal (1995) concludes that "poor inner-city neighborhoods, particularly communities of color, have unequal access to opportunities in numerous areas, including employment, credit and financial services, housing, neighborhood shopping, and social networks and services that provide access to information and resources" (169).

intervene on behalf of the common good) is low (Sampson, Rauden-bush, and Earls 1997). Wilson (1996) suggests that residents of neigh-borhoods with high jobless rates are cut off from role models and routines of life that can help socialize them for work. Ellen and Turner (1997) hypothesize that families with the most limited resources are especially vulnerable to the negative conditions in poor neighborhoods. All of these analyses are similar in suggesting that to understand the situation of the urban poor, it is necessary to take into account more than their individual characteristics. It is also necessary to understand the role of neighborhood conditions.[4]

Public housing developments can be viewed as an extreme example of the poor being socially isolated in neighborhoods with high rates of job-lessness and poverty. Consequently, hypotheses linking residency in such neighborhoods to reduced life chances may also apply, with partic-ular cogency, to public housing.

Certain features of public and assisted housing may further impede res-idents' employment. Traditionally, residents have paid 30 percent of their income (after certain deductions and disregards) for rent. Thus, as their income rises, so does their rent. This acts as a kind of tax on additional income, reducing tenants' economic incentive to work (New-man 1999). Public housing may also allow tenants to work less while maintaining the same lifestyle by keeping rents lower than in the pri-vate market (by about $200 a month in California, according to Ong 1998). The long waiting time for apartments in public housing (five years or more in some locations) may have additional negative effects on work effort. Painter (1997) argues that prospective tenants may not seek to increase their earnings for fear of becoming ineligible for hous-ing assistance; the waiting list also ties tenants to public housing devel-opments because if they give up an apartment to move closer to a job opportunity, they cannot easily fall back on public housing if they falter. (In response to widespread concern about these problems, the Quality of Housing and Work Responsibility Act of 1998 includes provisions for new rent policies that will reduce the financial disincentives to work by diminishing the connection between rent and income and by encour-aging public housing agencies (PHAs) to recruit more working fami-lies.) Finally, the stigma associated with public housing may lead employers to reject applicants who give public housing developments as their address (Reingold 1997) and may also contribute to low expec-tations of success on the part of residents.

---

[4] At the same time, studies show that the effects of neighborhood characteristics are weaker than the effects of individual and family characteristics (see Briggs 1998; Brooks-Gunn, Duncan, and Aber 1997; Galster and Killen 1995; Turner 1998).

In sum, the literature on the social effects of the increasing concentration of joblessness and poverty and analyses of conditions specific to public housing suggest that relative to living in other types of housing, living in public housing developments negatively affects residents' labor market success (although some of these same problems also apply to subsidized renters who live in privately owned housing).

Evidence on Whether Housing Status Affects Employment Outcomes

Four relatively recent studies offer a direct test of the relationship between housing assistance and employment among welfare recipients. In one small study, Reingold (1997) surveyed 138 African-American female AFDC recipients in Chicago. Compared with residents in unsubsidized private housing, public housing tenants were only somewhat less likely to be employed in the week before the interview (8.1 percent versus 9.6 percent), less likely to be self-employed (2.3 percent versus 3.8 percent), less likely to have engaged in informal work activities such as babysitting and fixing hair in the six months before the interview (19.8 percent versus 26.9 percent), and less likely to have ever held a steady job (53.5 percent versus 59.6 percent). None of these differences were statistically significant. On the basis of these results (and other findings), Reingold reports that "the differences are not large enough to conclude that the provision of public housing creates work disincentives or high rates of joblessness" (1997, 483).

In a larger study, Ong (1998) used a survey of more than 1,100 female AFDC recipients in four California counties. He found no difference between those in public housing developments and those in unsubsidized private housing in the percentage that worked the previous month (18 percent versus 16 percent). However, recipients with subsidies for private housing (which in California primarily take the form of Section 8 vouchers or certificates) were considerably more likely to work (29 percent) than the other two groups were.

Ong sought to determine whether this effect had something to do with Section 8 housing itself or with the kinds of tenants who live in that type of housing. Using regression analysis to control for the influence of resident characteristics such as age, race, schooling, time on welfare, and reported health problems, Ong found the same pattern: Residents in public housing or unsubsidized private housing did not differ in the number of hours they worked each month, while Section 8 residents worked about 11 hours more than these other groups, a statistically significant difference.

Ong suggests that the positive effect of subsidized private housing may, in some way, be due to the residential choice these tenants enjoy. They are better able to obtain jobs because they can relocate, while at the same time keeping their housing voucher.

Two other studies have used national data from the Survey of Income and Program Participation (SIPP) to explore the general relationship between the receipt of housing benefits and employment. Painter (1997) examined how much the labor force participation of working-age female heads of households with children was influenced by the receipt of public housing and Section 8 subsidies and by the length of time spent on a waiting list for housing assistance. Using data on over 2,500 people, he found that a greater reliance on housing benefits was associated with lower labor force participation, even after taking into account the estimated disincentive effects of receiving other government transfer benefits (AFDC, Food Stamps, and/or Medicaid).

In an analysis of nearly 12,000 working-age female heads of households with children, Currie and Yelowitz (1998) also observed a negative relationship between housing subsidies and labor market outcomes. Holding other factors constant, they found that these sample members were less likely to work, had lower earnings, and were more reliant on welfare income (1) if they lived in areas where the income limits that determine whether a family qualifies for housing subsidies (and which are based on area median income) were higher and (2) if they lived in areas where the estimated net cash value of the housing subsidies (which depends in part on local fair market rents) were higher.

In sum, these four studies do not paint a consistent picture of the relationship between housing benefits and employment outcomes. Moreover, the two national studies using SIPP data do not explicitly compare the relative work disincentive effects for people living in public, Section 8, or unsubsidized private housing. Nor do they show what the disincentive effects of housing benefits are for welfare recipients alone.

Evidence on Whether the Effectiveness of Employment Programs Varies by Housing Status

Few published studies are available on whether mainstream welfare-to-work or job training programs are any more or less effective for residents in public, Section 8, or unsubsidized housing. Some evidence does come from an evaluation of the national Job Training Partnership Act (JTPA), which examined the effects of several job-training approaches for low-income people. Over 18 months of follow-up, the programs tested had no statistically significant effects on the earnings of adult residents of public housing developments, but they did have positive earnings effects for the residents of "other" housing, a group that combined renters living in subsidized and unsubsidized private housing (Bloom et al. 1993).

The Present Study: Goals, Data, and Research Methods

This study uses data collected by the Manpower Demonstration Research Corporation (MDRC) on a sample of single-parent (mostly female) welfare recipients, nearly all of whom were African American, in Atlanta (Fulton County). This sample was part of a larger study: the National Evaluation of Welfare-to-Work Strategies (NEWWS), which is funded by the U.S. Department of Health and Human Services and the U.S. Department of Education and is examining, at seven sites across the country, the effects of alternative welfare-to-work programs initiated under the federal Job Opportunities and Basic Skills Training (JOBS) program of the Family Support Act of 1988. The JOBS program was targeted toward recipients of AFDC, which was replaced by TANF in 1996. Atlanta was chosen as the focus of the present study because it includes substantial proportions of single-parent AFDC recipients who live in public or assisted housing and because a broader range of data is available for that site than for some of the others.

In the Atlanta evaluation, AFDC applicants or recipients who were determined to be JOBS-mandatory (for example, whose youngest child was at least 3 years old and who did not meet exemption criteria such as having a serious illness) were required to attend an orientation session to learn about the JOBS program. However, before detailed explanations were given, orientation attendees were randomly assigned to one of two different program groups or to a control group. As described later in this chapter, the two program groups differed in their strategy for getting recipients employed. Those assigned to the control group did not have access to the assistance provided by either of these welfare-to-work strategies, although they were free to seek and take part in any other program in the community for which they were eligible. However, they were not required to look for work or prepare for work as a condition of receiving their full welfare benefits.

Using a sample of up to nearly 5,700 welfare recipients (depending on the analysis), the present study focuses on three main questions that grow out of the perception that residents of public housing are a particularly disadvantaged group:

1. Do welfare recipients who live in public housing have personal attributes or face circumstances that make them less employable than recipients who live in subsidized or unsubsidized private housing?

2. Do welfare recipients who live in public housing have worse employment and welfare outcomes than recipients in subsidized or unsubsidized private housing and, if so, can this be attributed to the individual characteristics of residents, or does the type of housing appear to have an independent effect?

3. Net of individual characteristics, are mainstream welfare-to-work programs less effective in improving the employment and welfare outcomes of recipients in public housing than they are for recipients in subsidized or unsubsidized private housing?

To address these questions, the analysis uses several types of data, including demographic and other background information, with an indicator of recipients' housing status on which validity tests were conducted.[5] These data were collected on all sample members just before random assignment. (The random assignment period was between January 1992 and January 1994.) Housing data are used to classify recipients into three groups: tenants in public housing developments, tenants in privately owned but government-subsidized housing (who will be referred to as the "Section 8" group), and tenants in unsubsidized private housing.

The pre–random assignment data also include recipients' responses to a two-page self-completed questionnaire, called the Private Opinion Survey, which covers a variety of work-related attitudes; expectations; and perceived social, situational, and psychological conditions that may impede working.

Administrative records were used to measure employment, earnings, and welfare receipt for three years after each sample member's random assignment date. (However, to obtain three years of follow-up in time for the present study, it was necessary to restrict the analysis of administrative records to an earlier cohort of sample members—those randomly assigned through March 1993.) These data come from automated county or state AFDC payment records and state unemployment insurance wage records. (See Hamilton et al. 1997.)

---

[5] A special quality control assessment verified the accuracy of this housing measure. See appendix 3A for details.

A few limitations of the sample and data should be noted. One is that the study sample is not representative of all AFDC recipients in Atlanta; it is limited to those who were deemed by the welfare department to be available and able to work and who were referred to the county's JOBS program. In addition, the follow-up period for the administrative records analyses covers only three of the five years that will eventually be included in the main study and, as noted, only an early cohort of the evaluation's full sample is being used. It is possible that the full sample and a longer follow-up would yield somewhat different results.[6]

Another limitation is that these administrative records do not capture employment in "under the table" jobs[7] or among people who leave the state.[8]

It is important to note that the housing variable used here does not distinguish between people receiving two different forms of Section 8 subsidies: tenant-based assistance (rent vouchers or certificates that "go with the tenant" for use in the private rental market) and project-based assistance (subsidies that are "attached" to specific housing units). In some respects, project-based assistance is akin to public housing in that subsidized tenants are concentrated in the same location. Thus, some of the differences (e.g., in background characteristics and

---

[6] Public use files with longer-term data will be available after the main evaluation is completed, permitting further analyses of the issues explored here.

[7] A comparison of survey and administrative records data on employment and earnings for the same individuals across 12 sites participating in the national evaluation of JTPA found that average survey-reported earnings were higher than average earnings found using unemployment insurance wage records. However, program impact estimates using each of these data sources were usually comparable. See Kornfeld and Bloom 1999.

[8] The wage records code people who moved out of state as having zero earnings, although they may have worked in their new state. Similarly, the welfare records do not distinguish between people who received no welfare payments and people who moved out of state. If tenants in public housing are less likely to move in general than those in private housing, it would be plausible to hypothesize that there is less out-of-state migration among tenants of public housing. If this hypothesis is correct, then our data may somewhat underestimate the earnings differences between public housing residents and those in private housing (subsidized or unsubsidized). This is because out-of-state migrants who actually do have earnings are coded as having none. Conversely, our estimates would somewhat overestimate welfare receipt differences, because some in-state residents who are coded as having zero welfare payments may be receiving welfare from another state. Data from HUD indicate that in 1993, about 20 percent of the households in public housing and project-based Section 8 housing moved the year before, compared with 30 percent of those with Section 8 vouchers and certificates (McGough 1997).

labor market experiences) reported in this study between welfare recipients living in public housing and those living in Section 8 housing may be less sharp than if it were possible to distinguish between the two different types of Section 8 housing. In the United States as a whole in 1996, 66 percent of AFDC recipients who received Section 8 subsidies had tenant-based assistance; in Georgia, the rate was 59 percent (Khadduri, Shroder, and Steffen 2003).

It is also important to note that this study examines the effects of the type of housing that welfare recipients were living in at the time of random assignment on their subsequent employment and welfare outcomes. This is an advantage in attributing causality to type of housing and may produce different results than cross-sectional studies, where any relationship might be due to employment histories affecting housing or housing affecting employment histories. However, there is also a likelihood that some recipients moved during the follow-up period. If they changed to a different type of housing, this might reduce the size of the effects found in parts of this study. Unfortunately, no information on how long sample members lived in public or other types of housing was available.

Welfare Recipients in Public Housing: Less "Work Ready" and Less "Work Oriented"?

Examining the background characteristics of Atlanta welfare recipients reveals a clear, substantial pattern of differences. On a number of variables, recipients in public housing are found to be the most disadvantaged, those in unsubsidized private housing are the least disadvantaged, and those in subsidized private housing are in between.[9] For example, as the first panel of figure 3.1 shows, 82 percent of recipients in public housing (black bar) had not worked in the year before entering the study, while this was true for 76 percent of those in Section 8 housing (gray bar) and 63 percent of those in unsubsidized private housing (white bar). (These and almost all other differences in background characteristics across the three housing groups are statistically significant as shown in tables 3B.1 and 3B.2. All tables are found in appendix 3B.)

Similarly, the public housing group had the highest proportion of long-term welfare recipients (see the second panel of figure 3.1), the highest

---

[9] The analysis in this section combines the program and control groups in order to maximize the number of sample points. Because the focus here is on the characteristics of sample members *before* random assignment, the research groups do not differ systematically on those measures.

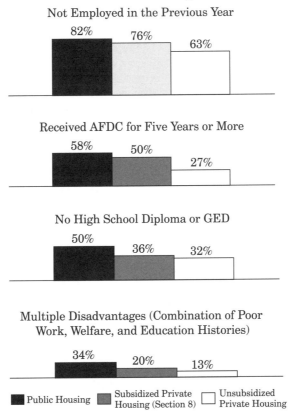

Figure 3.1. **Recipients' Employment, Welfare Receipt, and Education before Random Assignment**

Not Employed in the Previous Year

82% 76% 63%

Received AFDC for Five Years or More

58% 50% 27%

No High School Diploma or GED

50% 36% 32%

Multiple Disadvantages (Combination of Poor Work, Welfare, and Education Histories)

34% 20% 13%

■ Public Housing   ▨ Subsidized Private Housing (Section 8)   ☐ Unsubsidized Private Housing

Source: MDRC calculations from information routinely collected by welfare staff and from test data.

proportion of recipients lacking a high school diploma or General Equivalency Diploma (GED) (the third panel), and the highest proportion of multiply disadvantaged recipients (i.e., they did not work in the previous year *and* received welfare for more than the two previous years *and* did not have a diploma or GED) (the fourth panel). Recipients living in unsubsidized housing consistently had the smallest proportion of people with these characteristics. In addition, table 3B.1 shows that a higher proportion of recipients in public housing had larger families, grew up in AFDC households, and scored low on standardized reading and math tests administered by the welfare department at the time of entry into the study. (On some of these measures, recipients in Section 8 housing scored closer to those in public housing, but this varies greatly from measure to measure.)

In sum, compared with those living in unsubsidized private housing and, to a lesser extent, those living in Section 8 housing, residents of public housing in Atlanta have individual characteristics that can be expected to make it more difficult for them to secure and to retain employment. This evidence supports the view that they are a harder-to-employ group.

Some, but generally much smaller, differences are found across the three housing groups on variables from the Private Opinion Survey, which measured attitudinal, situational, and other barriers to employment, as figure 3.2 and table 3B.2 show. (However, given the large sample, most of the differences are statistically significant.) For example, slightly over two-thirds of public housing residents (68 percent) "agreed" or "agreed a lot" that "it is wrong to stay on welfare if you can get a job, even a job you don't like," a rate very close to the other two groups (67 percent for those in Section 8 housing and 73 percent for those in unsubsidized housing). There is only a 6 percentage point difference at most between the three groups in saying they "could not get a full-time or part-time job right now because of too many family problems." Transportation is more problematic, with 43 percent of public housing residents saying that they "could not go to school or a job training program right now" because they had "no way to get there every day," compared with slightly less than a third of the other two groups. Items or scales attempting to measure the strength of social support networks, depression, perceived personal efficacy, and recipients' selectivity about the jobs they would take reveal no major differences by type of housing. (See table 3B.2.) There was also little difference across groups on items attempting to measure their reservation wage.[10] Overall, these results do not make a case that public housing fosters an anti-work, pro-welfare environment for this sample.

Recipients in public housing are less optimistic about their prospects in the labor market. Fully 50 percent believe that "it will probably take them more than a year to get a full-time job and get off welfare," compared with 43 percent of those in Section 8 housing and 38 percent of those in unsubsidized housing (figure 3.2). Goodwin (1983) presents evidence suggesting that these types of expectations are important mediating variables that predict success in the job market.

---

[10] When asked to state the minimum amount of money per hour they would accept as a wage if someone offered them a full-time job with full medical benefits, from 82 percent to 84 percent of respondents in the three housing groups indicated that they would accept a job paying $7 or less. When the question referred to a full-time job with no medical benefits, from 56 percent to 58 percent indicated that they would accept such a job.

Figure 3.2. **Recipients' Work Attitudes and Expectations before Random Assignment**[a]

It is wrong to stay on welfare if you can get a job, even a job you don't like

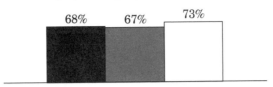

68%   67%   73%

Could not get a full- or part-time job right now because of too many family problems

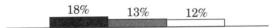

18%   13%   12%

Could not go to school or a job training program right now because they had no way to get there every day

43%   32%   30%

It will probably take more than a year to get a full-time job and get off welfare

50%   43%   38%

■ Public Housing   ■ Subsidized Private Housing (Section 8)   □ Unsubsidized Private Housing

Source: MDRC calculations from the Private Opinion Survey data.
[a] Sample members responded that they agreed or agreed a lot with the specified statement.

Effect of Housing Status on Success in the Labor Market

The finding that public housing welfare recipients in Atlanta appear to be more disadvantaged than their counterparts in other types of housing and that they have lower expectations of becoming self-sufficient suggest that they will rank lower on measures of subsequent employment and welfare receipt. This is what is observed.

Figure 3.3 presents findings on four key outcomes, with the control-group column in table 3B.3 (and in table 3B.4) providing data on additional measures. Unlike the foregoing analysis of recipients' background characteristics, this analysis includes only members of the control group and is intended to show the normal pattern of outcomes for each housing group in the absence of any special effort by the welfare department to require work or help recipients prepare for or look for it.

Estimates That Ignore Differences across the Three Housing Groups in Recipients' Background Characteristics

The graphs on the left-hand side of figure 3.3 present the control group's outcomes *before* statistically controlling for any differences in background characteristics among recipients in the different housing groups. In other words, they ignore the fact that recipients in public housing were a more disadvantaged, less job-ready group at the time of random assignment than those in the other housing groups.[11] Not surprisingly, the graphs show that over the following three years the public housing group had the poorest outcomes, while those living in unsubsidized private housing had the best ones. For example, only 58 percent of recipients living in public housing were ever employed during the follow-up period, compared with 72 percent of those living in unsubsidized housing. The average earnings of public housing residents (counting zero earnings for those never employed) were $3,290 lower ($4,965 versus $8,255), they accumulated $1,638 more in AFDC/TANF payments ($8,126 versus $6,488), and they were more likely (by 14 percentage points) to be on welfare at the end of the follow-up period (70 percent versus 56 percent). All of these differences are statistically significant.[12]

There is no support in these data for Ong's (1998) finding that Section 8 renters work more than members of the other housing groups do.[13] On all eight outcomes for the control group (see table 3B.4), Section 8

---

[11] The outcome estimates reported here are the control group means derived from separate ordinary least squares regression models used to estimate unconditional program impacts (discussed later in this chapter) for each housing group. See table 3B.5 for the models used when three-year earnings is the dependent variable.

[12] See table 3B.6 for the results of statistical significance tests applied to the differences between the groups on all outcome and impact measures.

[13] Possibly contributing to this difference across the two studies is the fact that in California, Section 8 renters on AFDC were more likely to receive tenant-based (rather than project-based) assistance than in Georgia (78 percent versus 59 percent, respectively, according to data presented in Khadduri, Shroder, and Steffen 2003).

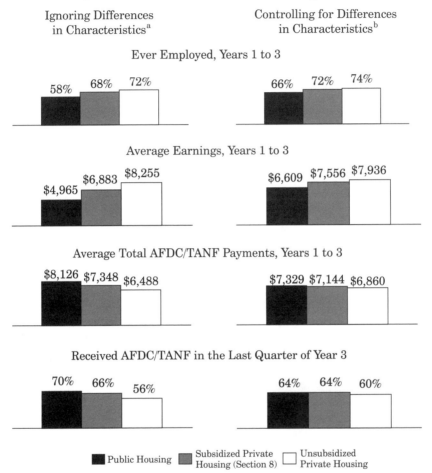

Figure 3.3. **Control Group's Employment and Welfare Outcomes within Three Years after Random Assignment**

Ignoring Differences in Characteristics[a]   Controlling for Differences in Characteristics[b]

Ever Employed, Years 1 to 3

58% 68% 72%   66% 72% 74%

Average Earnings, Years 1 to 3

$4,965 $6,883 $8,255 $6,609 $7,556 $7,936

Average Total AFDC/TANF Payments, Years 1 to 3

$8,126 $7,348 $6,488 $7,329 $7,144 $6,860

Received AFDC/TANF in the Last Quarter of Year 3

70% 66% 56%   64% 64% 60%

■ Public Housing ▨ Subsidized Private Housing (Section 8) ☐ Unsubsidized Private Housing

Sources: MDRC calculations from Georgia unemployment insurance earning records and AFDC records.
Note: See table 3B.6 for the statistical significance of the differences in outcomes between housing groups.
[a] Differences across the three housing groups in recipients' background characteristics are not controlled in making these estimates.
[b] These estimates reflect statistical adjustments to control for differences across the three housing groups in selected background characteristics of recipients.

renters fall between the other two groups, being closer to those in unsubsidized housing on some measures and closer to those in public housing on others.

Based on a large sample, a substantial follow-up period, and multiple outcome measures, the Atlanta findings provide strong evidence that welfare recipients living in public housing have poorer labor market outcomes than recipients in unsubsidized private housing and, to a lesser extent, than those living in Section 8 housing.

Estimates That Adjust for Differences across the Three Housing Groups in Recipients' Background Characteristics

The graphs on the right-hand side of figure 3.3 show the differences in outcomes for the control group by housing status *after* controlling for differences in the background characteristics among recipients in different types of housing.[14] This is an attempt to determine whether housing status per se influences labor market outcomes above and beyond any influence exerted by recipients' initial level of disadvantage or job readiness. By comparing the left and right column graphs for each outcome measure, one can see by how much, if at all, the differences in outcomes across the three housing groups are reduced by controlling for differences in the types of people in each group. If no substantial differences in outcomes remained across the groups after these statistical adjustments, it would suggest that the mere fact of living in public housing was not causing recipients to have worse labor market outcomes, but rather that recipients who have characteristics that lead to worse labor market outcomes were simply more likely to be living in public housing.

Figure 3.3 shows that controlling for a small set of background characteristics appears to explain much of the difference in outcomes by type of housing. For example, the original difference in average earnings between public housing recipients and those in unsubsidized housing had been $3,290; with background characteristics controlled, this difference is reduced by 60 percent to $1,327 ($7,936 minus $6,609), although the difference is still statistically significant. Reductions are also found on the other outcome variables.

After controlling for background variables, recipients living in Section 8 housing still fall between the other two groups. There is no indication that their employment rate or earnings are any higher than for welfare recipients living in unsubsidized housing.

---

[14] The control variables include age, race/ethnicity, marital status, number of children, age of youngest child, educational attainment, and a number of specifications of prior earnings, prior AFDC receipt, and prior food stamps receipt. Table 3B.7 presents the regression equation used to derive the control group means for three-year earnings after controlling for differences in these variables across housing groups.

The finding that some differences in earnings and other outcomes remain after controlling for important background characteristics suggests that not all of the differences are due to the types of people who live in particular types of residences. As an additional test, a broader set of variables, including the attitudinal, situational, and other variables from the Private Opinion Survey listed in table 3B.2 (those that produced statistically significant differences across the three housing groups), along with the demographic characteristics listed in footnote 14, were entered into a regression equation that had earnings as the dependent variable. This test reduced the difference in earnings between public housing and unsubsidized housing to the point where it was no longer statistically different from zero (data not presented).

From one perspective, these results lend weight to Reingold's conclusion that "the perception that public housing is contributing to high levels of unemployment and joblessness appears to be an illusion created by the concentration of human despair within many of these housing developments" (1997, 484). However, it is important to note that the lower ranking of public housing residents on some background variables at the time of random assignment may be a direct consequence of living in public housing *before* that point. If so, controlling for these characteristics might lead to underestimating the *total* effect of public housing. For example, if living in public housing partly explains why some residents had no high school diploma or GED certificate or had lower job expectations before they entered the study, then controlling for these factors would mask the earlier effect of public housing. Still, whatever disadvantages living in public housing might have imposed on recipients before random assignment, it had little *additional* negative effect on their subsequent earnings after controlling for differences in background characteristics across housing statuses.

Impacts of Atlanta's Welfare-to-Work Strategies

The next question to be addressed is whether mainstream welfare-to-work programs (programs not specifically targeted toward public or assisted housing residents) can help public housing residents. It may be that such programs are *less* effective for them simply because they are a harder-to-employ group, regardless of how they became that way.

The NEWWS tested two different program treatments at the Atlanta site (and other sites): a labor force attachment strategy, which emphasized quick entry into the labor force, and a human capital development strategy, which emphasized participation in education and training before people look for work in order to get a better job. In the former approach, recipients were typically directed into job club or job search activities as their first program assignment; those who did not find a job were then assigned to short-term education, training, or work experience activities. In the latter approach, recipients who did not have a high school diploma or GED (about 44 percent of the Atlanta sample overall) were usually assigned to longer-term remedial instruction in basic skills or preparation to take a GED examination, while others were directed toward vocational training programs or, to a lesser extent, college.[15]

Figure 3.4 shows the effects of both approaches separately. Each graph represents a program *impact*—that is, the *difference* between the outcomes for the program and control groups *within each housing status*.[16] (These "unconditional" estimates were made without statistically adjusting for differences across the housing groups in recipients' background characteristics.[17] For the full program and control group outcomes and impacts, and for impacts on additional outcome measures, see tables 3B.3 and 3B.4.)

A clear—and unexpected—pattern emerges from these data. For each outcome measure, the program impact is *larger* for recipients living in public housing than for the other two housing groups; this is true for both the labor force attachment and the human capital development approaches. For example, the impact of the labor force attachment program on average earnings for recipients in public housing (i.e., the treatment group–control group difference) was $2,115 over the three years of follow-up. The impact for recipients in unsubsidized private housing was less: $1,585. Thus, the impact was over 33 percent higher for the public housing group than for the unsubsidized housing group. The disparity is even greater for the human capital development approach, where the earnings impact for recipients living in public housing ($1,762) is more than twice that for recipients living in unsubsidized housing ($853, which is not a statistically significant program group–control group difference). (See table 3B.5.)

---

[15] For more detail on Atlanta's implementation of these two approaches, see Hamilton et al. 1997.

[16] Within each housing group, the estimated differences on outcome measures between the program and control groups may be subject to some uncertainty because various random factors might make those differences slightly positive or slightly negative even if there were no real differences caused by the program. To rule out chance, these outcome differences were tested statistically and were considered statistically significant if there was no more than a 10 percent probability that the measured differences could have been produced by chance and not as a result of the program.

[17] See table 3B.5 for the regression models used to estimate unconditional program impacts on three-year earnings for each of the three housing groups.

Figure 3.4. **Welfare-to-Work Program Impacts on Recipients' Employment and Welfare Outcomes**

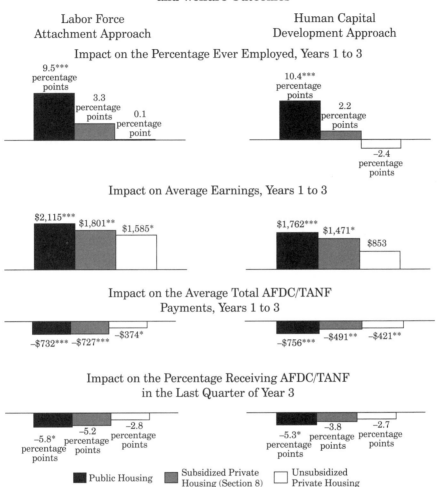

Labor Force
Attachment Approach

Human Capital
Development Approach

Impact on the Percentage Ever Employed, Years 1 to 3

9.5*** percentage points
3.3 percentage points
0.1 percentage point

10.4*** percentage points
2.2 percentage points
–2.4 percentage points

Impact on Average Earnings, Years 1 to 3

$2,115*** $1,801** $1,585*

$1,762*** $1,471* $853

Impact on the Average Total AFDC/TANF
Payments, Years 1 to 3

–$732*** –$727*** –$374*

–$756*** –$491** –$421**

Impact on the Percentage Receiving AFDC/TANF
in the Last Quarter of Year 3

–5.8* percentage points
–5.2 percentage points
–2.8 percentage points

–5.3* percentage points
–3.8 percentage points
–2.7 percentage points

■ Public Housing   ▨ Subsidized Private Housing (Section 8)   ☐ Unsubsidized Private Housing

Source: MDRC calculations from Georgia unemployment insurance earning records and AFDC records.
Notes: Rounding may cause slight discrepancies in calculating sums, averages, and differences. Impacts represent the difference between the outcomes of the program and control groups. Depending on the variable, impacts are represented either by percentage points or dollars. Positive impacts indicate that the program group's outcomes were higher than those of the control group, while negative impacts indicate the reverse. See table 3B.6 for the statistical significance of the differences in impacts between housing groups.
*$p = 0.1$. **$p = 0.05$. ***$p = 0.01$.

The impact on welfare payments and the likelihood of being on welfare at the end of the follow-up period are also larger for recipients living in public housing than for those in unsubsidized housing (figure 3.4).

The impact for recipients living in Section 8 housing generally falls between the other two groups, although the pattern varies depending on the outcome measure.

One way to summarize these data is to compare the number of statistically significant impacts that emerge for each housing group across the full range of outcome variables and across the two different treatment strategies. As shown in tables 3B.3 and 3B.4, out of 16 treatment group–control group comparisons for each housing group, there are 16 statistically significant impacts for residents of public housing, 10 for Section 8 renters, and only 3 for unsubsidized private renters. This pattern suggests that welfare-to-work programs, no matter what their emphasis, have a broader range of effects and larger effects on recipients living in public housing and, to a lesser extent, Section 8 housing than on those living in unsubsidized housing. When statistical significance tests are applied to the *differences* in impacts by housing status, the differences are significant in 4 of the 16 comparisons (those involving employment measures) between the public and unsubsidized housing groups (see table 3B.6, panel B, first and fourth columns). All other differences in impacts between these two groups, although not statistically significant (perhaps, in part, because of the relatively small sample size), are in the same direction: That is, they favor residents of public housing. This highly consistent pattern of results supports the conclusion that the variation in impacts by housing group is a true difference. (It is also worth noting that, overall, the results do not point to any clear advantage of the more intensive and higher-cost human capital development strategy over the labor force attachment approach. However, this conclusion could change with analyses of longer follow-up data; it might take longer for the human capital approach, with its longer up-front investment, to produce its full effects.)

What is driving these differences? Why should type of residence have a substantial, consistent effect on the impact of welfare-to-work programs? One possibility is that because welfare recipients in public housing are a more disadvantaged group, they have more to gain from the program's services and participation mandate. If this were the explanation, however, one would expect that controlling for differences across housing status in the work-relevant background characteristics of recipients would reduce the disparity in impacts. However, these "conditional" estimates (not presented here)[18] were virtually identical to the unconditional estimates presented in figure 3.4 and in tables 3B.3 and 3B.4.

---

[18] For conditional impacts, the regression equations include the background characteristics specified in table 3B.5, plus a set of terms that interact the research group dummy variables with three of the most important background factors: earnings in the previous year, AFDC payments in the previous year, and possession of a high school

A second possibility is that recipients living in public housing experience a more intensive welfare-to-work treatment than those living in other housing situations. An examination of participation rates in program activities (not shown here) offers inconsistent support for this hypothesis. According to recipient survey data, the impact of the labor force attachment program on participation in employment-related activities (particularly job search or job club) was larger for recipients living in public housing and Section 8 housing than for those living in unsubsidized private housing. However, this was not true for the human capital development approach, which had similar impacts on participation rates across the different housing groups but still produced a greater impact on employment for public housing residents.

Emerging Evidence from Other Locales

The types of people who live in public and Section 8 housing can vary greatly across cities, depending on the tightness of the private rental market, the supply and quality of public housing, the supply of vouchers, local rules and practices for selecting tenants for public and Section 8 housing, and other factors. The effects of welfare-to-work programs are also known to vary widely across states and localities. It is therefore important to ask whether the Atlanta findings are likely to represent a broader pattern. In this regard, it is helpful to consider emerging evidence from two other welfare-to-work evaluations conducted by MDRC.

One set of findings is from a study of a Columbus, OH, program, which, like the Atlanta program, was part of the NEWWS (Scrivener and Walter 2001). Data from that study were analyzed for this chapter. A second set of findings is from a state-sponsored evaluation of the Minnesota Family Investment Program (MFIP) (Miller et al. 2000). Both of these studies are large-scale random assignment evaluations.[19] The analysis by housing status in Minnesota is limited to longer-term welfare recipients (i.e., those who had received AFDC for at least two

---

diploma. (See table 3B.7.) Because the level of disadvantage among recipients differs by housing group and because the impacts of a welfare-to-work program might vary according to recipients' background characteristics, it is possible that any variation by housing group merely reflects the program's differential effectiveness for different types of people. Including the three interaction terms is an attempt to control for that possibility to estimate what the differences in impacts would be if the types of people in each housing group were similar.

[19] The data set for the Columbus study does not include the attitudinal and situational data available from the Private Opinion Survey, but most of the demographic variables and employment and welfare outcome data are the same. Minnesota's data are more similar to Atlanta's.

years before random assignment) who were living in urban areas, and the variable does not distinguish between recipients of public and Section 8 housing. Among sample members receiving any housing benefits, about 80 percent were in Section 8 housing, and the rest were in public housing (Miller 1998). Findings are currently available from analyses of follow-up data covering three years after random assignment in Atlanta and Columbus. In Minnesota, an in-depth analysis covers 18 months of follow-up (Miller 1998), but some three-year results are also available (Miller et al. 2000).

Both the Columbus and Minnesota studies reveal some patterns that are similar to and some patterns that contrast with the findings from the Atlanta study.

Columbus and Minnesota Recipients' Employment-Related Characteristics and Outcomes, by Housing Status

The analysis of pre–random assignment background characteristics of program and control group members suggests that, unlike the pattern in Atlanta, residents of Section 8 housing in Columbus are a somewhat more disadvantaged group than those in public or unsubsidized private housing, but the differences are not large or consistent across the range of available measures.[20] Moreover, the control group's average earnings over the follow-up period in Columbus differ less by housing status than in Atlanta.[21] Welfare payments do vary substantially by housing status in Columbus, but the Section 8 group has the highest payments.[22]

In the Minnesota study, while there are some differences in background characteristics and in the attitudes, problems, and situations measured by the Private Opinion Survey, the data do not consistently show recipients in the public/assisted housing group to be less job ready than those

---

[20] The Section 8 group had a higher proportion of people who had received welfare for five years or more (60 percent) than either the public housing or unsubsidized housing groups (42 percent and 39 percent, respectively). However, among all three groups, a similar proportion (41 percent to 43 percent) did not have a high school diploma or GED. The proportion of people who had not worked the year before entering the study was roughly the same for residents of public and Section 8 housing (78 and 80 percent, respectively), but lower (68 percent) for those in unsubsidized private housing.

[21] These ranged from $10,443 for the subsidized housing group to $11,207 for the unsubsidized housing group, a spread of only $764 over the three years after random assignment.

[22] These payments ranged from a low of $6,988 for the unsubsidized private housing group to a high of $8,533 for those in subsidized private housing, a difference of $1,545, which is close to the range observed in Atlanta.

in private unsubsidized housing. Also, among controls, the differences across these two housing groups in employment, earnings, and welfare outcomes over the follow-up period are neither consistent nor particularly large.[23]

These different patterns from Atlanta, Columbus, and Minnesota serve as a good warning not to assume that welfare recipients living in public housing are always a distinctly more difficult-to-employ group. This may be the case, as in Atlanta, but it apparently is not necessarily so. Similarly, recipients living in Section 8 housing may or may not be a systematically more disadvantaged group than those living in unsubsidized private housing. Even comparing just three studies, it is clear that the relationship between housing status and success in the labor market can vary substantially across cities and states, depending on local conditions.

Effects of the Columbus and Minnesota Welfare-to-Work Programs, by Housing Status

In Columbus, the larger NEWWS evaluation tested the effects of two different case management strategies. Under the traditional approach, income maintenance workers determined individuals' welfare eligibility, and other staff helped with employment-related services. By contrast, under the integrated approach, both sets of functions were assigned to the same staff member, who worked with smaller caseloads than staff using the traditional approach. Welfare recipients were randomly assigned to one of the two treatment groups (both of which emphasized human capital development) or to a control group that received no special employment services and faced no special requirements to prepare for or look for work.

When the results of the traditional case management approach are examined, the largest impacts are generally found for recipients living in public housing. For example, the three-year impact on average earnings for this group is a statistically significant $2,819, while it is –$20 for those in Section 8 housing and only $140 (and not statistically significant) for those in unsubsidized private housing. Statistically significant impacts on average welfare payments are found in all three

---

[23] For example (without controlling for differences across the groups in residents' background characteristics), recipients living in public/assisted housing were less likely than recipients living in unsubsidized housing to have been employed at all during the follow-up period (53 percent versus 62 percent), but had somewhat higher average earnings ($3,924 versus $3,780). They also received somewhat more in welfare payments ($10,563 versus $10,001) and were somewhat more likely to be on welfare in the last quarter of the follow-up period (82 percent versus 74 percent).

housing groups, but they are almost twice as large for recipients living in public housing as for those living in either Section 8 or unsubsidized private housing (these welfare reductions were $1,205, $629, and $607, respectively). The pattern of results for the integrated approach is similar. Thus, regardless of how case management was structured, the program was most effective during the three-year follow-up period for the public housing group.

The Minnesota study also tested two different treatments. One group was offered, among other things, an enhanced financial incentive to work through a higher earnings disregard, which allowed recipients to keep more of their welfare grant while working. The second group had access to the enhanced financial incentives, too, but "long-term recipients" (those who had received welfare for 24 of the preceding 36 months) were also required to look for work or participate in new work-preparation activities that were arranged and monitored by case managers who stressed the benefits of the new incentives as well. Welfare recipients were randomly assigned to one of these two groups or to a control group that had to abide by regular AFDC rules and had no participation mandate (but could access some employment services through the welfare department).[24]

The larger MFIP evaluation found that among long-term recipients living in urban areas at the time of random assignment, the largest impacts occurred for recipients assigned to the "full MFIP" research group, which combined incentives, services, case management, and a participation mandate. No statistically significant earnings effect was observed for the group receiving the enhanced incentives alone. Most important, for the full MFIP group, the impacts were largely concentrated among recipients living in public or Section 8 housing. While MFIP caused the average earnings of the public/subsidized housing group to increase by a statistically significant $2,041 during the 18-month follow-up period over what they would have been in the absence of the program, the impact on the earnings of recipients in unsubsidized private housing was only $426 and not statistically significant. MFIP's impact on welfare payments differed little by housing status (the program *increased* welfare payments during this period, which was a direct consequence of its enhanced financial work incentives).

Miller (1998) used a conditional regression analysis to test whether the program's impacts varied by housing status because of differences in the kinds of recipients living in public/subsidized and unsubsidized housing. Controlling for a variety of background characteristics barely changed the differences.

---

[24] The larger MFIP evaluation includes a third treatment group, but this group was not included in the housing analysis. See Miller et al. 1997.

Longer-term findings from the MFIP evaluation more recently became available and show a similar pattern of results. For example, among the urban long-term recipients in the public/subsidized housing subgroup, the full MFIP treatment increased average quarterly earnings in the third follow-up year by $304 relative to the earnings of comparable members of the control group (a statistically significant difference). By contrast, the impact on the unsubsidized private housing group was only $23. (See Miller et al. 2000.)

Taken together, the findings from the Atlanta, Columbus, and Minnesota studies point to an important and consistent result: All three mainstream welfare-to-work programs had their largest, most consistent employment and earnings impacts on welfare recipients who lived in public or Section 8 housing. The impact was smallest—and sometimes almost entirely absent—for recipients in unsubsidized private housing. While these three studies each tested different welfare-to-work strategies, they all yield the same general result. At the very least, these findings underscore the importance of examining the relative effects of welfare-to-work programs by housing status and the importance of research to try to understand what might be causing these consistent differences in impacts.

Limitations of Mainstream Welfare-to-Work Programs for Transforming Public Housing

Even though Atlanta's two welfare-to-work strategies had important positive effects on employment and welfare outcomes, it is important to understand that, like most such programs, overall effects were modest and left many recipients without sustained work, with low incomes, and still relying on welfare. Figure 3.5 and tables 3B.3 and 3B.4 show various outcomes for program group members. Despite the positive effects of these program strategies, almost a third of the welfare recipients living in public housing were never employed during the three-year follow-up period, a rate close to that of the other housing groups. Even more troubling, only about 40 to 46 percent of recipients in each housing group (and across the two program treatments) were working in the last quarter of the follow-up period, and still fewer (24 to 28 percent) worked in all four quarters of the third follow-up year (figure 3.5). In other words, sustained, steady employment was the exception, not the norm. At least half and usually more of the recipients in all groups were receiving AFDC/TANF in the last quarter of year 3 (figure 3.5).[25]

---

[25] Data from Columbus and Minnesota similarly point to the difficulty of achieving stable employment.

Figure 3.5. **Program Group's Employment Stability, Earnings, and Welfare Receipt within Three Years after Random Assignment**

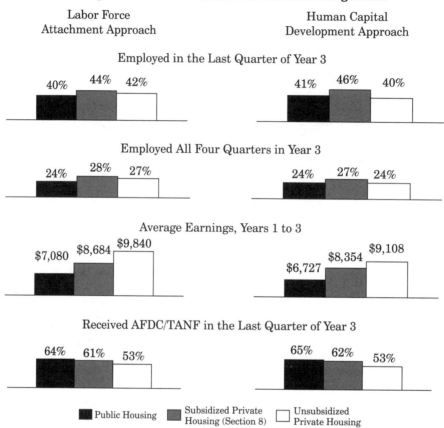

Source: MDRC calculations from Georgia unemployment insurance earning records and AFDC records.

Note: See table 3B.6 for the statistical significance of the differences in outcomes between housing groups.

If an important policy goal is to transform public housing developments from communities where many welfare recipients do not work steadily to places where many do, even relatively effective mainstream welfare-to-work programs fall far short. While there was a greater impact on recipients in public housing in Atlanta, it brought these recipients roughly up to the employment levels in the other housing groups, but steady employment in all three groups was still low. Thus, the findings point to the need to find more powerful ways to increase sustained employment.[26]

---

[26] The Jobs-Plus Community Revitalization Initiative for Public Housing Families, a research demonstration project in seven cities, is testing a new approach to increase steady employment among residents of public housing developments. The strategy

Conclusion

The major findings of the Atlanta data are:

1. Welfare recipients who live in public housing or, to a lesser extent, subsidized private housing have background characteristics and situations that make it more difficult for them to secure and retain jobs.

2. Type of housing is associated with subsequent labor market behavior and welfare receipt, but when background factors are controlled, these relationships are greatly diminished.

3. Mainstream welfare-to-work programs are more effective for public housing residents and least effective for those living in unsubsidized private housing, even when differences in background factors are controlled.

In addition, data from two other welfare-to-work evaluations—in Columbus, OH, and in urban areas of Minnesota—add detail to these findings. First, there is considerable variation across the study sites in whether recipients in public or Section 8 housing are more or less disadvantaged than those in unsubsidized housing in terms of their background characteristics and circumstances. Second, despite the fact that these studies were testing different types of welfare-to-work programs in different locations, they consistently show that the impact of the programs is smallest (and sometimes negligible) for recipients living in unsubsidized housing; both the Atlanta and Columbus data (which distinguish between public and Section 8 housing as well as unsubsidized private housing) show that the impact is greatest for those in public housing.

These findings suggest important questions about how welfare-to-work programs are working and how they might be improved. For example, if the success of these programs in some cities were concentrated among recipients who live in public housing, this would limit the chances of widespread effects, since most welfare recipients do not receive housing assistance. At the very least, the findings point to the need for a much better understanding of *why* program effects vary by housing status. It is also important to consider how program treatments might be adapted for recipients in different types of housing in order to increase a program's overall effectiveness.

---

combines the use of employment and training services, enhanced financial incentives to work, and new social supports for work targeted toward all working-age residents in these developments. See Riccio 1999.

Finally, it is important to emphasize that while mainstream welfare-to-work programs in some cities are more effective for public housing residents than for other housing groups, the Atlanta data show that these programs brought the public housing group's employment rates and average earnings only up to the levels of the other groups. Steady employment among all groups was still low, highlighting a difficult problem for which further program innovation is warranted, regardless of the housing status of welfare recipients.

Appendix 3A

Measuring Housing Status

Before random assignment, orientation staff completed a client characteristics form based on one-on-one interviews with each welfare applicant and recipient referred to Fulton County's welfare-to-work program. Included on the form was the following item: "What is your current housing status?" The possible responses were "public housing," "subsidized housing," "emergency/temporary shelter," and "none of the above." Very few reported living in emergency housing (1.1 percent of the sample of persons randomly assigned in the evaluation), and they are excluded from the analysis. About a third (32.1 percent) reported living in public housing, and 21.6 percent said they lived in subsidized housing; 45.2 percent chose "none of the above" and are assumed to have been living in unsubsidized private housing.

Because housing information is key to this analysis and comes from self-reports, the accuracy of these data needs to be considered. Shroder and Martin (1996) have reported that a substantial number of respondents in the American Housing Survey misreported their housing status when asked whether they were living in private, public, or other subsidized housing. In the present study, sample members' self-reports should be more accurate for two reasons. First, the sample is limited to a welfare population, which is likely to be more aware of major government benefit programs that might apply to people like them. Second, the information was not obtained from a self-administered questionnaire but from a program intake interview during which welfare staff could help respondents who did not understand the categories.

Two partial tests of the validity of this housing item for the Atlanta sample were conducted. The first involves a stratified random subsample of Atlanta recipients who were interviewed in their homes two years after random assignment. In the interview, respondents were asked a similar question about their type of housing. After the interview, the interviewer was asked whether or not the respondent lived in public housing. Thus, the respondent's own characterization of her housing can be compared with the interviewer's characterization. Where respondents reported living in public housing, interviewers agreed in 92 percent of the cases; where recipients did not report a public housing residence, interviewers agreed in 95 percent of the cases.

A second test comes from the home addresses that respondents supplied during their intake interview. For a subsample of respondents who said they lived in public housing, telephone calls to staff in several of the PHAs in Fulton County verified that these addresses were indeed public housing properties.

These two results suggest that answers about public housing projects are substantially correct. It is still possible that some respondents confused subsidized private housing and unsubsidized private housing, although this would seem to be a less likely mistake.

Appendix 3B

Supplementary Tables

Table 3B.1 **Selected Characteristics of the Atlanta Sample before Random Assignment**

Characteristic at Baseline	Public Housing	Subsidized Private Housing (Section 8)	Unsubsidized Private Housing
African American (%)	97.8	97.5	91.3 ***
Average age (years)	32.6	32.3	33.1 ***
Never married (%)	65.0	65.7	53.0 ***
Has three or more children (%)	38.4	26.3	24.4 ***
Currently employed (%)	5.2	7.2	9.4 ***
Not employed in the previous year (%)	81.6	75.9	62.6 ***
Never worked full-time for one employer for 6 months or more (%)	37.4	25.2	21.2 ***
In first spell of AFDC receipt (%)	3.9	4.6	14.4 ***
Received AFDC for 5 years or more (%)[a]	58.0	50.0	27.0 ***
Received AFDC for 10 years or more (%)	32.0	22.0	13.0 ***
Raised as a child in a household receiving AFDC (%)	32.6	27.9	20.4 ***
Low reading test score (%)	65.4	54.8	45.6 ***
Low mathematics test score (%)	71.2	63.1	52.5 ***
No high school diploma or GED[b] (%)	50.0	36.0	32.0 ***
Any current or recent education and training (%)	12.7	19.8	15.6 ***
Multiple disadvantages (prior employment, welfare, and education)[c] (%)	33.9	20.2	13.2 ***
Moved in the past 2 years (%)	49.0	55.7	66.1 ***
Sample size	1,886	1,329	2,454

Source: MDRC calculations from information routinely collected by welfare staff and from test data.

Note: Residents living in temporary or emergency housing are excluded from the sample.

[a] This refers to the total number of months accumulated from one or more spells on an individual's own or spouse's AFDC case. It does not include AFDC receipt under a parent's name.

[b] This credential is given to those who pass the GED test and is intended to signify knowledge of high school subjects.

[c] This category refers to people who did not work in the year before random assignment, had received welfare for longer than the two previous years, and did not have a high school diploma or GED.

*p = 0.1. **p = 0.05. ***p = 0.01.

Fannie Mae Foundation

Table 3B.2. **Attitudes and Situational Problems of the Atlanta Sample before Random Assignment**

Attitude or Situation at Baseline	Public Housing (%)	Subsidized Private Housing (Section 8) (%)	Unsubsidized Private Housing (%)
Weak social support network	20.3	19.0	21.1
High score on the depression scale	11.1	12.4	13.6 *
Low score on the efficacy scale	28.3	21.1	21.4 ***
Reported health and emotional barriers (self or family member)	29.4	23.1	20.9 ***
Agreed or agreed a lot that they could not go to school or a job training program right now because they had:			
No way to get there every day	42.7	31.6	30.1 ***
Too many family problems	30.4	22.7	24.2 ***
Reported family problems as a barrier to JOBS participation and working	14.3	10.0	8.7 ***
Agreed or agreed a lot that they could not get a job right now because they had too many family problems for full- or part-time work	18.0	13.2	11.7 ***
Agreed or agreed a lot that it will probably take them more than a year to get a full-time job and get off welfare	50.2	42.9	37.5 ***
If they had a choice, would prefer to work			
Part-time	23.5	21.6	14.4 ***
Full-time	76.6	78.4	85.7 ***
Selective attitude about taking jobs	31.6	34.4	29.0 ***
Agreed or agreed a lot that			
It is unfair to make people on welfare get a job if they don't want to	16.2	11.6	10.4 ***
It is wrong to stay on welfare if you can get a job, even a job you don't like	68.0	66.7	72.7 ***
Sample size	1,886	1,329	2,454[a]

Source: MDRC calculations from the Private Opinion Survey data.
Note: Residents living in emergency or temporary housing are excluded from the sample.
[a]Public Opinion Survey data were not collected for 726 sample members, in many cases because intake into the study sample started before this instrument began to be used.
p = 0.1. **p* = 0.05. ****p* = 0.01.

Table 3B.3. **JOBS Atlanta Three-Year Impacts of the Labor Force Attachment Approach (LFA) by Housing Status**

Outcome	LFA Group	Control Group	Difference (Impact)	Percent Change
Public Housing				
Ever employed, years 1 to 3 (%)	67.5	58.0	9.5***	16.41
Employed all four quarters of year 3 (%)	23.5	18.2	5.3**	29.24
Employed in the last quarter of year 3 (%)	39.6	34.4	5.2*	15.1
Average quarters employed, years 1 to 3	4.00	3.02	0.98***	32.41
Average earnings, years 1 to 3	$7,080	$4,965	$2,115***	42.59
Received AFDC/TANF in the last quarter of year 3 (%)	64.3	70.1	−5.8*	−8.27
Average number of months receiving AFDC/TANF, years 1 to 3	26.87	29.07	−2.21***	−7.59
Average total AFDC/TANF payments, years 1 to 3	$7,394	$8,126	−$732***	−9.01
Sample size (total = 921)	477	444		
Subsidized Private Housing (Section 8)				
Ever employed, years 1 to 3 (%)	71.0	67.7	3.3	4.86
Employed all four quarters of year 3 (%)	28.4	21.6	6.9**	31.83
Employed in the last quarter of year 3 (%)	43.5	37.0	6.5*	17.63
Average quarters employed, years 1 to 3	4.50	3.75	0.74**	19.8
Average earnings, years 1 to 3	$8,684	$6,883	$1,801**	26.16
Received AFDC/TANF in the last quarter of year 3 (%)	60.8	66.0	−5.2	−7.85
Average number of months receiving AFDC/TANF, years 1 to 3	25.59	27.93	−2.34***	−8.38
Average total AFDC/TANF payments, years 1 to 3	$6,621	$7,348	−$727***	−9.89
Sample size (total = 629)	317	312		
Unsubsidized Private Housing				
Ever employed, years 1 to 3 (%)	71.8	71.8	0.1	0.08
Employed all four quarters of year 3 (%)	27.2	24.4	2.8	11.41
Employed in the last quarter of year 3 (%)	42.0	38.8	3.2	8.14
Average quarters employed, years 1 to 3	4.52	4.38	0.14	3.2
Average earnings, years 1 to 3	$9,840	$8,255	$1,585*	19.2
Received AFDC/TANF in the last quarter of year 3 (%)	53.1	55.9	−2.8	−5.03
Average number of months receiving AFDC/TANF, years 1 to 3	23.81	24.65	−0.84	−3.42
Average total AFDC/TANF payments, years 1 to 3	$6,114	$6,488	−$374*	−5.77
Sample size (total = 868)	395	473		

Source: MDRC calculations from Georgia unemployment insurance earning records and AFDC records.
Notes: Samples for impact analyses consist of individuals who were randomly assigned from January 1992 to March 1993. Dollar averages include zero values for sample members not employed or not receiving welfare. Estimates are regression adjusted using ordinary least squares, controlling for pre–random assignment characteristics of sample members. Rounding may cause slight discrepancies in calculating sums and differences. A two-tailed *t*-test was applied to differences between experimental and control groups.
Percent Change equals Difference divided by Control Group and multiplied by 100.
*p = 0.1. **p = 0.05. ***p = 0.01.

Table 3B.4. **JOBS Atlanta Three-Year Impacts of the Human Capital Development Approach (HCD) by Housing Status**

Outcome	HCD Group	Control Group	Difference (Impact)	Percent Change
Public Housing				
Ever employed, years 1 to 3 (%)	68.4	58.0	10.4***	17.97
Employed all four quarters of year 3 (%)	23.9	18.2	5.6**	30.92
Employed in the last quarter of year 3 (%)	40.9	34.4	6.5**	18.94
Average quarters employed, years 1 to 3	3.86	3.02	0.83***	27.52
Average earnings, years 1 to 3	$6,727	$4,965	$1,762***	35.48
Received AFDC/TANF in the last quarter of year 3 (%)	64.8	70.1	–5.3*	–7.56
Average number of months receiving AFDC/TANF, years 1 to 3	27.43	29.07	–1.64**	–5.64
Average total AFDC/TANF payments, years 1 to 3	$7,370	$8,126	–$756***	–9.3
Sample size (total = 921)	477	444		
Subsidized Private Housing (Section 8)				
Ever employed, years 1 to 3 (%)	69.9	67.7	2.2	3.26
Employed all four quarters of year 3 (%)	27.2	21.6	5.6*	26.17
Employed in the last quarter of year 3 (%)	45.9	37.0	8.9**	24.16
Average quarters employed, years 1 to 3	4.25	3.75	0.49	13.12
Average earnings, years 1 to 3	$8,354	$6,883	$1,471*	21.37
Received AFDC/TANF in the last quarter of year 3 (%)	62.3	66.0	–3.8	–5.7
Average number of months receiving AFDC/TANF, years 1 to 3	26.67	27.93	–1.26	–4.51
Average total AFDC/TANF payments, years 1 to 3	$6,857	$7,348	–$491**	–6.68
Sample size (total = 619)	307	312		
Unsubsidized Private Housing				
Ever employed, years 1 to 3 (%)	69.4	71.8	–2.4	–3.29
Employed all four quarters of year 3 (%)	24.2	24.4	–0.2	–0.85
Employed in the last quarter of year 3 (%)	40.2	38.8	1.4	3.51
Average quarters employed, years 1 to 3	4.48	4.38	0.10	2.22
Average earnings, years 1 to 3	$9,108	$8,255	$853	10.33
Received AFDC/TANF in the last quarter of year 3 (%)	53.2	55.9	–2.7	–4.88
Average number of months receiving AFDC/TANF, years 1 to 3	23.69	24.65	–0.96	–3.88
Average total AFDC/TANF payments, years 1 to 3	$6,067	$6,488	–$421**	–6.5
Sample size (total = 905)	432	473		

Source: MDRC calculations from Georgia unemployment insurance earning records and AFDC records.

Notes: Samples for impact analyses consist of individuals who were randomly assigned from January 1992 to March 1993. Dollar averages include zero values for sample members not employed or not receiving welfare. Estimates are regression adjusted using ordinary least squares, controlling for pre–random assignment characteristics of sample members. Rounding may cause slight discrepancies in calculating sums and differences. A two-tailed *t*-test was applied to differences between experimental and control groups.

Percent Change equals Difference divided by Control Group and multiplied by 100.

*$p = 0.1$. **$p = 0.05$. ***$p = 0.01$.

Table 3B.5. **Estimated Regression Coefficients for Three-Year Earnings Impacts in Atlanta (Unconditional Estimates)**

Regressor or Statistic	Public Housing	Subsidized Private Housing (Section 8)	Unsubsidized Private Housing
Human Capital	1761.645 ***	1470.964 *	852.864
Development group	(596.309)	(849.142)	(832.597)
Labor Force Attachment	2114.519 ***	1800.561 **	1584.950 *
group	(598.218)	(842.886)	(853.519)
Employed in the previous	2006.612 **	520.127	1619.576
year	(821.112)	(1154.389)	(1126.718)
Employed before quarter 1	−634.930	1871.505	−390.362
	(1184.229)	(1517.705)	(1377.862)
Previous year's earnings	0.701 **	0.629	0.856 **
	(0.314)	(0.401)	(0.397)
Previous year's earnings	−0.000 ***	0.000 ***	−0.000
squared	(0.000)	(0.000)	(0.000)
Earnings before quarter 1	6.331 ***	2.236 *	4.540 ***
	(0.949)	(1.171)	(0.908)
Received AFDC before	7153.257 *	−3908.284	2191.522
quarter 1	(4156.468)	(4128.238)	(4778.106)
Received AFDC in the	−2886.220	15280.000 ***	5551.940
previous year	(4997.344)	(5829.509)	(5693.165)
Average AFDC per month	−4.334	−14.507	−7.768
received	(6.228)	(9.557)	(8.567)
Number of months receiving	−263.106	−261.003	−396.859 ***
AFDC in the previous year	(163.760)	(195.104)	(153.242)
Single parent ever married or	828.904	2267.138 ***	830.680
married and living with	(556.649)	(782.101)	(763.101)
spouse			
Has two children	509.070	1448.143	308.312
	(662.905)	(889.396)	(877.053)
Has three or more children	−76.324	2451.394 *	1226.485
	(885.360)	(1258.049)	(1235.872)
Has any children 0 to	−470.480	653.360	−298.499
5 years old	(539.518)	(779.575)	(778.287)
White	−948.724	6959.819	−201.725
	(9314.173)	(6790.010)	(4912.807)
Black	17.262	6076.865	−376.040
	(9066.510)	(6149.606)	(4764.565)
Hispanic	1955.386	4198.197	3521.916
	(9692.647)	(6901.264)	(6066.551)
Asian/Pacific Islander	−738.735	—	−5253.056
	(10476.374)	—	(8689.669)
Age at random assignment	−162.724 ***	−206.938	−47.098
	(41.631)	(63.612)	(59.136)
Female	2274.453	−861.291	2723.689
	(1800.289)	(2629.696)	(1608.009)
Received high school	2901.099 ***	3553.488 ***	4219.488 ***
diploma or GED	(494.257)	(713.171)	(752.892)
Intercept	9362.999	−2112.890	88.539
	(9698.696)	(7669.877)	(5827.706)
R square	0.2133	0.3008	0.1719
F statistic	16.944	18.723	12.047
Sample size (total = 3,634)	1,398	936	1,300

Source: MDRC calculations using Atlanta data collected as part of the NEWWS. See tables 3B.1, 3B.3, and 3B.4.

Note: A two-tailed *t*-test was applied to each coefficient estimate.
*$p = 0.1$. **$p = 0.05$. ***$p = 0.01$.

Table 3B.6. **Statistical Significance of the Differences in Outcomes and Impacts across Housing Groups**

A. Comparison of Outcomes (Ignoring Differences in Characteristic across Housing Groups)

Variable	Control Group			Labor Force Attachment Group			Human Capital Development Group		
	Public vs. Unsubsidized Housing	Public vs. Section 8 Housing	Section 8 vs. Unsubsidized Housing	Public vs. Unsubsidized Housing	Public vs. Section 8 Housing	Section 8 vs. Unsubsidized Housing	Public vs. Unsubsidized Housing	Public vs. Section 8 Housing	Section 8 vs. Unsubsidized Housing
Ever employed, years 1 to 3 (%)	***	***	ns	ns	ns	ns	ns	ns	ns
Employed all four quarters of year 3 (%)	**	ns	ns	ns	ns	ns	ns	ns	ns
Employed in the last quarter of year 3 (%)	ns	ns	ns	ns	ns	ns	ns	ns	*
Average quarters employed, years 1 to 3	***	***	**	**	*	ns	***	ns	ns
Average earnings, years 1 to 3 ($)	***	***	*	***	**	ns	***	**	ns
Received AFDC/TANF in the last quarter of year 3 (%)	***	ns	***	***	ns	**	***	ns	***
Average number of months receiving AFDC/TANF, years 1 to 3	***	ns	***	***	*	**	***	ns	***
Average total AFDC/TANF payments, years 1 to 3	***	***	***	***	***	**	***	**	***

Table 3B.6. **Statistical Significance of the Differences in Outcomes and Impacts across Housing Groups** *(continued)*

B. Comparison of Impacts (Unconditional Estimates)

Variable	Labor Force Attachment Group			Human Capital Development Group		
	Public vs. Unsubsidized Housing	Public vs. Section 8 Housing	Section 8 vs. Unsubsidized Housing	Public vs. Unsubsidized Housing	Public vs. Section 8 Housing	Section 8 vs. Unsubsidized Housing
Ever employed, years 1 to 3 (%)	**	ns	ns	***	*	ns
Employed all four quarters of year 3 (%)	ns	ns	ns	ns	ns	ns
Employed in the last quarter of year 3 (%)	ns	ns	ns	ns	ns	ns
Average quarters employed, years 1 to 3	**	ns	ns	**	ns	ns
Average earnings, years 1 to 3 ($)	ns	ns	ns	ns	ns	ns
Received AFDC/TANF in the last quarter of year 3 (%)	ns	ns	ns	ns	ns	ns
Average number of months receiving AFDC/TANF, years 1 to 3	ns	ns	ns	ns	ns	ns
Average total AFDC/TANF payments, years 1 to 3	ns	ns	ns	ns	ns	ns

Source: MDRC calculations from Georgia unemployment insurance earning records and AFDC records.
Note: A means difference test was applied to differences between outcomes and impacts.
*p = 0.1. **p = 0.05. ***p = 0.01. ns = not significant.

Table 3B.7. **Estimated Unstandardized Regression Coefficients Used to Derive Three-Year Earnings Impacts in Atlanta (Conditional Estimates[a])**

Regressor or Statistic	Estimates[b]
HCDs in public housing	−1276.272
	(1825.056)
HCDs in subsidized private housing	−1542.703
	(1828.206)
HCDs in unsubsidized private housing	−2105.618
	(1649.698)
LFAs in public housing	−1199.187
	(1738.026)
LFAs in subsidized private housing	−1567.304
	(1747.000)
LFAs in unsubsidized private housing	−2016.198
	(1602.539)
Section 8—subsidized housing	947.127
	(801.944)
Private unsubsidized housing	1327.731*
	(742.304)
HCDs by earnings in the previous year	0.374
	(0.254)
HCDs by total AFDC received during the previous year	0.680
	(0.479)
HCDs with a high school diploma	1313.880
	(899.397)
LFAs by earnings in the previous year	0.810***
	(0.182)
LFAs by total AFDC received during the previous year	0.667
	(0.460)
LFAs with a high school diploma	1687.833*
	(902.526)
Employed in the previous year	1314.957**
	(586.100)
Employed before quarter 1	576.764
	(782.734)
Previous year's earnings squared	0.000
	(0.000)
Earnings before quarter 1	4.183***
	(0.553)
Received AFDC before quarter 1	1183.195
	(2531.363)
Received AFDC in the previous year	4423.788
	(2958.873)
Number of months received AFDC in the previous year	−56.217
	(178.921)

Table 3B.7. **Estimated Unstandardized Regression Coefficients Used to Derive Three-Year Earnings Impacts in Atlanta (Conditional Estimates[a])** *(continued)*

Regressor or Statistic	Estimates[b]
Received food stamps in the previous year	−1302.953
	(2141.428)
Average food stamps per month received	3.858
	(3.641)
Number of months received food stamps in the previous year	94.239
	(111.934)
Previous year's earnings	0.311
	(0.228)
AFDC in the previous year	−1.629***
	(0.545)
Received high school diploma or GED	2513.476***
	(637.033)
Single parent ever married or married living with spouse	1158.483***
	(403.265)
Has two children	658.583
	(484.388)
Has three or more children	984.961
	(711.548)
Any child 0 to 5 years old	−112.403
	(400.725)
Black	208.059
	(999.980)
Not black or white	345.175
	(−1869.336)
Age at random assignment	−130.267***
	(−31.22)
Female	704.468
	(−1064.002)
Intercept	4532.720
	(3003.373)
R square	0.2141
F statistic	28.003
Sample size	3,634

Sources: MDRC calculations using Atlanta data collected as part of the NEWWS. See tables 3B.1, 3B.3, and 3B.4.

Notes: HCD refers to the human capital development group. LFA refers to the labor force attachment group.

[a] This model is used to derive estimates of the control group's outcomes and the program's impacts after adjusting for differences in selected background characteristics across housing groups.

[b] It should be noted that the coefficients for the first six variables do not by themselves indicate the conditional program impacts for the individuals in each group; these require additional calculations to be derived from this equation. However, the difference in the coefficients between any two housing groups within each treatment stream (e.g., between HCDs in public housing versus HCDs in subsidized private housing) reflects the difference in conditional impacts between each group.

*$p = 0.1$. **$p = 0.05$. ***$p = 0.01$.

Authors

James A. Riccio is a Senior Fellow at the Manpower Demonstration Research Corporation. Alan Orenstein is a consultant.

The authors are grateful to the following people for assistance on various parts of this chapter: Susan Bloom, Jevon Nicholson, Electra Taylor, Seble Tareke, Cynthia Miller, and the late Daniel Friedlander. We would also like to thank Howard Bloom, Amy S. Bogdon, Jeffrey M. Lubell, Anu Rangarajan, Barbara Sard, and two anonymous reviewers for helpful comments on earlier drafts. Funding for the study was provided by the Fannie Mae Foundation, with additional support from the Jobs-Plus Community Revitalization Initiative for Public Housing Families, a demonstration research project sponsored by the Rockefeller Foundation, the U.S. Department of Housing and Urban Development, the U.S. Department of Health and Human Services, the U.S. Department of Labor, the James Irvine Foundation, the Joyce Foundation, the Northwest Area Foundation, the Surdna Foundation, and the Anne E. Casey Foundation.

References

Abramson, Alan J., Mitchell S. Tobin, and Matthew R. VanderGoot. 1995. The Changing Geography of Metropolitan Opportunity: The Segregation of the Poor in U.S. Metropolitan Areas, 1970 to 1990. *Housing Policy Debate* 6(1):45–72.

Bloom, Howard S., Larry L. Orr, George Cave, Stephen H. Bell, and Fred Doolittle. 1993. *The JTPA Study: Title II–A Impacts on Earnings and Employment at 18 Months*. Research and Evaluation Report, Series 93–C. Washington, DC: U.S. Department of Labor, Employment and Training Administration.

Briggs, Xavier de Souza. 1998. Brown Kids in White Suburbs: Housing Mobility and the Many Faces of Social Capital. *Housing Policy Debate* 9(1):177–221.

Brooks-Gunn, Jeanne, Greg J. Duncan, and J. Lawrence Aber, eds. 1997. *Neighborhood Poverty. Vol. II: Policy Implications in Studying Neighborhoods*. New York: Russell Sage Foundation.

Currie, Janet, and Arron Yelowitz. 1998. Public Housing and Labor Supply. Working Paper No. 8. Joint Center for Poverty Research.

Dickens, William T. 1999. Rebuilding Urban Labor Markets: What Community Development Can Accomplish. In *Urban Problems and Community Development*, ed. Ronald F. Ferguson and William T. Dickens, 381–435. Washington, DC: Brookings Institution Press.

Ellen, Ingrid Gould, and Margery Austin Turner. 1997. Does Neighborhood Matter? Assessing Recent Evidence. *Housing Policy Debate* 8(4):833–66.

Galster, George C., and Sean P. Killen. 1995. The Geography of Metropolitan Opportunity: A Reconnaissance and Conceptual Framework. *Housing Policy Debate* 6(1):7–43.

Goodwin, Leonard. 1983. *Causes and Cures of Welfare: New Evidence on the Social Psychology of the Poor*. Lexington, MA: Lexington Books.

Hamilton, Gayle, Thomas Brock, Mary Farrell, Daniel Friedlander, and Kristen Harknett. 1997. *National Evaluation of Welfare-to-Work Strategies: Evaluating Two Welfare-to-Work Program Approaches; Two-Year Findings on the Labor Force Attachment and Human Capital Development Programs in Three Sites*. Washington, DC: U.S. Department of Health and Human Services, Administration for Children and Families and Office of the Assistant Secretary for Planning and Evaluation; and U.S. Department of Education, Office of the Under Secretary and Office of Vocational and Adult Education.

Ihlanfeldt, Keith R., and David L. Sjoquist. 1998. The Spatial Mismatch Hypothesis: A Review of Recent Studies and Their Implications for Welfare Reform. *Housing Policy Debate* 9(4):848–92.

Jargowsky, Paul A. 1997. *Poverty and Place: Ghettos, Barrios, and the American City*. New York: Russell Sage Foundation.

Kain, John F. 1992. The Spatial Mismatch Hypothesis: Three Decades Later. *Housing Policy Debate* 3(2):371–460.

Khadduri, Jill, Mark Shroder, and Barry Steffen. 2003. Can Housing Assistance Support Welfare Reform? In *A Place to Live, a Means to Work: How Housing Assistance Can Strengthen Welfare Policy*, ed. Barbara Sard and Amy S. Bogdon, 23–62. Washington, DC: Fannie Mae Foundation.

Kingsley, G. Thomas, Joseph B. McNeely, and James O. Gibson. 1997. *Community Building: Coming of Age*. Washington, DC: Development Training Institute, Inc., and Urban Institute.

Kornfeld, Robert, and Howard S. Bloom. 1999. Measuring Program Impacts on Earnings and Employment: Do Unemployment Insurance Wage Reports from Employers Agree with Surveys of Individuals? *Journal of Labor Economics* 17(1):168–97.

Massey, Douglas S., and Nancy A. Denton. 1993. *American Apartheid: Segregation and the Making of the Underclass*. Cambridge, MA: Harvard University Press.

McGough, Duane T. 1997. *Characteristics of HUD-Assisted Renters and Their Units in 1993*. Washington, DC: U.S. Department of Housing and Urban Development, Office of Policy Development and Research.

Miller, Cynthia. 1998. Explaining MFIP's Impacts by Housing Status. Unpublished paper. Manpower Demonstration Research Corporation.

Miller, Cynthia, Virginia Knox, Patricia Auspos, Jo Anna Hunter-Manns, and Alan Orenstein. 1997. *Making Welfare Work and Work Pay: Implementation and 18-Month Impacts of the Minnesota Family Investment Program*. New York: Manpower Demonstration Research Corporation.

Miller, Cynthia, Virginia Knox, Lisa A. Gennetian, Martey Dodoo, Jo Anna Hunter, and Cindy Redcross. 2000. *Reforming Welfare and Rewarding Work: Final Report on the Minnesota Family Investment Program. Vol. 1: Effects on Adults*. New York: Manpower Demonstration Research Corporation.

Naparstek, Arthur J., Dennis Dooley, and Robin Smith. 1997. *Community Building in Public Housing: Ties That Bind People and Their Communities*. Washington, DC: U.S. Department of Housing and Urban Development.

Newman, Sandra J. 1999. Introduction and Overview. In *The Home Front: Implications of Welfare Reform for Housing Policy*, ed. Sandra J. Newman, 1–28. Washington, DC: Urban Institute Press.

Newman, Sandra J., and Joseph Harkness. 1999. The Effects of Welfare Reform on Housing: A National Analysis. In *The Home Front: Implications of Welfare Reform for Housing Policy,* ed. Sandra J. Newman, 29–80. Washington, DC: Urban Institute Press.

Newman, Sandra J., and Ann B. Schnare. 1997. "…And a Suitable Living Environment": The Failure of Housing Programs to Deliver on Neighborhood Quality. *Housing Policy Debate* 8(4):703–41.

Ong, Paul. 1998. Subsidized Housing and Work among Welfare Recipients. *Housing Policy Debate* 9(4):775–94.

Painter, Gary. 1997. Low-Income Housing Assistance: Its Impact on Labor Force and Housing Program Participation. *Journal of Housing Research* 12(1):1–26.

Reingold, David A. 1997. Does Inner-City Public Housing Exacerbate the Employment Problems of Tenants? *Journal of Urban Affairs* 19(4):469–86.

Riccio, James A. 1999. *Mobilizing Public Housing Communities for Work: Origins and Early Accomplishments of the Jobs-Plus Demonstration.* New York: Manpower Demonstration Research Corporation.

Sampson, Robert J., Stephen W. Raudenbush, and Felton Earls. 1997. Neighborhoods and Violent Crime: A Multilevel Study of Collective Efficacy. *Science* 277:918–24.

Scrivener, Susan, and Johanna Walter. 2001. *National Evaluation of Welfare-to-Work Strategies: Evaluating Two Approaches to Case Management: Implementation, Participation Patterns, Costs, and Three-Year Impacts of the Columbus Welfare-to-Work Program.* Washington, DC: U.S. Department of Health and Human Services, Administration for Children and Families and Office of the Assistant Secretary for Planning and Evaluation; and U.S. Department of Education, Office of the Under Secretary and Office of Vocational and Adult Education.

Shroder, Mark, and Marge Martin. 1996. New Results from Administrative Data: Housing the Poor, or, What They Don't Know Might Hurt Somebody. Paper presented at the midyear meeting of the American Real Estate and Urban Economics Association, Washington, DC, May 29.

Turner, Margery Austin. 1998. Moving out of Poverty: Expanding Mobility and Choice through Tenant-Based Housing Assistance. *Housing Policy Debate* 9(2):373–94.

U.S. Department of Housing and Urban Development. 1998. Characteristics of Households in Public and Assisted Housing. Table prepared by the Office of Policy Development and Research, February.

Vidal, Avis C. 1995. Reintegrating Disadvantaged Communities into the Fabric of Urban Life: The Role of Community Development. *Housing Policy Debate* 6(1): 169–230.

Wilson, William Julius. 1996. *When Work Disappears: The World of the New Urban Poor.* New York: Knopf.

Part III—The Role of Housing Providers

CHAPTER 4

The Role of Housing Providers in an Era of Welfare Reform

Barbara Sard
Center on Budget and Policy Priorities

Abstract

The current era of welfare reform transforms the environment in which housing programs for families with children operate, making it imperative that housing agencies reassess their role in relation to their tenants' economic well-being. This chapter presents the case for agencies to play an active role in helping their tenants work. Rather than being helpless bystanders to welfare reform, agencies can act strategically to help their tenants and thereby help themselves and their communities.

Work-promoting activities may entail little if any additional cost if they build on housing agencies' strategic advantages and involve advocacy to increase available resources, the substitution of new means to carry out already funded activities, and partnerships with other agencies. Special funds to support work-promoting activities are uniquely available to agencies annually from the Department of Housing and Urban Development, but without apparent justification, they are disproportionately limited to use for public housing tenants.

Keywords: Low-income housing; Welfare

Introduction

The current era of welfare reform transforms the environment in which housing programs for poor families with children operate. Time limits on welfare assistance, coupled with work requirements for most parents, including those with very young children, are changing many families' lives. More adult tenants are working, though not necessarily consistently or for more than poverty-level wages. More children may be left unattended. And for the first time since the right to welfare benefits became a reality some 30 years ago, there is a serious risk that a substantial number of families will be left without any reliable source of income.

Such a transformation in the environment makes it imperative that housing agencies reassess their role in relation to their tenants'[1] economic well-being. Although some have urged that housing agencies respond by transforming themselves into engines of "self-sufficiency," others point to the need for caution based on the perceived limits of what housing agencies can do while continuing to perform their primary role of providing decent, affordable housing (Basgal 2000; Bratt and Keyes 1997; Manpower Demonstration Research Corporation [MDRC] 1996; National Housing Conference [NHC] Panel 1998). This chapter presents the case for housing agencies to play an active role in helping their tenants work. Rather than being bystanders to the changes brought on by welfare reform, agencies can act strategically to help their tenants and thereby help themselves and their communities.

The first part of the chapter articulates in detail the rationale for an active role for housing agencies in promoting employment. It analyzes why such a role may be in their self-interest as well as beneficial for their tenants and communities. In addition, it assesses the inherent advantages that housing agencies have in trying to increase tenant employment and prevent the destitution that may otherwise befall some families as a result of welfare reform. The second part discusses eight specific activities that housing agencies can undertake to help tenants replace welfare income with wages. This section illustrates the broad range of advocacy, partnership, and direct provision of service approaches that build on the strategic advantages of housing agencies and the lessons of welfare-to-work research.

The third part focuses on the cost implications of an active role for housing agencies in promoting tenant employment. It highlights how agencies can use low-cost or no-cost strategies to increase tenant employment. Such strategies involve advocacy to increase available resources, the substitution of new means to carry out already funded activities, or partnerships with other agencies. In addition, it discusses the funding streams uniquely available to housing agencies, as well as other grant programs that reward their participation. This part demonstrates that about three-quarters of the special funding available to housing agencies from the U.S. Department of Housing and Urban Development (HUD) to support work-promoting activities must be used for public housing tenants, despite the fact that only about 30 percent of the families that receive welfare and housing assistance live in public housing. The chapter concludes with a set of recommendations on work-promoting activities by housing agencies.

---

[1] As used in this chapter, "tenants" includes both families that are tenants of the housing provider, as in the public housing and project-based Section 8 programs, and participants in Section 8 voucher programs, who are technically tenants of the private landlords from whom they rent.

The focus of this chapter is on agencies that administer the three primary federal housing programs serving poor families with children: public housing agencies (PHAs) for the public housing and tenant-based Section 8 programs; and private owners, both for-profit and non-profit, for the project-based Section 8 program. (For simplicity, the chapter refers to private owners as "agencies" regardless of their organizational structure or profit-making status.) These programs provide the vast majority of the federal housing assistance to families that receive welfare cash benefits through the Temporary Assistance for Needy Families (TANF) block grant in addition to HUD housing assistance (Khadduri, Shroder, and Steffen 2003).[2]

The Rationale for an Active Role for Housing Agencies in Helping Tenants Work

There are three major reasons to actively promote the employment of tenants who receive federal housing assistance:

1. Families that fail to make up for the loss of welfare income with earnings from work may become destitute. This will have adverse consequences for the families themselves, the communities they live in, and the housing agencies that provide their subsidies.

2. In addition to the benefit to tenants and their families from increased employment and earnings, other families in their developments and surrounding communities may also benefit from healthier local economies and safer and better-maintained housing. Housing agencies that can "grow incomes" within their developments may benefit financially and can achieve mixed-income communities without restricting access to scarce housing subsidies by those families that need them most.

3. Activities to promote work among tenants may improve the reputation of housing agencies in their communities and increase public support for housing programs. PHAs in particular may benefit from improved assessment scores, an increased likelihood of receiving HUD grants, and avoidance of legal sanctions.

---

[2] Owners of private rental units with substantial numbers of families that receive TANF benefits but not Section 8 subsidies may be hurt more than subsidized owners if welfare changes result in declines in income for a substantial number of families. Consequently, private owners, too, may wish to undertake activities to help their tenants secure or retain employment. A recent study found that of the relatively small share of tenants of community development corporations with TANF income (the median share was 13 percent), a majority have Section 8 or other rent subsidies (Wright, Ellen, and Schill 2001).

This section first explains these reasons for promoting tenant employment and then discusses why housing agencies are well positioned to undertake such efforts in light of their nature and programs.

Adverse Effects of Destitution from the Loss of Welfare Benefits without Replacement Earnings on Families, Their Communities, and Their Housing Agencies

The TANF block grant that replaced the Aid to Families with Dependent Children (AFDC) program imposes time limits on welfare benefits for families with children, coupled with work requirements while families receive aid.[3] Available evidence indicates that these new policies will result in a significant number of families failing to replace lost welfare income with wages or other sources of income.[4] Not surprisingly, families that have lost welfare benefits report a higher incidence of lack of sufficient food, problems paying rent or utility bills, and homelessness (Loprest 1999; Sherman et al. 1998).

Tenants in assisted housing programs may fare worse than families without housing assistance in attempting to replace welfare income with earnings. Before welfare reform was initiated in most states, families receiving welfare and housing assistance were less likely to have

---

[3] The Personal Responsibility and Work Opportunity Reconciliation Act of 1996 placed a five-year time limit on the federally funded welfare benefits a family may receive under the TANF block grant. States may impose a shorter time limit on TANF benefits, and about 20 have done so. Families receiving federal TANF benefits must work no later than 24 months after they begin to receive assistance unless they have been exempted from work requirements; some states have elected shorter time periods. Families that do not comply with state-established work requirements are subject to reduction or termination of benefits. The Urban Institute's summary of state policies on time limits, work requirements, and sanctions in each state as of October 1997 is contained in Gallagher et al. (1998).

[4] In a survey based on a national sample, the Urban Institute (Loprest 1999) found that 25 percent of the families that left welfare without returning from 1995 to 1997 were not working and had no working partner. About half of these nonworking families—or about 12 percent of all families surveyed—had no reported source of cash income. (The other nonworking families had been able to replace at least some of their welfare income with child support and/or disability benefits.) Findings were not significantly different for those who left later—between 1997 and 1999—and were not receiving welfare benefits at the time of the 1999 survey (Loprest 2001). Available data from other so-called leaver studies do not indicate whether families were without any cash income, but they do show that between 25 and 38 percent had no reported employment in the 12 months after leaving welfare and that, according to three studies, between 60 and 75 percent were not employed in all four quarters (U.S. Department of Health and Human Services [HHS], Office of the Assistant Secretary for Planning and Evaluation 2000). None of these HHS-funded studies isolates results for the subgroup of welfare families with housing assistance. See also Primus et al. (1999).

been recently employed and had been getting welfare benefits longer than families receiving welfare but not housing assistance (Newman and Harkness 1999). The isolated location of some public housing and Section 8 developments in neighborhoods of concentrated poverty may exacerbate some families' difficulties in obtaining employment (Khadduri, Shroder, and Steffen 2003; Newman and Schnare 1997).[5] In addition, it is possible that the reduced economic gain that families receiving housing assistance generally derive from working compared with families not receiving assistance acts as a disincentive to work even in the face of welfare work requirements and time limits, unless these "sticks" are accompanied by programs that provide supports for work (Lubell, Nelson, and Sard 2003).[6] Families that left welfare in Cuyahoga County, OH (Cleveland), because of that state's three-year time limit were significantly more likely to live in subsidized housing than families that left welfare voluntarily (Bania et al. 2001).

Few studies compare outcomes for TANF leavers with and without housing assistance. A recent study of persons leaving welfare in Massachusetts in early 1999 found that, 6 to 15 months after their welfare cases closed, those who had housing subsidies when they left welfare had a higher employment rate (74.2 percent) than those who did not (67.7 percent). Welfare leavers in subsidized housing had this higher employment rate despite being more likely than people in unsubsidized housing to be long-term welfare recipients and to have two or more children and substantially more likely (59.2 percent versus 26.0 percent) to be black or Hispanic—factors normally correlated with less successful employment outcomes.

In addition, unassisted leavers were substantially more likely to have another adult in the household (59.5 percent versus 31.0 percent) than assisted leavers. Despite their higher rate of employment and lower average payments for housing, assisted leavers were somewhat more likely than unassisted leavers to report a worsening in their financial

---

[5] An analysis of the Tenant Data Files of the New York City Housing Authority showed that welfare families living in projects in neighborhoods that have higher crime rates and higher rates of female-headed household poverty and that are isolated from transportation and job centers are significantly less likely to leave welfare than similar families in better-located New York City housing projects (Boushey and Ding 2000).

[6] Generally, the rent for families in public housing and Section 8 goes up 30 cents for every dollar increase in their income (Sard 2000). The housing tax is less severe, however, than the tax on earnings imposed by most states' TANF programs (Lazere and Daskal 2003). For more details about provisions in the Quality Housing and Work Responsibility Act (QHWRA) that limit rent increases in public housing that would otherwise result from an increase in income, see Lazere and Daskal (2003).

situation after leaving welfare, perhaps because they were less likely to benefit from the income of another adult (Nagle 2001).[7]

There is evidence that a significant number of families living in subsidized housing are unlikely to maintain steady employment after five years of receiving welfare. The probability that some families will become destitute poses financial risks for housing agencies, even if they do not experience a *net* reduction in tenant rent payments. Efforts to predict the likely impact of welfare changes on housing program revenues have tentatively concluded that agencies in some areas are likely to suffer a net loss, while other agencies will see the increase in the earnings of some tenants offset the loss of income by others (Connell, Devine, and Rubin 1998; Newman and Harkness 1999; U.S. General Accounting Office [GAO] 1998a). A neutral or positive result is most likely for housing agencies in areas where the overall unemployment rate is low and tenants face little competition for jobs they can reach (Connell, Devine, and Rubin 1998).

Federal law requires housing agencies to reduce to zero the rent due from families that lose welfare benefits because of time limits and have no other income (Sard 2000; Sard and Lubell 1998). As a result, tenants who lose welfare benefits for this reason are likely to remain in assisted housing. Extreme destitution may cause some members of such families to vandalize property or steal from other residents, which in turn would increase maintenance and security costs and decrease the quality of life for other tenants.

However, public housing tenants and families with tenant-based Section 8 subsidies that fail to comply with work requirements (or commit welfare fraud) will not see their rent obligations reduced despite their loss of income (Sard 2000). But with reduced or no income, such families may not be able to pay their rent and risk eviction and possible homelessness.

Relative to agencies administering a component of the Section 8 program, PHAs operating public housing have more to lose from a net decrease in tenants' incomes. PHAs do not generally receive any

---

[7] While both groups worked an average of 33 hours a week at their main job, unassisted leavers with earnings had somewhat higher hourly wages than assisted leavers with earnings (median of $8.50 versus $8.15). Differences in employment rates and hourly earnings were statistically significant at the 10 percent level. There was no statistically significant difference in average weekly wages. It is important to note that the study did not employ an experimental design and therefore cannot control for unobserved characteristics of the two groups that may affect their outcomes. HUD will soon be publishing other local studies that compare outcomes for welfare leavers with and without housing assistance.

additional federal subsidy during a year in which they experience a net decrease in revenue, and recent history suggests that there is no guarantee that their subsidy will increase the following year to compensate for reduced revenue. By contrast, agencies operating either of the Section 8 programs are relatively insulated from decreases in tenants' incomes, since their subsidies will increase to offset any loss. Both private subsidized owners and PHAs operating public housing, however, face some financial risk if their costs increase because of vandalism or crime, since federal subsidies generally do not vary with changes in agencies' year-to-year expenses. Agencies administering a tenant-based Section 8 program may be hurt if private landlords become less willing to rent to Section 8 families because of the risk that they will not be able to pay their share of the rent. These different financial consequences are caused by the different federal funding rules that apply to each program (see appendix 4A).

The Benefits of Increased Tenant Employment and Earnings to Families and Communities

The possibility of avoiding hardships such as hunger, loss of stable housing, or homelessness, along with the prospect of improving families' lives through increased self-esteem and financial gain from work, are significant reasons for housing agencies to take an active role in promoting employment. More working families may make public and assisted housing developments better places to live.[8] When their spending power increases, families can support more local businesses, which in turn improve the quality of life through additional neighborhood conveniences (GAO 1997; Sexton 1997).

Promoting mixed-income communities from within may be more successful than an admissions strategy and has the additional advantage of preserving newly available units for families in greater need of housing assistance (see Lubell, Nelson, and Sard 2003). Many knowledgeable observers believe that strategies to raise the employment rate of current residents—and not admissions strategies—are likely to offer the only realistic alternative for sustaining public housing (Bailey and Wallace 1997; Diaz 1997). If families with higher incomes and more choices consider the location of public housing and project-based Section 8

---

[8] While the literature on the actual effects of mixed-income housing on lower-income residents is inconclusive, many people, including federal policy makers, are convinced that it is superior to traditional public housing (Rosenbaum, Stroh, and Flynn 1998; Schwartz and Tajbakhsh 1997; Vale 1998). In QHWRA, Congress required PHAs to deconcentrate public housing through a mixed-income strategy. Implementation of this requirement has been controversial, however, causing HUD to change its rules several times.

developments undesirable, PHAs and private owners can do little to alter these dynamics. In addition, attracting higher-income families may require capital improvements that PHAs and owners cannot afford. Even if agencies succeed in attracting some new tenants with higher incomes, only about 13 percent of the units in public housing or project-based Section 8 developments become available each year (Lubell, Nelson, and Sard 2003). A work-promoting strategy may more effectively increase the number of tenants that are employed.

Since 2001, PHAs operating public housing have been permitted to retain 50 percent of the net increase in tenant rent revenues without seeing a reduction in their federal operating subsidy (HUD Office of Public and Indian Housing [PIH] 2001). These funds can be reinvested in the agency's developments to improve physical conditions and can also be used to provide tenants with work-promoting services. Consequently, it is in PHAs' self-interest to try to achieve an increase in the incomes of public housing tenants, and success may create a funding stream for future investment.

Ways That Activities to Increase Tenants' Employment and Earnings Confer Additional Benefits on Housing Agencies and Programs

Housing agencies that have sponsored work-promoting activities tend to believe that they are "good for the real estate" (NHC 1998; Rojas 1997). The perception that such activities enhance the value of the housing itself, while helping families and enabling them to pay higher rents, appears to be due to two factors. First, programs to promote employment and increase tenants' earnings may stabilize developments, reduce maintenance costs and crime, and generally strengthen the community (GAO 1996; Hecht 1996; MDRC 1996; U.S. Department of Labor [DOL] 1992). Second, such improvements in the property, as well as the lure of the programs themselves, are believed to make a development more attractive to working applicants and people striving to get ahead. Being able to attract such tenants can help ensure the long-term viability of a development (CommonBond 1998; Mendes 1998).

Agency programs to promote work may also confer more generalized benefits on housing programs as a whole, as well as on applicants waiting for housing assistance. Success stories that link assisted housing programs with families leaving the welfare rolls for decent-paying jobs have been shown in focus groups and surveys to increase public support for low-income housing programs (National Low-Income Housing Coalition 1998). Since the mid-1980s, there has been a growing political consensus that housing programs must help deliver on the goal of increasing families' economic independence from government assistance (Bratt 1996; Rohe and Kleit 1997; Shlay 1993). Only by increasing public support for low-income housing programs will additional funds be appropriated so more families can benefit from affordable housing.

For reasons explained in detail later, work-promoting activities may also result in tangible benefits to housing agencies, particularly PHAs operating public housing, in the form of improved management ratings or higher scores on competitive grant applications. In addition, such activities may prevent the imposition of sanctions for failure to comply with legal requirements. These benefits can accrue largely from agencies' efforts, regardless of their results. In addition, agencies that succeed in increasing their rent revenues can now retain half the increase without an offsetting reduction in their federal operating subsidies.

Effect on HUD assessment of agency performance. PHAs that operate public housing must now be evaluated in part on their activities to coordinate or provide effective programs and activities to promote the economic self-sufficiency of residents.[9] This change in HUD's system for assessing PHA performance was mandated by the Quality Housing and Work Responsibility Act (QHWRA) (Sard and Lubell 1998). It is too soon to tell whether this change in how HUD scores performance will affect PHAs' activities. Nonetheless, it is significant that for the first time, PHAs are being expected not only to provide decent-quality housing and manage their funds efficiently, but also to undertake other nonhousing activities to improve the lives of their tenants. By contrast, HUD's evaluation system for tenant-based Section 8 agencies does little to encourage activities to promote tenant employment.[10] Activities by private owners to promote work have no role in how HUD assesses their effectiveness.

---

[9] 24 C.F.R. §902.43(a)(6). PHAs' efforts to promote the economic self-sufficiency of public housing residents are worth 7 out of 100 points in the Public Housing Assessment System (HUD PIH 2000b). At this point, however, this factor is self-rated by PHAs without any objective measures and may apply only to PHAs that receive special funding from HUD. As part of the larger overhaul of the system, the department may change how the points are awarded under the economic self-sufficiency subindicator.

[10] The only economic self-sufficiency indicator used to assess PHA performance for the tenant-based Section 8 program applies to less than half the administering agencies. These are the PHAs that are required to enroll families in the Family Self-Sufficiency (FSS) program, an initiative begun in the early 1990s that combines case management services with a special savings feature. (See notes 24 and 25.) These PHAs are evaluated in part on whether they are enrolling at least 80 percent of the required number of families and whether at least 30 percent or more of enrollees have increased their earnings and are accumulating savings as a result. Few PHAs are required to enroll more than a small fraction of their Section 8 participants in the FSS program.

Effect on the receipt of HUD competitive grants. HUD has structured
some of its competitive grants to reward agencies for promoting tenant
employment. The criteria used to award the 50,000 fiscal year (FY)
1999 Welfare-to-Work vouchers benefited those agencies that could
demonstrate an understanding of the barriers to employment faced by
current or recent TANF recipients in their area and that had developed
working partnerships with welfare and other human service agencies.
Similarly, a PHA with a record of success in work-promoting activities,
particularly in partnership with other community agencies, is likely to
score far better when competing for HUD's largest public housing
grants—HOPE VI revitalization funds—than another PHA with
equally deteriorated housing and an equally good physical rehabilitation proposal. Competitions for funds under some other HUD programs, such as the Resident Opportunities and Self-Sufficiency (ROSS)
Program, reward PHAs with experience and proven success in managing or partnering with other agencies to operate programs that
promote resident self-sufficiency (HUD 2000b). HUD's criteria for
selecting PHAs to receive new housing vouchers in 2002 include the
operation of an FSS program (HUD 2002b).

Compliance with Section 3 hiring obligations. Recipients of HUD
housing and community development funds must give priority "to
the greatest extent feasible" to certain individuals and firms for the
employment, training, and contracting opportunities generated by the
HUD funds.[11] The most extensive requirements apply to PHAs for the
benefit of public housing tenants, who must be given first preference
by PHAs and their contractors for work funded by all HUD moneys:
capital and operating formula subsidies, as well as competitive grants.
Priority for jobs and contracts funded by operating subsidies is particularly important, since these jobs include such functions as bookkeeping,
janitorial services, and landscaping, which may appeal to female tenants more than construction jobs. Operating subsidy–funded jobs are
also more likely to be year-round rather than seasonal.

---

[11] Section 3(b) of the Housing and Urban Development Act of 1968, 12 U.S.C. 1701u(b)
states:

> It is the policy of the Congress and the purpose of this section to ensure that the
> employment and other economic opportunities generated by Federal financial
> assistance for housing and community development programs shall, to the great-
> est extent feasible, be directed toward low- and very low-income persons, particu-
> larly those who are recipients of government assistance for housing.

These requirements were significantly strengthened in 1992 and by HUD's interim
final regulations issued in 1994. See 24 C.F.R. Part 135. This is a simplified description
of the complex requirements of HUD regulations.

PHAs that fail to hire, or have their contractors hire, public housing residents for at least 30 percent of the new jobs generated by all of the HUD funds they receive may be subject to enforcement actions by HUD or by residents. In addition, PHAs are expected to award at least 10 percent of the dollar amount of building trades contracts and 3 percent of all other contracts that result from HUD funds to businesses that are majority-owned by public housing residents or whose workforce includes at least 30 percent public housing residents. Qualifying contractors may enforce these requirements. PHAs that fail to meet these requirements are subject to administrative and judicial orders regarding future hiring, training, and contracting and may be disqualified from receiving competitive HUD funds. Private Section 8 owners that receive new HUD funds for construction or rehabilitation are subject to similar obligations and enforcement actions.

Although some PHAs hire and contract with residents beyond these minimum levels, most PHAs are likely not in compliance with Section 3. In the past, HUD has done little to enforce these requirements or monitor compliance (Allan 1995; Caftel and Haywood 1994; HUD, Office of Fair Housing and Equal Opportunity [FHEO] 1995; MDRC 1996; National Housing Law Project [NHLP] 1993; Wood et al. 1999). The work obligations created by welfare reform, coupled with the new requirement that PHAs report on their Section 3 activities as part of the annual plan process, may increase efforts by residents to generate job opportunities by enforcing their rights under Section 3 (Pollack and Schlossberg 1999).

Housing Agencies' Strategic Advantages in Promoting Employment

Not only is increasing tenant employment and earnings good for the tenants, their communities, and their housing agencies, but agencies and programs are well positioned to make uniquely valuable contributions to this effort. Housing agencies have four sets of strategic advantages to prevent tenant destitution and promote tenant employment.

1. Place-based programs facilitate the efficient provision of services and may be more effective at promoting employment for families with multiple barriers to work.

2. Housing programs, particularly tenant-based programs, may provide access to neighborhoods with better job opportunities.

3. Housing agencies are more likely than welfare agencies to help families increase their incomes above the poverty level and to prevent vulnerable families from falling through the cracks.

4. Housing agencies and programs can increase job opportunities and the availability of other resources to promote work.

An important threshold question is whether the welfare agency, alone or in combination with other service providers and employers in the community, is adequately meeting the employment and work support needs of a housing agency's tenants. If a welfare agency has adopted a comprehensive program that is aimed at helping families get out of poverty and that includes a careful assessment of individual needs, referral to appropriate, available services and jobs, and tracking of individual results, a housing agency may need to do no more than help make sure that its tenants understand the new rules and how to take advantage of the available resources. With such minor efforts, a housing agency could be reasonably confident that its welfare tenants will be employed rather than destitute when they lose their benefits.[12] Such individualized, comprehensive approaches by welfare agencies, however, are not common. Because most housing agencies cannot count on the necessary help being available for their tenants without some effort on their part, it is important to address how agencies may best be able to meet their tenants' needs.

Advantages of place-based programs. Such programs facilitate the efficient provision of services and may be more effective at promoting employment for families with multiple barriers to work. In providing employment and work supports, housing programs that attach assistance to particular buildings, such as public housing and project-based Section 8 programs, have a number of advantages in addition to the possible disadvantages their location may entail. Given the sizable pool of eligible individuals in a single location, concentrations of poor families currently or recently on welfare may attract organizations and employers to provide services and recruit workers efficiently (Khadduri, Shroder, and Steffen 2003). As an added inducement, PHAs or private owners may be able to make space available to service providers or lease commercial space to potential employers, on the condition that services and jobs be provided to residents.

---

[12] The demonstration phase of the Minnesota Family Independence Program is an example of such a comprehensive state program that has had dramatic, positive effects on increasing employment and earnings, particularly for families receiving housing assistance (Knox, Miller, and Gennetian 2000).

There is substantial anecdotal evidence that tenants make better use of on-site services than of equivalent programs requiring even minimal travel (Cohen et al. 2001; Riccio 1999b).[13] Some data also indicate a higher rate of employment among tenants at public housing developments with child care centers than among comparable families at otherwise similar developments (Boushey and Ding 2000; Robins 1988). By eliminating travel time, on-site training and child care programs and case management services facilitate so-called wrap-around programs to enhance tenants' skills and resolve personal problems. Such programs combine quick-attachment work strategies with training and case management services in the evenings and on weekends (Fleischer and Sherwood 2000). By locating services where the family lives, some of the site-based programs appear to facilitate a focus on the entire family and the service needs of all its members, rather than on the family head who needs to become employed (DOL 1992; Kramer 2000; Shlay 1993). For some families, children's behavioral or health problems are a serious barrier to employment; in these cases, such a focus may be key to making real progress toward employment (DOL 1992; Olson and Pavetti 1996; Shlay 1993).[14]

Many knowledgeable observers believe that place-based settings are more effective at helping welfare families with the most severe barriers enter and remain in the labor force (Cohen et al. 2001; Fleischer and Sherwood 2000; Kramer 2000; Riccio 1999b; Welfare Information Network 1999). Proponents of these approaches have labeled them "saturation" employment programs or "vocationalizing" the housing (Fleischer and Sherwood 2000; Riccio 1999b). Among the highlighted features of place-based settings are greater ease of utilization, the availability of case managers on a drop-in basis when tenants have problems, the potential for case managers to be aware of and to try to remedy barriers that other family members pose to employment, the possibility that families trying to work can encourage one another, and more flexibility in providing supported employment-type settings. While none of these features is unique to a housing development—for example, supported employment is frequently provided in freestanding

---

[13] An extreme but nonetheless real example of increased participation in on-site services was the lack of attendance by tenants from the Benwood/McMechen Housing Authority in West Virginia at basic education classes at a community college literally one block away, while 27 tenants enrolled in a general education diploma (GED) program when the college brought its courses (along with a range of assessment and support services) to the housing complex (Toloken 1997).

[14] An early evaluation of the Family Development Center at the Lafayette Courts development in Baltimore, which was the precursor to the Family Investment Centers, found no change in families' economic circumstances, but did find some hopeful signs that educational and attitudinal improvements would yield long-run positive outcomes (Shlay 1993).

employment settings (Nightingale et al. 2000)—supporters of place-based employment programs argue that the combination of these features in a single location renders the totality of the services significantly more effective than if they were provided independently.

Access to neighborhoods with better job opportunities. Opportunities for employment vary dramatically depending on where families live. As self-evident as this proposition may seem, welfare agencies and other policy makers are only slowly recognizing its importance (U.S. Departments of Health and Human Services, Labor, and Transportation 2000). There are three types of strategies to overcome this spatial mismatch: transportation strategies to bring the people to the jobs, economic development strategies to bring more jobs to the people, and housing mobility/relocation strategies to help the people move to areas of expanding job opportunities (Hughes 1995).

Locating new affordable housing in job-rich areas can play an important role in a housing mobility/relocation strategy. Similarly, preferences favoring families making the transition from welfare to work for admission to existing well-located developments may promote employment as well (Lubell, Nelson, and Sard 2003).

Families with tenant-based Section 8 vouchers may be able to use them to move closer to jobs or to better transportation to jobs. Partly because policy makers recognized the need to overcome welfare recipients' geographical barriers to employment, in FY 1999, at HUD's request, Congress funded 50,000 new housing vouchers that targeted families moving from welfare to work (Lubell and Sard 1999). While new housing resources can aid additional families, approximately one out of every six TANF families—more than half of the TANF families with housing assistance—already have inherently mobile tenant-based subsidies.[15]

Ability to help families increase their incomes above poverty level and prevent them from falling through the cracks. Housing agencies are more likely than welfare agencies to encourage and help residents participate in programs that may increase their incomes above the poverty

---

[15] As of March 2001 (the latest data available), approximately 2.1 million families were receiving monthly cash benefits under the TANF program. In May 2001, HUD's data from its Multifamily Tenant Characteristics System indicated that about 340,000 families with tenant-based Section 8 subsidies had some income from TANF or general assistance, as did 190,000 families in public housing and 103,000 families in units with project-based Section 8 assistance. (I adjusted the reported data somewhat based on conversations with HUD staff.) The chapter by Khadduri, Shroder, and Steffen in this volume contains data on the combined receipt of welfare and housing assistance in each state in late 1996 and early 1997, as well as some later data.

line, rather than aiming only to achieve sufficient income to be ineligible for TANF. Housing programs have an interest in seeing families increase their incomes to higher levels, either to retain them as higher rent-paying role models or to enable them to move to private-market housing and relinquish a unit or subsidy to another family.[16] In addition, welfare agencies may cease to be concerned about whether families whose welfare benefits have been terminated because of failure to comply with work requirements or time limits obtain replacement income, but such families remain the housing agencies' tenants, at least for a while. Housing agencies may thus perceive that tenants facing work obligations and time limits may need work-promoting services when the welfare agency does not identify or act on such a need.

Further, welfare agencies are likely to lose contact with families once their benefits are terminated (Sweeney 2000). Such families have no reason to report a change of address to the welfare agency, and staff have no reason to find out how families are faring unless they are located in one of the few states that have special follow-up programs in place (Goldberg and Schott 2000). By contrast, housing agencies, as part of their core mission, need to keep track of where tenants live. Families that have lost income are likely to contact their housing manager to request that their rent be reduced. Even if they do not, managers of public housing or Section 8 developments may be aware of the families' misfortune.[17] Destitute families are likely to remain in their assisted housing as long as they are allowed to. As a result, housing agencies, in the regular course of their business, have multiple ways to stay in touch with families that have lost welfare benefits and then fallen through whatever safety net the community may have in place.

---

[16] Public housing tenants may remain as tenants no matter how much they earn as long as they are willing to pay 30 percent of their income for rent (or a lower ceiling or flat rent if the PHA has set one) (NHLP 1994). In the Section 8 programs, families become ineligible for housing assistance when 30 percent of their income equals or exceeds the subsidy amount or the gross rent, whichever is lower. A family that becomes financially ineligible may remain as a tenant in a Section 8 project and pay market rent unless all units in a development have project-based Section 8 subsidies. See Lazere and Daskal (2003) for a discussion of the relatively rapid phase-out of TANF and food stamp benefits compared with housing assistance when tenants go to work.

[17] The Milwaukee Housing Authority (MHA) employed two public housing tenants as employment coordinators at its Hillside Terrace HOPE VI development. They were responsible for reaching out to and following residents who were otherwise likely to "fall between the cracks" of the TANF system, in the words of the then MHA director, Ricardo Diaz (Naparstak et al. 2000, 43). In a different model, a South Bronx nonprofit developer has partnered with a local community development corporation to help tenants who have lost welfare benefits because of work-related sanctions (some had tenant-based Section 8 subsidies) (Cohen et al. 2001).

Ways to increase job opportunities and the availability of other resources to promote work. Housing agencies can prefer their own tenants for available jobs and encourage their contractors to employ tenants. In addition, agencies can increase the availability of work-promoting services to their tenants by tapping grant programs uniquely available to them and using their assets and prestige to increase the services available in the community and to their tenants.

Every housing agency—even if it administers only the tenant-based Section 8 program—is also an employer. It has office staff who perform basic tasks related to selecting new tenants and determining financial eligibility and rent levels. In addition, agencies that are also land-lords—PHAs that own public housing or private owners that operate Section 8 project-based units—must carry out functions such as rent collection, basic maintenance of buildings and grounds, and evictions. Either directly or through contractors, the agency may also undertake substantial rehabilitation when needed or new construction when funds permit. Many housing agencies provide tenants with special security and other services as well. All of these essential functions generate both employment and training possibilities.

It is reportedly rare for welfare agencies to target funds or programs to residents of assisted housing developments (GAO 1998a). Housing agencies have unique access to a number of HUD-funded programs to promote work, such as ROSS, Family Self-Sufficiency (FSS), and HOPE VI Community and Supportive Services. (These programs are discussed in the third part of this chapter and in appendix 4B.) In addition to the funds made available by these programs, these grants may leverage services from other agencies. Housing agencies may also leverage additional services and employment opportunities for tenants through the "carrot" of new housing funds, such as HOPE VI revitalization grants or welfare-to-work vouchers. Through advocacy efforts, alone or in coalition with other groups, housing agencies may be able to expand the employment-promoting resources available in the community. In addition, through partnerships with other agencies or case management services, staff can link their tenants more effectively with existing community services. They may also be able to persuade human service agencies to focus scarce resources on their tenants, on the grounds that families with stable housing may benefit more from services than other welfare families (Lubell, Nelson, and Sard 2003; Riccio and Orenstein 2003).

There are a number of predictable responses to these reasons why housing agencies should undertake work-promoting activities. Some people may question whether such activities will be effective. It is true that only limited data are available to show that work-promoting activities led by or based at housing agencies can be effective (Bogdon 1999;

Riccio 1999a) or, perhaps most important, that they are any more effective than similar activities undertaken by employment and training agencies. Moreover, few relevant research efforts are under way.[18] However, a growing number of experienced housing managers point to their own apparently successful experiences promoting tenant employment (see, for example, Andrews 1998; Basgal 2000; Bratt and Keyes 1997; Naparstek et al. 2000; NHC 1998). Since the possible adverse consequences of state welfare reform policies are fairly immediate, housing agencies will have to decide about their role on the basis of available information.

Others may assert that housing agencies lack expertise as job developers, trainers, and social service providers and that work-promoting activities take time, money, or both—resources that are in short supply at housing agencies. To demonstrate that housing agency staff may not need such expertise to operate or coordinate effective programs and to lay the groundwork for the discussion of costs and resources, the next section contains examples of some of the most potentially effective work-promoting activities that housing agencies have used.

Strategies That Respond to Welfare Reform by Building on the Advantages of Housing Agencies and Programs

Housing providers can undertake myriad activities to attempt to address barriers their tenants face in becoming and remaining employed. It is helpful to categorize these activities into three types of strategies: advocacy, partnership, and direct provision.[19]

---

[18] The Jobs-Plus Demonstration will shed light on the impact of place-based saturation employment strategies in public housing developments compared with the prevailing level of generally available services in the community, but the study is not designed to contrast comparable levels of services by housing and other agencies (Riccio 1999b). Similarly, the Moving to Opportunity Demonstration will study the effects on employment and welfare receipt of using tenant-based subsidies to move to low-poverty neighborhoods, but the comparison is only with families that use tenant-based subsidies in other types of neighborhoods or remain in high-poverty public housing or project-based Section 8 developments (HUD Office of Policy Development and Research 1999). The evaluation of the Welfare-to-Work vouchers will compare families with and without housing vouchers, but families with Section 8 vouchers may receive work-promoting services not available to comparison families (HUD PIH 2000b).

[19] Agencies' rent policies may be another potentially important vehicle to encourage work. While public housing managers now have substantial flexibility in designing their rent policies, the only discretion currently permitted in the Section 8 program is to avoid immediate rent increases by limiting them to the annual recertification. For the tenant-based Section 8 program, families can accumulate savings equivalent to the increased rent payments due to earnings through FSS program escrow accounts (Sard 2001a). See Lazere and Daskal (2003) for further discussion of rent policy options.

In *advocacy* activities, the staff or board of a housing agency, alone or in concert with others, can urge local or state policy-making bodies to adopt policies or programs or appropriate funds that will help meet tenants' needs. The agency may also help tenants learn to advocate on their own behalf. Advocating on issues of primary concern to the tenants rather than programs or budgets requires a major role shift for many agencies. But the effort may yield positive results with relatively little investment of time. Housing agencies are frequently respected and influential players in their local communities. PHAs generally have either an elected board of commissioners or are part of city or county (or, less frequently, state) government and thus have political connections. To advocate effectively at the state level, small agencies and owners may join other housing agencies in statewide trade groups. Private owners of project-based Section 8 developments may have a common link through the state housing finance agency.

Through *partnerships*, housing agencies and one or more government or private-sector agencies or employers collaborate to carry out activities leading to employment or related services. The housing agency may be the facilitator, or it may respond to others' initiatives. Ideally, the housing agency will get more in value for its tenants from a partnership arrangement than it has to pay. For example, it may contribute resources or services that are relatively cost-free, such as space for a child care center or job training program.

When a housing agency acts as the employer or provides services through its own staff or contractors, it is using a *direct provision* approach. It is the doer, rather than the facilitator or the advocate. Although direct provision strategies are often assumed to be expensive, they do not involve significant additional costs when they use alternate means to carry out existing functions. Direct provision and partnership approaches are often combined.

To illustrate the range of potentially effective strategies that housing agencies can undertake to promote tenant employment, this section briefly discusses eight strategies to meet the three primary needs of families seeking to replace welfare income with earnings.

1. Strategies to increase the availability of jobs:
    — Direct provision of jobs by housing agencies and their contractors
    — Partnerships between PHAs or private owners and community economic development corporations to create jobs
    — Direct and partnership strategies by PHAs to help TANF families use their tenant-based Section 8 subsidies to move closer to jobs

2. Strategies to help tenants prepare for work, increase their earnings, and avoid welfare sanctions:
    — Direct and partnership strategies to provide on-site training linked to employment
    — Leveraging of training and supportive services through service coordinators and on-site multiservice centers
    — Advocacy and services to ameliorate TANF sanctions

3. Strategies to help tenants obtain the support services they need to work:
    — Partnerships with child care agencies and direct support for tenants' in-home child care businesses to increase the availability of care outside of normal working hours
    — Advocacy to increase available transit services connecting concentrations of assisted tenants with job opportunities

Three important caveats should be noted about the following discussion. First, with a few exceptions, little empirical research has established the effectiveness of these strategies, *when used by housing agencies*, to promote employment. The selection is derived from best practices reports in light of the lessons of welfare reform research and the strategic advantages of housing agencies. Second, a combination of strategies in a comprehensive approach may be more effective than any single strategy (Brown 1996; Pitcoff 1997). Third, before instituting any work-promoting agenda, a housing agency should carefully assess the employment barriers its tenants face, given local labor market conditions and available services. The skill levels of assisted housing tenants receiving welfare benefits vary substantially by location, as do the requirements for and the relative number of available jobs (Connell, Devine, and Rubin 1998).[20] There is also likely to be considerable variation in the extent of unmet need for skill-building programs and for child care and transportation assistance.

Strategies for Housing Agencies to Increase the Availability of Jobs for Recipients of Housing and Welfare Assistance

The primary need for families facing work obligations and time limits is a job. The need for additional jobs may be particularly great when assisted housing is located in neighborhoods that are geographically isolated both from available employment opportunities for which tenants are qualified and transportation to such employment (Connell,

---

[20] HUD's analysis of eight communities found that the ratio of entry-level job seekers to available entry-level jobs in the metropolitan area ranged from 1.7:1 in Richmond, VA, to nearly 13:1 in Toledo, OH (Connell, Devine, and Rubin 1998).

Devine, and Rubin 1998). PHAs and private owners operating assisted
housing programs can increase the number of suitable jobs available to
their tenants through a range of approaches.

Direct provision of jobs by housing agencies and their contractors. While
housing programs alone cannot fill the job gap that will likely appear
as time limits take effect, they can be an important source of jobs. By
increasing the share of agency jobs that go to tenants and contracts
that go to tenant-controlled businesses, as well as imposing tenant hiring requirements on contractors, agencies can directly increase the
number of tenants with earnings. Such a strategy has been labeled
"housing-led economic development" (Hecht 1996).

Some housing agencies have been highly successful in generating jobs
for residents. For example, the Housing Authority of Baltimore City
(HABC) collaborated with the local welfare agency to hire more than
60 TANF recipients living in their family developments to work as
groundskeepers. Their wages ($6.50 per hour) were partially paid
through a TANF grant diversion program. HABC staff members who
previously did the work were redeployed to unit maintenance (Wood et
al. 1999). The Danbury (CT) Housing Authority reports that about half
of its employees, including the deputy director, are current or former
public housing residents. The agency has worked with local colleges to
design courses that equip employees to meet the technological demands
of their jobs and reimburses employees for tuition. In addition, faced
with the likelihood that some residents would not have jobs when
Connecticut's 21-month TANF time limit began to take effect in 1998,
Danbury leveraged jobs from vendors with which it does substantial
business, such as area banks ("Job Readiness, Upgraded Skills"1999).
Other housing agencies (Jersey City, NJ, and Tampa, FL) also report
that half or more of their employees or the workers hired by their contractors are residents (MDRC 1996; "Section 3 Employment Efforts"
1998).

Through a variety of hiring and contracting strategies, the Housing
Authority of the City of Los Angeles (HACLA) created an estimated
1,000 jobs for its public housing residents between 1994 and 1996
(Leavitt and Ochs 1997). Following HUD's Step-Up model, PHA efforts
are frequently coupled with paid union apprenticeship programs in the
maintenance and construction trades, which may also lead to outside
jobs (Allan 1995; GAO 1996; MDRC 1996; Strawn 1998).[21] A recent

---

[21] Similar on-the-job training programs in the residential and building trades are operated by some housing agencies without the union apprenticeship link (see Andrews
[1998], which describes efforts to help formerly homeless tenants in San Francisco).
It is not clear whether wage gains are as substantial for tenants in these nonunion
efforts.

example is the partnership between the Oakland Housing Authority and the Carpenters and Painters Union that trained 35 residents, 90 percent of whom became employed in these trades at salaries ranging from $10.40 to $30.50 per hour (Naperstek et al. 2000). Average hourly earnings ($8.28 per hour) were reported for female graduates of Baltimore's Step-Up program, which is estimated to have saved the state $120,000 in welfare payments over two years (Wood et al. 1999).

Some PHAs have focused on tenant microenterprises. The Chicago Housing Authority (CHA) helped create 130 resident-owned businesses with contracts in excess of $42,000,000 (Carter 1998). In addition to their other projects, some of these businesses contracted with CHA to provide maintenance services, while others provided resident services, such as transportation to jobs. These businesses became a substantial source of jobs for other residents: Most of the 792 employees hired by the resident businesses at CHA in 1996–97 were tenants who had been on welfare ("CHA Promotes Resident Businesses" 1997).[22]

The San Antonio Housing Authority (SAHA) has also emphasized the development of resident businesses. In its first three years, the SAHA economic development program helped develop 19 resident-owned businesses that employed 60 to 100 public housing tenants, depending on the season. The agency contracts with 18 of these 19 businesses (Center for Community Change [CCC] 1999).

A related approach is to lease space to commercial enterprises at a discount in return for agreements to hire residents (Fleischer and Sherwood 2000; Kramer 2000). Alternatively, housing agencies can use government loan guarantees and other funds to persuade retail enterprises that both train and hire residents to locate at their sites ("Mobile Public Housing Effort" 1999).

Such housing-led economic development is vital for tenants when they lack any previous work experience or are geographically isolated from job opportunities. If a housing agency can provide that hardest-to-get first job for tenants with no work experience, the job may then open doors in the private labor market (Kramer 2000; Strawn 1998). The CHA consciously targets residents who have never been employed for

---

[22] According to the CHA, the businesses owned by its residents in 1998 together employed more welfare families than any company in the state (Carter 1998). Watkins (1993) describes programs to help develop business opportunities for tenants at five urban and rural PHAs. MDRC (1996) contains additional case studies of PHA efforts to develop tenant-run microenterprises, although the MDRC report is skeptical of the potential of such businesses. For an excellent discussion of the potential benefits and pitfalls of family day care businesses, and the potential role of housing agencies, see McKay and Lopez (1997).

certain of its clerical and administrative jobs ("CHA Promotes Resident Businesses" 1997). Also, helping tenants with their first job is a cornerstone of the strategies used by supportive housing providers to help formerly homeless tenants and others (Fleischer and Sherwood 2000). In another case, faced with a 26 percent unemployment rate in the surrounding community, the Housing Authority of the City of Nogales, AZ, decided to form its own construction company, which trained and hired residents instead of paying out-of-town contractors to bring crews to that remote area (National Association of Housing and Redevelopment Officials 1998).

Most of those facing work requirements and time limits are single mothers with children. As a result, a vital question is the extent to which these jobs will benefit women. Many are in occupations that traditionally employ few women, but agencies have made successful efforts to overcome the stereotypes held by contractors, unions, and residents. For example, 40 of the 60 participants in a joint project of the Baltimore Housing Authority; the American Federation of State, County, and Municipal Employees; and other agencies to train residents for maintenance and repair jobs with the housing authority are single mothers with children (MAHN [Meeting America's Housing Needs] Conference/Dialogue 1998). Nonetheless, opening up housing agency jobs to women remains an uphill effort (HUD FHEO 1995; MDRC 1996).

Despite the unique and significant role that housing programs could play in creating jobs for residents and the legal requirements of Section 3, relatively few agencies appear to be realizing this potential or complying with the law. Public housing projects run by resident manager corporations appear to have been more successful in this regard (Kingsley, McNeely, and Gibson 1997; MDRC 1996). Together with the very effective efforts of some PHAs, this suggests that obstacles to resident hiring can be overcome.

Partnerships between PHAs or private owners and community economic development corporations to create jobs. Another promising strategy is for housing agencies that do not themselves have a formal economic development role to partner with community economic development corporations to foster local job-creating initiatives (Weiss and Kelly 2000; Zdenek 1998). For example, the New York City Housing Authority has collaborated with the South Brooklyn Local Development Corporation to establish several thrift shops that provide entry-level jobs for local public housing residents who receive welfare benefits and have little or no work experience ("Brooklyn Thrift Stores" 1997). Similarly, a local community housing development organization in Los Angeles trained neighborhood residents for construction jobs on its projects.

Residents at a public housing project in the neighborhood proposed that HACLA provide additional funding to the community development corporation (CDC) to enable it to expand its program and train more residents (Leavitt and Ochs 1997).

Direct and partnering strategies by PHAs to help TANF families use their tenant-based Section 8 subsidies to move closer to jobs. Families' need to find employment as a result of welfare reform requires increased attention to helping those with Section 8 subsidies move to areas with better access to job opportunities. The increasing suburbanization of entry-level jobs compounds the barriers to job access created by living in neighborhoods of concentrated poverty (Ellen and Turner 1997; GAO 1998b).

While welfare families with tenant-based rental assistance generally live in neighborhoods with substantially less concentrated poverty, few such families appear to have used their subsidies to move to neighborhoods with better job opportunities (Khadduri, Shroder, and Steffen 2003). Many choose to stay because of familiarity or a desire to remain close to existing support networks. But for others, such a decision may not reflect a true choice, because of lack of awareness of the right to move beyond city or county boundaries, an absence of rental units in better neighborhoods that are affordable even with a voucher, transportation barriers, and discrimination in the housing market.

There are a number of ways PHAs can help families make informed choices about whether to move to areas with more jobs. To make housing in job-rich areas accessible, agencies must use their discretion under new program rules to adjust subsidy amounts (Sard 2001b). PHAs should ensure that Section 8 families understand that they can use their rental subsidy to move to other cities. Also, families need to be made aware of the potential to increase their access to jobs. It is likely many are unaware of the metropolitan geography of job opportunities.

In addition, experience has shown that two components of housing mobility programs that use tenant-based Section 8 subsidies are key: counseling for families and outreach to landlords. Counseling helps families become acquainted with unfamiliar parts of the city or metropolitan area. Outreach to landlords in areas where job or transportation opportunities are better is critical to soliciting participation by new owners who may not know how the program operates (Peterson and Williams 1995; Sard 1993; Turner 1998).

Combining mobility efforts with programs that help families obtain cars and provide other services to support work may enhance the likelihood of successful employment. A number of PHAs participating in

HUD's Regional Opportunity Counseling Program or in the new Section 8 Welfare-to-Work voucher program are partnering with other government and nonprofit agencies to link families to the services they need to be able to work (HUD FHEO 2000; HUD PIH 2000c).[23]

Strategies to Help Tenants Prepare for Work, Increase Their Earnings, and Avoid Welfare Sanctions

To illustrate the range of available options, this part discusses three different types of work-preparation activities that build on housing agency attributes.

Direct and partnership strategies to provide on-site training linked to employment. Research has shown that the most effective training programs for welfare recipients are either on-the-job or otherwise directly linked with particular employers or a job sector (DOL 1992; Strawn 1998; Zdenek 1998). Housing agencies can interest employers in partnerships to generate training and jobs by turning their concentration of poor tenants into a strategic advantage as an efficient source of trainees.

Two multisite examples include efforts by PHAs and Walgreens drug store chain, and by Mercy Housing Corporation, a nonprofit developer of housing with many tenants receiving project- or tenant-based Section 8 assistance. Drawing on an initial effort in Chicago, Walgreens plans to provide on-site training at dozens of public housing developments undergoing renovation as part of HUD's HOPE VI program. Tenants who successfully complete training are offered employment at local stores (Naparstek et al. 2000). Mercy Housing Corporation has found that in areas with extremely low unemployment, employers needing additional workers are interested in providing tenants with training. The housing agency in effect reduces the employer's recruitment costs by mustering a large group of potential trainees and future workers (NHC Panel 1998).

---

[23] Despite greater proximity to employment as a result of moving to the suburbs, tenants without cars may still find suburban jobs inaccessible. In the Gautreaux program, families that used their Section 8 subsidies to move to the suburbs experienced greater transportation barriers to employment than city movers (Rosenbaum and Popkin 1991). The Cincinnati Metropolitan Housing Authority, as part of its Regional Opportunity Counseling Program, works with a nonprofit that supplies cars to low-income residents who need them for employment (HUD FHEO 2000). Families participating in the FSS program may use their escrowed funds to purchase cars (Rohe and Kleit 1999; see also note 24), and some FSS programs (Clearwater, FL, for example) provide loans for car purchase (Wood et al. 1999).

A large PHA or Section 8 owner may develop and provide an employer-linked training program for its own tenants. For example, the Madison Park Development Corporation (MPDC), the nonprofit owner of a 546-unit, project-based Section 8 development in Boston in which one-third of the tenants receive TANF benefits, developed a highly successful 15-week customer service training program that was designed and operated in conjunction with area employers in the higher education, health care, financial services, and merchandise delivery/courier sectors. Most graduates have been placed in jobs in the targeted industries, at an average salary of $22,000 a year (MPDC 1998).

Leveraging of training through service coordinators or on-site multi-service centers. Most housing-led efforts appear to use an individual or entity that functions as a service coordinator (CCC 1999; Naparstek et al. 2000; Wood et al. 1999). Typically, the service coordinator identifies the work-preparation services in the community and links tenants needing particular services with appropriate programs. The assessment of tenants' barriers to work may be done by this coordinator or by a partner agency. The effectiveness of such a strategy depends on the availability and responsiveness of service-providing partners (GAO 1992).

The service coordinator may also act as a case manager, helping tenants troubleshoot problems as they arise, whether they are directly connected to work preparation, are family related, or appear after the tenants have begun working (Riccio 1999a; Rohe and Kleit 1997). To avoid wasting scarce resources and subjecting tenants to time-consuming and possibly conflicting obligations, however, it is important to avoid the duplication of case management functions by housing and welfare agencies.

A service coordinator model can be freestanding (CommonBond 1998; Franco 1995; Tull 1996) or combined with a multiservice center that contains training or computer facilities (CCC 1999; Wood et al. 1999). The freestanding model is best suited to geographically dispersed tenants with mobile Section 8 subsidies (GAO 1992, 1993).

HUD's primary program to help PHA tenants move from welfare to work, the FSS program, uses primarily the freestanding service coordinator model. FSS does not provide funding for services. The case manager works with each family to develop an FSS contract and help access supportive services such as child care, transportation, credit and money counseling, and educational programs. The other main feature of FSS is an escrow account.[24] As of late 2000, there were roughly 54,000 FSS participants at approximately 1,400 PHAs; most of them had tenant-based Section 8 subsidies (Sard 2001a). Many more families could be enrolled in FSS if more PHAs complied with legal requirements on enrollment or operated voluntary programs.[25] While no national data on FSS employment outcomes are available, 126 San Diego participants succeeded in replacing welfare income with wages; more than half had full-time jobs. The average annual earnings increase for families that made the transition from welfare to work was $10,687 (Wood et al. 1999).[26]

Establishing a housing site–based center as a focus for attracting partners to provide work-preparation services to tenants (and possibly youth-related, medical, and child care services as well) has been at the core of a number of HUD initiatives, such as Family Investment and Neighborhood Networks Centers.[27] As part of its Bridging the Digital Divide initiative, HUD expanded the concept of computer-based

---

[24] If an FSS participant increases her earnings from work, an amount equal to 30 percent of her net increase in income (or 30 percent of her increased *earnings*, whichever is lower) will be deposited into an escrow account. If the participant graduates from FSS, she will receive all of the funds in her escrow account. If the housing agency agrees, the participant may also withdraw funds for certain work-related expenses while still in FSS. If the participant fails to complete the program, she loses the funds in the account. PHAs receive additional funding from HUD to cover their contributions to FSS escrow accounts. See Rohe and Kleit (1999) and Sard (2001a).

[25] PHAs that received additional funding from HUD for incremental Section 8 certificates or vouchers or public housing units from FY 1993 until October 21, 1998, were required to operate FSS programs for the equivalent number of tenants. (FSS is not available to families in the project-based Section 8 program.) Any PHA may operate an FSS program, and agencies may operate larger FSS programs than they are obligated to run. HUD estimates that as of the fall of 1998, 139,500 FSS slots were required nationwide (Sard 2001a).

[26] See Sard (2001a) for a discussion of the available data on the effect of FSS participation on employment and earnings, and a comparison with the predecessor Gateway program on which FSS was partly modeled.

[27] The Neighborhood Networks initiative initially focused on HUD-subsidized or -insured multifamily developments, to encourage the use of space for resource and computer learning centers. As of early 2002, more than 800 project-based Section 8 and other HUD-insured multifamily developments had Neighborhood Networks Centers (HUD 2002a). While this is not a grant program, the department permits owners of projects with an approved Neighborhood Networks plan to draw funds from the project's residual receipts account and to borrow funds from the replacement reserve account. In certain limited cases, owners may also get a rent increase to help cover costs. However, owners are expected to obtain grants from outside sources and to leverage services from other community agencies. The rules governing Neighborhood Networks are contained in HUD 1997a.

learning centers from multifamily housing, where it originated, to public housing sites. In FY 2002, for the first time, Congress provided funding for Neighborhood Networks Centers, but only in public housing (Sard 2002).

Site-based centers have also been used by housing agencies initiating their own programs or working in collaboration with city agencies or community-based organizations (CommonBond 1998; DOL 1992; "High-Rise Project Rehabilitated" 1998). State housing finance agencies have promoted the addition of computer learning centers in multifamily assisted developments (National Council of State Housing Agencies [NCSHA] 1998). Some PHAs have succeeded in persuading workforce development agencies to locate new one-stop centers that provide access to federally funded job training in public housing developments (Riccio 1999b). By taking advantage of the concentration of potential program participants and eliminating transportation and other barriers, such site-based centers can benefit service providers as well as tenants (DOL 1992; Johnson 1998).

Advocacy to ameliorate TANF sanction policies and direct provision of services to help families cure or correct sanctions. As a condition of receiving TANF benefits, parents must comply with state-imposed work requirements as well as a number of behavioral conditions, such as cooperation with enforcement of child support obligations. Depending on state rules, noncompliance results in a partial reduction or termination of benefits.[28] State sanction rates vary substantially, but 25 to 30 percent or higher is apparently not unusual (Golden 1998). From 1997 through 1999, approximately 540,000 families across the country lost their entire TANF grant because of sanctions (Goldberg and Schott 2000). No national data are available on the sanction rate for TANF families in assisted housing.[29] There is some reason to believe that the rate may be just as high or higher. Studies of sanctioned families have shown that noncompliance is more common among families with limited work experience, lengthy periods of welfare receipt, and multiple

---

[28] In 1999, 13 states and the District of Columbia partially reduced TANF grants for noncompliance with work requirements, regardless of the number of instances of noncompliance; 22 states partially reduced the grant for the initial sanction but after repeated instances terminated the entire grant; and 15 states terminated the entire grant whenever the family failed to comply with work requirements (GAO 2000). Some states impose less severe penalties for noncompliance with other TANF requirements (GAO 2000).

[29] One study of welfare leavers living in low-income neighborhoods of Boston, Chicago, and San Antonio found that families that left welfare because of sanctions were somewhat more likely than other leavers to have housing subsidies (Moffitt and Roff 2000). However, another local study of an urban Michigan county found no difference in sanction rates based on whether leavers received assistance (Corcoran and Heflin 2002).

barriers to work (GAO 2000; Goldberg and Schott 2000). As noted earlier, families receiving federal housing assistance are more likely than other welfare families to have such characteristics.

Noncompliance often results from a failure to understand notices or requirements (GAO 2000; Golden 1998; Sweeney 2000). Tenants with various disabilities, such as limited literacy or substance abuse or mental health problems, are particularly vulnerable to sanctions based on nonwillful actions. Also, adults with such disabilities are among those least likely to find employment when they lose benefits (Goldberg and Schott 2000; Sweeney 2000). Other tenants may be subject to sanction and loss of welfare benefits if they choose to complete training programs in which they are enrolled in order to improve their future earning capacity rather than drop out to meet welfare program work requirements.

Housing agencies may be able to use their influence as major institutions to successfully advocate for changes in state or county sanction policies or local practices. The staff of the Housing Authority of the City of Milwaukee negotiated exceptions to Wisconsin's "work first" requirement to permit residents to retain their welfare assistance while they pursue certification as nursing or pharmacy assistants (Wood et al. 1999). Housing agencies could also advocate for special intervention or conciliation policies before welfare benefits are terminated. For example, actual contact with noncompliant families by a staff person from the welfare agency or a specially contracted service provider, including a home visit if necessary, could be required before benefits are terminated.[30] In addition, parents with learning disabilities, limited literacy, or mental health or substance abuse problems could be permitted to meet work requirements by participating in programs to address these personal barriers to work (Herr, Wagner, and Halpern 1996), or else such families could be exempted from work requirements and time limits on hardship grounds.

Frequently, agency staff become aware that a family has lost TANF benefits when a tenant requests a rent reduction. As part of its response, the agency could help tenants, directly or through referrals, take the actions necessary to comply with TANF requirements and get the sanction lifted. In about half the states, compliance results in reinstatement of benefits (GAO 2000). Work opportunities sponsored by the housing agency could enable families to comply with requirements. Alternatively,

---

[30] Tennessee and several other states require home visits before a sanction is imposed, if other attempts to ensure that a family understands what is required have failed. The Customer Service Review Program in Tennessee resulted in retention of TANF benefits for about one-third of the cases originally subject to closure in 1999 (Goldberg and Schott 2000).

if families believe that the sanction should not have been imposed, they could be referred to appropriate social service or legal aid agencies for assistance in determining whether the decision was correct under federal and state TANF rules and what could be done to reverse it.

The Milwaukee Housing Authority reports that it uses both of these strategies. PHA staff meet with families that have been found to be noncompliant and refer parents to employment agencies operating in their development or to legal aid or other resources to challenge the sanction (NHLP 1999). Some CDCs also help sanctioned families by referring them to agencies that can help them reinstate their TANF benefits (Wright, Ellen, and Schill 2001).

Strategies to Enable Tenants to Obtain the Support Services They Need to Work

Many tenants will need one or more support services, most commonly child care and transportation, to help them secure and retain employment (DOL 1992). Two strategies that housing agencies may be uniquely well positioned to implement are, first, partnerships with child care agencies and direct support for tenants' in-home child care businesses to increase the availability of care outside of normal working hours and, second, advocacy to increase available transit services connecting tenants with job opportunities.

Partnerships with child care agencies and direct support for tenants' in-home child care businesses. Some tenants seeking work will not be able to obtain the help they need through family or friends and so will need to turn to formal child care services. In some communities, the supply of such services is inadequate, particularly outside of regular working hours.[31] On-site child care services can save commuting time and are especially critical during the night.

Two studies have shown that having child care centers at public housing developments increases tenants' rate of employment and probability of leaving welfare. Drawing on data gathered in 1985 from a sample of PHAs, Robins (1988) concluded that the availability of an on-site child care center capable of serving a relatively large number of families results in an increase in tenants' likelihood of working, hours of work, and annual earnings, and in a decreased probability of receiving

---

[31] Studies indicate that one-quarter to one-half of employed leavers in particular states or counties work nontraditional hours—weekends, nights, early mornings, or split or changing shifts (Richer, Savner, and Greenberg 2001). A 13-state study of parents who left welfare between 1995 and 1997 found that more than one-quarter of employed leavers worked at night (Loprest 1999).

welfare benefits. These effects were particularly strong for parents of preschool children, regardless of whether they actually used the center. Using data from the Tenant Data Files of the New York City Housing Authority, Boushey and Ding (2000) concluded that the presence of a day care program in a development increases the probability of tenants leaving welfare within four years and overcomes the negative effects of particular neighborhoods on welfare exits.

Many housing agencies—for-profit as well as nonprofit—improve the availability of child care services by contributing space for such facilities to a local child care agency in return for operating the on-site program (NHC Panel 1998; Wright, Ellen, and Schill 2001). The challenge in some communities may be to have such on-site centers provide care for children outside of regular daytime working hours. Because of the likely difficulty of such arrangements, a housing agency program that trains and supports a network of tenants who provide quality day care in their units may better meet this need (Ebb 1997; Lombardi 1996; McKay and Lopez 1997). A family day care strategy has the benefit of preserving all units for residential use and providing a source of employment for tenants. Housing authorities in six cities and a number of counties in rural Alabama have recently partnered with the Consortium for Worker Education and local child care organizations to create the National Satellite Childcare Project. Under this DOL-funded initiative, public housing tenants will be trained as in-home child care providers. The family day care programs will be developed as satellites of existing child care centers, affording tenants the security of regular employee status and ongoing supervision and training, including through the use of private computer networks (DOL 1999).

Advocacy to increase available transit services connecting concentrations of assisted tenants with job opportunities. Two-thirds of new entry-level jobs are in the suburbs, while three-quarters of welfare recipients live in central cities or in rural areas (U.S. Department of Transportation [DOT] 2000). In addition, only 1 in 20 welfare families has reported having a car (GAO 1998b). Mass transit systems are often inadequate to take central-city residents to suburban jobs, particularly if an intermediate stop is necessary because of child care (HUD 1997b; Hughes 1995). For many families in public housing and Section 8 project-based units, it is vital to develop transportation solutions to the mismatch between where they live and where the jobs are, since these families cannot move without losing their affordable housing (Connell, Devine, and Rubin 1998).

Through advocacy, a housing agency can seek to persuade a local or metropolitan public transit provider to alter or increase bus routes or other transit services to provide more efficient links between its developments and transportation hubs or the locations of concentrated job opportunities. An important new focus of such advocacy efforts is influencing what proposals are generated locally and endorsed by the metropolitan planning organization or governor for special funding under the recent federal Access to Jobs initiative, for which housing agencies are eligible grantees (Rothman, Beckwith, and Stolz 1998).

Alternatively, state-level advocacy may result in additional funding for special transportation services for welfare recipients. Influenced by research from the Center on Urban Poverty and Social Change at Case Western University that demonstrated the significant transportation barriers faced by welfare families, including those in public and project-based assisted housing (Coulton, Leete, and Bania 1999), Ohio enacted a special transportation initiative as part of its welfare reform legislation. Some $5 million dollars in TANF funds were set aside for programs designed by each county in consultation with a local working group that was to include housing agency representatives.

Costs of an Active Housing Agency Role in Promoting Employment and How to Meet Them

For many housing agencies, a major deterrent to work-promoting activities is the belief that they are costly and will require expending the limited resources needed for basic operations. Neither premise is necessarily true. This part first analyzes the types of activities that may not entail additional costs and then reviews the special funding opportunities available. Comparing the special funds made available to housing agencies by HUD to promote work with the proportion of the population receiving both housing and welfare assistance reveals some surprising results. While 70 percent of the families that received both housing and welfare assistance in 2001 were in the Section 8 programs, a maximum of only about one-quarter of HUD's special funds may serve these families. There is no apparent policy justification for this disproportionate allocation of resources.

Some Work-Promoting Strategies That Need Not Involve Additional Costs

Advocacy strategies generally do not cause housing agencies to incur additional costs, nor is hiring additional staff likely to be required. Except for the staff time involved in meetings and conversations with relevant groups and decision makers, few resources need to be expended. By contrast, depending on their design, partnership and direct provision approaches may or may not mean additional costs.

Advocacy approaches. Advocacy approaches entail no measurable financial cost for housing agencies, since these efforts are likely to involve only redirecting some staff time. For example, the director of special projects for the Providence (RI) Housing Authority estimated that she spent about seven hours a week over the previous two years chairing the advisory commission to the legislature on the state's welfare reform bill, but no additional staff were hired nor did she receive additional compensation.[32] As states struggle to get the hardest-to-employ welfare recipients into the workforce, they may be willing to reexamine their policies and programs with prompting from advocates. In addition, housing agencies may be able to use their political influence to bring needed city services to their tenants (CCC 1999).

Compared with partnership and direct provision strategies, advocacy approaches such as the transportation example discussed earlier can best increase the overall level of resources committed to solving the problems of lack of employment, low earnings, and inadequate support services for welfare families facing work requirements and time limits. Also, because advocacy approaches are likely to yield results that benefit many welfare families (and not just the tenants of a particular development), these approaches are more likely to benefit families with tenant-based Section 8 assistance than many partnership or direct provision strategies. Depending on local circumstances, however, without a more comprehensive strategy, advocacy approaches may not succeed or may not result in sufficient increases in jobs and services for tenants.

Taking on an advocacy role to promote the economic well-being of their tenants will be a major change for most housing agency leaders. Few now advocate on issues other than those that directly affect their core housing mission, and few PHA staff or private owners have much experience working with state agencies and legislative bodies. Where housing agencies are supported primarily by federal contracts, they may have felt little need to become players in resource allocation decisions at the state or local level. Even CDCs, which are locally rooted, have historically confined their advocacy to issues such as the Low-Income Housing Tax Credit or compliance with the Community Reinvestment Act, which they have seen as most directly connected to their success (Nowak 1998).

Partnership approaches. This type of approach may also be essentially cost-free if housing agency staff can arrange for partner organizations, such as human service agencies and employers, to target the agency's

---

[32] Interview with Marcia Sullivan, April 24, 2000. She judged this advocacy role to be a "great" use of her time, both with regard to the changes accomplished and the additional knowledge she was able to bring to her work at the housing agency.

tenants at their own cost. As is the case with advocacy approaches, additional staff time will be required to work out such arrangements, but hiring additional staff should not be necessary unless the relationships to be negotiated are numerous or particularly problematic, as in the Jobs-Plus demonstration in public housing (Kato and Riccio 2001). Some of the union apprenticeship programs, employer-provided training efforts, and on-site location of referral resources such as the One-Stop Career Centers mentioned earlier were made available to tenants at no cost to the housing agencies.

Agencies may be best able to enter into cost-free work-promoting partnerships by providing free space to training or child care programs or reduced rentals to commercial enterprises that commit to hiring residents. PHAs will generally suffer no loss and may increase their revenue from such agreements.[33] By contrast, if a project-based Section 8 owner has only residential space available, it will lose subsidies for the off-line units. PHAs and private owners are, however, responsible for any capital costs involved in converting existing space to a work-promoting use and do not receive additional funds from HUD for this purpose.

Some agencies may be able to leverage services for their tenants by agreeing to allocate available units or Section 8 subsidies to families that are a priority for the partner agency. This is essentially the program model of the new Welfare-to-Work vouchers. HUD provided funding only for the vouchers (and the usual administrative fee), but gave preference in the competition to PHAs that could leverage services from community partners. Similarly, eight PHAs in Utah agreed to give top priority for admission to public housing to families enrolled in the state's welfare/job training program (the Family Employment Program) in exchange for the state's agreeing to allow existing public housing tenants to participate in the special training program ("Public Housing: Utah" 1997).

---

[33] Under certain conditions, HUD rules permit PHAs to continue to receive operating subsidies for public housing units converted to nondwelling use for economic self-sufficiency programs (24 C.F.R. §990.108[b][2]) and for use in conjunction with an FSS program (HUD PIH 2001). The lack of tenant rent payments for such units will be fully offset (starting in the following year) by an increase in the federal subsidy received, unless Congress has not fully funded the operating subsidy account. See appendix 4A. If space leased to a commercial enterprise would otherwise have been used as a residence, only the rent actually received is considered in determining the PHA's operating subsidy. Consequently, reducing the rent charged to a commercial enterprise to encourage tenant employment does not result in a net loss of revenue to the PHA. A PHA that leases nondwelling space to a commercial facility can retain any income earned as a result without a HUD offset (HUD PIH 2000a).

In addition to the potential to provide needed services or employment to tenants at little or no cost, partnership approaches have the
important benefit of bringing expertise to the housing agency's work-
promoting strategies. By forging connections, partnerships may bring
agencies new fund-raising contacts for both government and private
funding streams (GAO 1996). The relationships developed through
partnerships can also give housing agencies a competitive advantage in
applying for HUD grants that increasingly require evidence of partnerships with community agencies.

Partnerships among various housing agencies in a neighborhood, city,
or metropolitan area also have important advantages. In major cities
with a concentration of welfare families, there are typically one or more
PHAs, numerous privately owned project-based Section 8 developments, and a significant number of CDCs or other community-based
organizations that provide housing to many families receiving welfare
benefits, including those with tenant-based Section 8 subsidies. Despite
the increased efficiency and other likely advantages of larger-scale collaborations for employment strategies, economic development efforts,
and capital-intensive or specialized services, such cross-housing activities appear to be uncommon. One important direction for future policy
would be to develop mechanisms to promote collaborations among
housing agencies in an area, as well as among housing agencies, the
welfare agency, and job training agencies.

But partnerships are not a panacea. As noted earlier, policy changes
may be vital to sustain the safety net for families with serious barriers
to work or to expand resources to meet their needs. Many human service agencies or employers will not be willing or able to shoulder the
additional costs of providing new services to housing agencies' tenants.
Even if an agency chooses to use partnerships to promote work among
its tenants, it may still face funding problems.

Direct provision approaches. If a housing agency can promote work by
adjusting how it performs a function that it would have to perform anyway, there is likely to be little or no additional cost to the agency. For
example, every PHA and private owner of assisted housing must do
maintenance and rent recertification. Maintenance tasks can become a
means of employing and training residents. Rent recertification interviews can be combined with advice on how to avoid or correct benefit
reductions or terminations and appropriate referrals related to new obligations under the state TANF plan. PHAs administering the tenant-
based Section 8 program can provide clearer information to families
about where the most job growth is anticipated in the surrounding area
and their right to use their subsidies to move to such areas. Agencies
that are constructing or rehabilitating housing may be able to place

residents in on-the-job training or regular employment slots generated by these activities.

For real gains from an aggressive hiring strategy to be possible, however, agencies may need to provide training to equip residents to take jobs with the agency or its contractors or to start their own businesses. Such training may entail additional costs. Imposing and enforcing resident hiring obligations on contractors may also entail higher costs for contracted services (MDRC 1996) as well as for monitoring compliance.

But employing its own residents may also reduce a housing agency's expenses. When residents work on maintenance, their stake in the property increases, and as a result they may enforce social norms against the destruction of property on other residents, thereby avoiding maintenance costs that would otherwise have been incurred (MDRC 1996; "Section 3 Employment Efforts" 1998). Savings may also result from residents' performing higher-quality work because they care about their community. The Housing Authority of Savannah, GA, found that contracting out janitorial service to the resident association rather than other commercial firms resulted in cleaner buildings (GAO 1996). Resident employees or contractors may also be less costly than other private contractors, possibly because of the reduction in travel time to rural areas, as in the Nogales (AZ) example discussed earlier.

For activities other than those that housing agencies can do as part of their existing functions, a direct provision approach is likely to be both costly and less uniquely appropriate. In these cases, advocacy and partnering approaches would generally be preferable to draw on nonhousing resources, to bring housing agencies and tenants into collaborations with other groups, and possibly to expand the total resources available for welfare-to-work activities. But if advocacy and partnerships are deemed unlikely to succeed, a direct provision approach may be worthwhile. Some of the side-benefits of partnerships—building collaborations and helping integrate the tenants into the surrounding neighborhood—can still be achieved by contracting for some or all of the services with other agencies and allowing site-based programs to serve other community residents.

The importance of considering the net costs of work-promoting activities. Even if work-promoting activities require increased expenditures, they will not have a *net* cost if expenditures are offset by savings or increased revenue. Just as resident hiring may reduce expenses, other strategies that prevent destitution and increase tenant employment and earnings may reduce vandalism and crime, resulting in lower maintenance and security costs.

Such a reduction in actual expenses results in real financial gain for agencies managing public housing and project-based Section 8 programs, since their HUD subsidies are unaffected by reduced costs. If tenants get jobs (or paid trainee positions) or increase their earnings, they may pay increased rents. HUD's costs for the Section 8 programs will be reduced if tenant rents increase, but local agencies and owners are not permitted to realize a net gain in revenue.

Since FY 2001, PHAs have been permitted to retain half of the additional revenue generated by increased rent payments by public housing tenants, and use the funds to improve maintenance or for resident self-sufficiency programs (HUD PIH 2001). The payoff from the investment in work-promoting activities may take some years to be realized, however, so additional resources will still be needed in the short run to fund activities that are cost-neutral or advantageous over the long-term.

Resources Housing Agencies Can Access to Meet Additional Costs of Work-Promoting Activities

While much of the regular funding that housing agencies receive from HUD can be used for these activities, most agencies will be willing or able to provide such costly services only if they can obtain additional funding (Johnson 1998; NHC Panel 1998). Because of inadequacies in HUD's subsidy formulas and congressional underfunding of formula-determined need in recent years, many PHAs consider operating and capital funds to be insufficient to cover their basic costs (Council of Large Public Housing Authorities [CLPHA] 2000; see appendix 4A). Similarly, after recent reductions in the administrative fees that PHAs receive to operate the tenant-based Section 8 program and the rescission of most program reserves, some PHAs contend that they do not have the funds to pay for services for families with tenant-based subsidies. The costs of services may not be included in the rent allowed in project-based Section 8 developments.[34]

HUD provides funds through a number of special programs, available only to housing agencies, to help meet the costs of work-promoting activities. In addition, agencies are well positioned to access HUD and other federal funds that are distributed to local and state governments or available through competition and that may be used for

---

[34] In the project-based Section 8 program, HUD permits owners and managers to use available funds in certain accounts for job training programs and Neighborhood Networks Centers, but it is unlikely that many projects will have such funds or be able to tap them (HUD 1997a, 1997c; Rojas 1997).

work-promoting activities. Finally, housing agencies may be able to raise money from corporations and foundations to fund their non-housing activities.

HUD funds available only to housing agencies. The primary HUD special or competitive grant programs that may be used to defray the costs of work-promoting activities are the ROSS Program, the Community and Supportive Services component of HOPE VI (HUD's program to revitalize seriously distressed public housing), the FSS program, and, beginning in FY 2002, Neighborhood Networks.[35] Funds are distributed on a competitive basis for ROSS, HOPE VI, and Neighborhood Networks. HUD has made it a priority in these competitions to fund programs designed to help tenants who are welfare recipients become employed.[36] HUD funds the cost of one service coordinator for each public housing FSS program. Each Section 8 FSS program with 25 or more participants may also receive additional funds for at least one service coordinator; large programs can receive up to one coordinator for each 50 approved slots. (See appendix 4B.)

Approximately $187 million, which housing agencies can use to promote work among assisted tenants receiving TANF benefits (and others), has been available annually through these special HUD programs. Table 4.1 shows the maximum amount estimated to be available annually from these four programs to assist families in public housing and in the two Section 8 programs.

---

[35] Before 2002, some private owners of HUD-assisted multifamily housing and larger PHAs managing public housing received substantial funding from HUD's Drug Elimination Program (DEP), which could be used for work-promoting activities. In the HUD appropriation for FY 2002, Congress acceded to the administration's request to eliminate this program. PHAs will receive some additional operating subsidies as a result, but are under no obligation to use these funds for activities related to drug elimination. In recent years, HUD estimated that PHAs used about 45 percent of formula DEP grants (or about $100 million) for prevention and treatment, much of it possibly for work-promoting activities (HUD 2000a). Within the overall DEP appropriation, $16.25 million was formerly set aside for competitive application among private owners of multifamily housing; some of this money was used for work-promoting activities. In the short term, PHAs and owners may still have unexpended DEP funds from previous years that they can use to promote work.

[36] Descriptions of these programs are available in Sard (2002) and Wood et al. (1999).

Table 4.1. **HUD Funds for Housing Agencies for Work-Promoting Activities**

HUD Programs	Total Available Each Year	Maximum for Public Housing	Maximum for Tenant-Based Section 8	Maximum for Project-Based Section 8
ROSS	$30	$30	$0	$0
HOPE VI Community and Supportive Services	$73	$73	?	$0
FSS Coordinators	$64.245	$17.845	$46.4	$0
Neighborhood Networks	$20	$20	$0	?
Total funds available	$187.245	$140.845	$46.4	$0

Notes: All dollars are in millions. For an explanation of the figures in this table, see appendix 4B.

Other government funds. The HUD grants earmarked for housing agencies for work-promoting activities are far from sufficient to meet the need.[37] Frequently, a combination of funding from a number of sources will be necessary for a housing agency to undertake work-promoting activities. For example, the customer service training program discussed earlier is operated by a nonprofit Section 8 owner, the MPDC, and was funded by a combination of Drug Elimination Program funding from HUD (no longer available), funds originally paid as a subsidy to the owner by HUD (this money had been saved in a project reserve account), and two state job development grants (MPDC 1998).

To obtain additional funding for work-related services, housing agencies may turn to other federal agencies or state or local government agencies. For example, housing agencies may receive grants from the state or local agencies that distribute HUD Community Development Block Grant (CDBG) funds[38] or other job training moneys, as well as from child care and transportation agencies.

Housing agencies were quite successful in the national competitions for DOL welfare-to-work grants that funded a wide range of employment-related services for families deemed to have severe barriers to employment. About a quarter of the grants, including the grant to the

---

[37] This is not to suggest that the work-related service needs of assisted tenants should be met primarily through the HUD budget, rather than through other sources. Funding such activities primarily through HUD could reduce the funding that would otherwise be available to provide housing assistance that itself can support welfare reform efforts, as well as meet other serious housing needs.

[38] Of the more than $4 billion of CDBG funding distributed annually to states and to cities with a population of 50,000 or more, up to 15 percent—a total of approximately $630 million annually—may be spent on services (Gramlich 1998).

Consortium for Worker Education discussed earlier, targeted residents of public or assisted housing, and housing agencies were the lead grantee for several multimillion dollar grants (DOL 1999). Housing agencies may be sought-after partners for the competitive Job Access and Reverse Commute grants administered by DOT. Applicants receive additional points if they have included housing agencies in the planning process, and certain HUD funds can be used for the required 50 percent match (DOT 2000).

As more states approach their time limits on TANF assistance, state and county welfare agencies may increasingly see housing agencies' requests for resources as an efficient means of reaching families with substantial barriers to employment. Both the Massachusetts and New Jersey welfare agencies have made grants of TANF funds to the respective agencies that administer a statewide Section 8 program. In Massachusetts, the infusion of TANF funds made it possible for the state Section 8 agency to hire the additional case managers needed to expand its FSS program to the 2,000 new families receiving vouchers under the Welfare-to-Work Program. In New Jersey, TANF funds are used to help TANF families that receive Section 8 vouchers locate suitable housing. Kentucky provides TANF funds to a local PHA as part of a comprehensive employment and training program for public housing tenants.

Private funds. In addition to obtaining grants from HUD and other federal, state, and local government sources, agencies can raise money from businesses or foundations. Nonprofit housing owners appear to be substantially more adept at private fund-raising than PHAs or for-profit owners, since they are used to having to raise money simply to perform their core function (NHC Panel 1998). For example, the non-profit CommonBond Communities, which operates some 2,400 affordable rental units in 35 developments in Minnesota (mostly units with project-based or tenant-based Section 8 subsidies), allocates $1 million of its $13 million budget to on-site multipurpose Advantage Service Centers. Nearly 80 percent of the cost of the centers comes from private fund-raising from corporations, foundations, church groups, and others (CommonBond 1998).

Unequal Allocation of Resources to Promote Work among Tenants of Federal Housing Programs

Despite the fact that about 70 percent of the families receiving TANF benefits and housing assistance have Section 8 subsidies (see table 4.2), three-quarters of HUD's special grant funds for work-promoting activities are restricted to families living in public housing. There does not seem to be a sound justification for this mismatch.

Table 4.2. **Relative Availability of HUD Funds for Welfare-to-Work Activities to Help TANF Families in Different Housing Programs**

Housing Program	Percentage of All HUD-Assisted Families Receiving TANF Benefits[a]	Percentage of HUD Special Funding for Work-Promoting Activities[b]
Public Housing	30	75
Project-Based Section 8	16	0
Tenant-Based Section 8	54	25

[a]See data in footnote 15.
[b]Based on table 4.1 and explained in appendix 4B.

As shown in table 4.1, of the roughly $187 million available each year through the four major HUD programs providing funds directly to housing agencies for employment-related programs—ROSS, HOPE VI Community and Supportive Services, FSS Coordinators, and Neighborhood Networks—nearly $141 million, or 75 percent of the total funds available, may be used only for public housing tenants. The only funds reserved for Section 8 families consist of $46.4 million for FSS coordinators for families in the tenant-based program. Approximately 16 percent of the families that receive both TANF and HUD assistance are in the project-based Section 8 program (see table 4.2); these families are not eligible for any of HUD's special work-promoting funds. The largest group of families receiving both TANF and HUD assistance— the 54 percent in the tenant-based Section 8 program—receive the benefit from only about 25 percent of these special grant funds.[39]

To the extent that geographic isolation from job opportunities and concentrated poverty are rationales for concentrating scarce resources and required employment opportunities on public housing tenants, these rationales apply equally to families in some project-based Section 8 developments (Khadduri, Shroder, and Steffen 2003; Newman and Schnare 1997).

Section 8 families, particularly those in the tenant-based program, are less likely to be served by other work-promoting activities by housing agencies. Few PHAs or for-profit Section 8 owners are likely to engage in fund-raising on behalf of Section 8 tenants because of the way these agencies see their role vis-à-vis the tenants and their financial calculus. In addition, for-profit owners are likely to be oriented toward making

---

[39] Until 1999, HUD made available less than one-third of the current amount for Section 8 FSS coordinators. As a result, the share of the total special grant funds received by Section 8 families was substantially lower.

money, not raising it. Few PHAs that also operate public housing programs see Section 8 tenants as "theirs" the way they do public housing tenants. (PHAs committed to their Section 8 FSS programs may be an exception.) Financially, PHAs and private owners administering Section 8 programs do not have the exposure that PHAs may have—and, more important, think they have—in their public housing programs if families' net rent payments decrease. In the Section 8 programs, it is reasonably certain that HUD will make up the shortfall.[40] As a result, PHAs are likely to be less motivated to ensure that Section 8 tenants have earnings to replace the TANF benefits they may lose.

Compounding the disproportionately small amount of HUD funds that may be used to help Section 8 tenants work and the limited likelihood that agencies will engage in other fund-raising for work-promoting activities is the fact that adults in Section 8 programs receive no special consideration and thus are unlikely to receive jobs as a result of Section 3 hiring and contracting requirements. They are in the same preference category as any other low-income person residing in the metropolitan area (or nonmetropolitan county).[41] The broad targeting of preferential hiring and contracting requirements under Section 3, except for public housing funds, is likely to be more disadvantageous for families in the tenant-based rather than the project-based program. Despite the absence of any legal requirement to hire their tenants, agencies that own and manage project-based Section 8 housing may do so anyway. Because of their role, such agencies have more jobs and contracting opportunities than agencies that administer only the tenant-based program.

In short, it is likely that housing agencies will not expend much effort to help the largest number of families with TANF income and HUD assistance—those in the tenant-based Section 8 program—secure and

---

[40] See appendix 4A. In light of its obligation to make up any difference between tenants' rent payments and the full amount due private owners under project-based Section 8 contracts, HUD would appear to have the greatest financial interest in making sure that the incomes of project-based Section 8 tenants do not suffer a net reduction because of welfare reform. (Owners, however, and not HUD, are at risk if their expenses increase as a result of more vandalism or crime.) Yet as discussed earlier, HUD has done little to protect this interest. Neighborhood Networks is the only HUD work-promoting initiative directed at project-based Section 8 tenants, and no additional funds are available for centers serving these families.

[41] A family is considered low income if its income is within 80 percent of the area median income for its family size, as adjusted by HUD. HUD regulations permit, but do not require, recipients of community development funds to provide priority in hiring, relative to other low-income residents of the area, to "recipients of certificates or vouchers under the Section 8 housing assistance program, within the service area or neighborhood where the Section 3 covered project is located" (24 C.F.R. §135.34[a][4]).

retain employment. Indeed, PHAs appear to have enrolled only about 40 percent of the required number of Section 8 families in FSS programs.[42] Moreover, there is no national evidence that heads of households with children in the tenant-based Section 8 program have fewer personal barriers to work than families in public housing.[43]

It is possible, however, that families in the tenant-based program, regardless of personal characteristics, have less need for such services. Families dispersed in the community may be better served by other community-based services that promote employment, either because they live closer to where such services are located or because they are more willing to travel to reach them. While this may be the case, I do not know of any evidence to support it. Even without work-promoting services, families with vouchers may be better able to replace welfare income with wages by using their housing vouchers to move closer to available jobs. Some evidence from the Gautreaux and Moving to Opportunity (MTO) studies suggests that this is true for some families (Ludwig, Duncan, and Pinkston 2000; Rosenbaum 1995; Rosenbaum and DeLuca 2000), but there is not yet sufficient evidence from the MTO Demonstration to know whether this result is predictable.[44] Most important, few PHAs help families move to neighborhoods with the

---

[42] As of the fall of 2000, PHAs had enrolled approximately 54,000 of the required 139,500 families in the FSS program. See note 25.

[43] Data collected in 1997 indicated that the percentage of families with children in the public housing and tenant-based Section 8 programs with income primarily from welfare (about half) or primarily from employment (36 percent) was nearly identical (HUD Office of Policy Development and Research 1998). (As used by HUD in compiling these data, welfare income includes AFDC/TANF, state general assistance, and supplemental security income [SSI].) A higher percentage of families with children in the project-based Section 8 program had wages as their primary source of income (40 percent), and fewer relied primarily on welfare (38 percent), but the latter figure is not strictly comparable to the data for public housing and tenant-based Section 8 programs because it excludes SSI benefits. There is some local evidence from California of higher rates of employment among families that had children and received tenant-based Section 8 assistance than among families that had children and lived in public housing (Ong 1998). Riccio and Orenstein (2003) report data from the early 1990s on families receiving welfare benefits and housing assistance in Atlanta and Columbus (OH). Section 8 families in Atlanta were somewhat more likely to have worked in the previous year than families in public housing, but the opposite was true in Columbus.

[44] Some families need assistance to overcome skill deficits and other personal barriers to work and/or to meet work-related needs; others may need financial incentives or the threat of sanctions to outweigh reluctance to work. Welfare reform initiatives that have comprehensively addressed all of these barriers have shown remarkable success, particularly among families with tenant-based subsidies (Lubell, Nelson, and Sard 2003; Riccio and Orenstein 2003).

highest rate of job growth, and without such help, few families do so (Turner and Williams 1998).[45]

Conclusion

Available experience suggests that efforts by housing agencies to promote work and prevent destitution among their tenants facing work obligations and time limits under welfare reform can have significant benefits for tenants and their communities, as well as for the agencies themselves. In deciding what efforts to undertake, agencies should first assess how their tenants are faring in response to welfare reform policies and identify the gaps in locally available services. To help meet the gaps, agencies should strive to adopt strategies that take advantage of the inherent attributes of housing agencies and programs and that do not require a trade-off with basic operating funds. Such strategies may include the following:

1. Engaging in advocacy for improved welfare reform policies and additional resources and services

2. As part of rent recertification or other regular functions, identifying families having difficulties complying with welfare program requirements and providing appropriate referrals for services

3. Giving preference to tenants for the housing agency's job openings and contracting opportunities and encouraging its contractors to hire tenants, particularly those in need of job experience

4. Using available HUD moneys and other government grants that reward housing agency participation to fund additional costs and leverage other resources

5. For project-based programs, providing site-based comprehensive services that particularly target families with multiple barriers to work

---

[45] The Urban Institute has identified 54 programs that seek to improve the mobility potential of tenant-based Section 8 subsidies. All but 6 are either funded by HUD through the Regional Opportunity Counseling Program (16 sites), public housing vacancy consolidation (15 PHAs), or the MTO Demonstration (five areas) or required by litigation settlements. The remaining 6 programs use their regular administrative fees (Turner and Williams 1998). The cost of the mobility services provided by these programs ranges from about $1,000 to about $3,500 per family. Some of these programs also use HUD or other funds to provide training and services to families to help them work (HUD FHEO 2000). Agencies that do not have sufficient funds to carry out effective programs to promote mobility could seek TANF or other funds to do so.

6. For tenant-based programs, engaging in efforts to promote tenant mobility to areas with greater job opportunities and providing case management services (and the opportunity to accumulate savings) through expanded FSS programs

To promote efficiency, reduce costs, and use available expertise, housing agencies should endeavor, where appropriate, to collaborate with other housing agencies in their area as well as with welfare agencies, employers, and service providers. HUD's policies and competitive grant programs should reward such collaborations. Other federal agencies and local funders, governmental and private, should also encourage collaboration.

Finally, HUD and others concerned about housing and welfare policy should examine the disproportionate allocation of funds to promote work among families served by its primary housing programs and determine whether additional funds to serve Section 8 families are warranted.

Housing agencies cannot afford to be passive as welfare reform transforms their tenants' lives. At least in some states, the recent precipitous declines in the welfare rolls have increased the proportion of welfare families that live in assisted housing. This trend could provide an easy scapegoat for welfare officials or state legislators seeking to explain why families have not found employment; officials may try to claim that the cushion housing programs provide softens work requirements, time limits, and the resulting benefit reductions and terminations (McIntire 1998). Blaming housing programs for problems that could arise in welfare reform could serve the agenda of those who seek to shift resources from low-income housing to other program areas that they favor more, or to tax cuts.

Those who support an affirmative role for government in housing should be concerned that housing programs may be seen as the next trap for poor families rather than as an important part of the safety net. If housing programs are not seen as part of the solution, they will be seen as part of the problem.

Appendix 4A

Financial Consequences to Housing Agencies of Changes in Tenants' Incomes

Because rent obligation is generally based on income, agencies' rent revenues will fluctuate depending on changes in tenants' incomes. Also, if tenant hardship or the absence of supervision for youth after school causes more vandalism and crime, maintenance and security costs will naturally increase (Wright, Ellen, and Schill 2001). Conversely, if working tenants maintain their units and common areas better, operating costs will decrease.[46] Fluctuating incomes may also result in an increase in administrative costs to make interim rent adjustments. However, fluctuations in revenue or costs will affect the agency only if HUD does not adjust its subsidy. Different funding rules apply to different federal housing programs.

Public housing. For PHAs operating public housing, federal operating subsidies should in theory (but with some exceptions) cover the difference between their assumed expenses, determined by formula, and actual revenues in the previous year. In other words, a PHA should receive increased operating subsidy in the following year if it experiences a net decrease in rent revenues.[47] (A year-end adjustment is possible, but only if HUD has the funds.) In five out of six years (between 1996 and 2001), appropriations for federal operating subsidies have not been large enough to close the gap between projected revenues and assumed costs; in two of these six years, the shortfall was substantial.[48]

---

[46] Rosenbaum, Stroh, and Flynn (1998) provide some evidence of reductions in operating costs when more tenants are employed.

[47] HUD bases the operating subsidy calculation on the amount of rent that a PHA is supposed to collect for a particular month in the previous year, not on actual collections. As a result, if families that have lost welfare income do not pay the full rent they owe, a PHA receives no additional subsidy from HUD.

[48] In FY 1996, the funds appropriated by Congress for operating subsidies for public housing were sufficient to meet only 89 percent of the gap between PHAs' needs, as determined by HUD's performance funding system (PFS) formula, and tenants' rent payments. In FY 1997, because of increased tenant rent payments, operating subsidies met 99 percent of need (GAO 1997), and in FY 1998, the same subsidy amount was sufficient to meet 100 percent of need. But in FY 1999, the adequacy of the operating subsidy dropped again to 92.5 percent of need, although it recovered substantially in FY 2000 to 98.5 percent and in FY 2001 to 99.5 percent of need as determined by the PFS formula (HUD PIH 1997, 1999, 2000a, and 2001). PHAs have long maintained that HUD's PFS formula significantly understates the actual gap between their operating costs and their revenues, in part because of the recent practice of assuming that actual average tenant revenues will increase by 3 percent the following year (CLPHA 2000).

If an agency's expenses increase because of maintenance or security costs, increased evictions, additional rent redeterminations, or other cause, no adjustment is made.[49]

Since FY 2001, however, PHAs that have experienced a net increase in tenant rent revenues have been permitted to retain 50 percent of it without a reduction in their federal operating subsidy (HUD PIH 2001). Consequently, it is in their interest to try to prevent a decrease and to achieve an increase in tenants' incomes.

Project-based Section 8. HUD is contractually obligated to pay the difference between the approved rents for units and tenant contributions. But like PHAs, private owners generally cannot get an increase in their federal subsidies if their costs go up. Moreover, the project-based Section 8 program has no mechanism to allow owners to retain any share of increased rent revenues. Thus, project-based Section 8 owners are insulated from the short-term financial consequences of a net change in tenants' incomes. However, over the long term, if units become less attractive to prospective tenants for whatever reason, owners may incur a loss from prolonged vacancies as well as from increased operating costs.

Tenant-based Section 8. While the PHA's subsidy payment to the landlord must increase if a tenant's income and required contribution decrease, recent HUD funding rules essentially hold PHAs harmless from a net decrease in rent contributions.[50] But if welfare recipients with Section 8 vouchers cannot pay their rent and are leaving landlords with uncollectible debts and additional costs for evictions, landlords may become wary of renting to families with vouchers.[51] If a PHA is

---

[49] The use of formula factors to determine the allowable expense level for public housing has been a long-standing feature of the PFS. The negotiated rulemaking required by QHWRA resulted in few changes to the expense side of the formula. Instead, HUD has commissioned a cost study, which is not expected to be completed for several years (CLPHA 2000).

[50] Nearly all contracts between HUD and PHAs for Section 8 subsidies are now renewed annually. Regulations effective in 2000 require HUD to renew these contracts based on the PHA's actual average costs for a guaranteed number of families. If costs increase because of decreased tenant contributions, the next year's funding from HUD will increase to close the gap. In the initial year in which the cost increase occurs, a PHA is permitted to draw on its reserve to meet the additional costs (Sard 2001c).

[51] The risk that a family with a voucher may be unable to pay its share of the rent is particularly great when the required payment is more than 30 percent of its adjusted income. There are three situations in which this could occur. First, if a family has leased a unit that has a rent in excess of the maximum a PHA will pay (known as the PHA's payment standard), the tenant remains liable for the excess portion regardless of a decrease in income (24 C.F.R. §§ 982.505, 982.515). Second, if a family loses welfare income as a result of a work-related sanction or welfare fraud, a PHA must not reduce

not able to use all its vouchers, it loses administrative fees and is at risk of having its total allocation of vouchers permanently reduced. Conversely, if tenants increase their incomes and must therefore pay more of the rent, the PHA may be able to use the funds it saves for more vouchers and thereby earn additional administrative fees.[52] Having more working families participating in its program may make it easier for a PHA to use its allocated vouchers, since owners may be more willing to rent to working families and more units will be within their reach.

Appendix 4B

Explanation of Table 4.1, HUD Funds to Housing Agencies for Work-Promoting Activities

The four HUD programs listed in table 4.1 (ROSS, HOPE VI Community and Supportive Services, FSS coordinators, and Neighborhood Networks) are the only funding streams available solely or virtually entirely to public housing or Section 8 agencies that are not intended for regular housing operations and can be used for work-promoting activities. With the exception of Neighborhood Networks, each has had annual appropriations for long enough to be considered reasonably permanent.[53] The information in table 4.1 and this appendix is derived from Sard (2002) and sources cited therein and from HUD notices of FY 2001 funding availability and documentation supporting its FY 2002 budget request (HUD 2001a, 2001b).

The total amount available from each funding stream for tenants in each of the three main housing programs was derived as follows:

---

the family's rent (Sard 2000; 24 C.F.R. §5.615). Third, a family may be subject to a minimum rent of up to $50 per month.

[52] The amount of administrative fees PHAs receive for the tenant-based Section 8 program is based on the number of families leasing units in a particular month (24 C.F.R. §982.152). The new renewal funding rule authorizes HUD to permanently reduce the funds allocated to a PHA that fails to lease 90 percent of its allocated vouchers (or use 90 percent of its allocated funds.) It also authorizes PHAs, subject to certain conditions, to maximize leasing above the allocated number of vouchers but within overall budget authority. The tenant-based Section 8 renewal rule is explained in Sard (2001c).

[53] Because they lack recurring annual appropriations, some recent programs are excluded from table 4.1, including the Jobs-Plus Demonstration, which provides comprehensive services funded by HUD, foundations, and local partners to tenants in six public housing developments at five PHAs, and the Regional Opportunity Counseling Program, which used $20 million appropriated in FY 1995 to fund mobility services in 16 metropolitan areas. (HUD received an additional $10 million for this program in FY 1999 and issued a notice of the availability of these funds in 2001.)

1. For ROSS, I estimated that $30 million was the maximum available
    annually to provide work-promoting services to families currently
    or recently receiving welfare benefits. Although $55 million has
    been appropriated by Congress in each of the past several years
    (ROSS previously was called the Economic Development and Sup-
    portive Services Program), about $20 million has been reserved
    each year for service coordinators for elderly and disabled tenants.
    In FY 2000 and FY 2001, HUD also reserved $5 million for capacity
    building for resident organizations. While not all of the remaining
    $30 million must or is likely to be used for work-promoting services,
    I had no reliable means of setting another figure. All program par-
    ticipants must be residents of conventional public or Indian hous-
    ing. (Before FY 2001, one-quarter of ROSS funds could be used, at
    a PHA's discretion, for Section 8 families.)

2. For HOPE VI Community and Supportive Services, the $73 million
    in the second column is 15 percent of the estimated $487,485,000
    that HUD is likely to make available to PHAs for public housing
    revitalization grants in FY 2002. Of the $573.735 million appropri-
    ated by Congress for HOPE VI for FY 2002, $11.25 million is set
    aside for technical assistance and for Neighborhood Networks. I
    have assumed that HUD will reserve $75 million for demolition-
    only grants, as it did in FY 2001, leaving $487,485,000 for public
    housing revitalization. PHAs are permitted to, but not required to,
    spend up to 15 percent of HOPE VI revitalization grants for serv-
    ices. Such services are likely to emphasize work but may include
    youth- or elder-directed services. I have assumed that PHAs receiv-
    ing revitalization grants will spend the maximum amount—15 per-
    cent—on work-promoting services. This estimate may be high. It
    does not include non-HOPE VI funds that may be required as a
    match. (If a PHA spends more than 5 percent of its grant for serv-
    ices, it must provide a dollar-for-dollar match for these additional
    expenditures, but the match may be soft—that is, provided in kind
    or through volunteer services.) Nor does it include any of the demo-
    lition-only funds that may be spent on work-promoting services,
    despite HUD's requirement that half of any relocation funds that
    PHAs receive as part of a demolition-only grant be spent to promote
    the self-sufficiency of displaced residents. I attributed the full
    amount of funds available for services under HOPE VI to public
    housing tenants. While PHAs are supposed to make services avail-
    able to families that originally resided in revitalized public housing
    and relocated using tenant-based Section 8 subsidies, I know of no
    data concerning how much if any of the HOPE VI funds PHAs
    spend on such families. (No portion of the HOPE VI program is
    available to families in the project-based Section 8 program.)

3. For FSS coordinators, $64.245 million is the total of the $17.845
    million that HUD indicated it will spend for public housing FSS
    coordinators in FY 2002 (as a supplement to the operating subsidy
    it provides to PHAs) and the $46.4 million that it received for ten-
    ant-based FSS coordinators for FY 2002. This amount does not
    include additional HUD expenditures as a result of the escrow
    feature of the FSS program. Project-based Section 8 families
    are excluded by statute.

4. Congress appropriated funds for Neighborhood Networks ($20 mil-
    lion) for the first time in FY 2002. Within the Public Housing Capi-
    tal Fund, Congress designated $15 million in competitive grants
    for Neighborhood Networks Initiatives to establish and operate
    computer centers. In addition, Congress set aside another $5 mil-
    lion that will be competitively awarded to PHAs for the establish-
    ment and initial operation of computer centers in conjunction with
    FY 2002 HOPE VI awards. (The administration had proposed
    $80 million for community technology centers in low-income areas
    that would not have been restricted to public housing residents.)
    In theory, PHAs could allow Section 8 families to use the centers
    and notify them of that fact, but are not required to do so. Conse-
    quently, I have not assumed that any of these funds benefit
    Section 8 families. In 2000, Congress amended the statutory provi-
    sions governing public housing operating and capital funds to
    authorize their use for Neighborhood Networks, but did not appro-
    priate additional money for this purpose.

Author

Barbara Sard is Director of Housing Policy at the Center on Budget and Policy
Priorities.

References

Allan, Richard S. 1995. Step-Up: Old Values, New Opportunities. *Journal of Housing
and Community Development* 52(6):31–36.

Andrews, Nancy O. 1998. Housing Affordability and Income Mobility for the Poor: A
Review of Trends and Strategies. Paper presented at Meeting America's Housing Needs
(MAHN): A Habitat II Follow-Up Project. Philadelphia, April 30.

Bailey, Maxine, and John Wallace. 1997. *An Overview of the Jobs-Plus Community Revitalization Initiative for Public Housing Families.* New York: Manpower Demonstration
Research Corporation.

Bania, Neil, Claudia Coulton, Nina Lalich, Toby Martin, Matt Newburn, and Cara J. Pasqualone. 2001. *A Comparison of Time-Limited and Non-Time-Limited Welfare Leavers in Cuyahoga County, Ohio*. Cleveland: Case Western Reserve University, Center on Urban Poverty and Social Change, Mandel School of Applied Social Sciences.

Basgal, Ophelia B. 2000. Welfare Reform: Should Housing Have a Role? *Journal of Housing and Community Development* 57(1):19–21.

Bogdon, Amy S. 1999. What Can We Learn from Previous Housing-Based Self-Sufficiency Programs. In *The Home Front: Implications of Welfare Reform for Housing Policy*, ed. Sandra J. Newman, 149–74. Washington, DC: Urban Institute Press.

Boushey, Heather, and Bai Ding. 2000. *Leaving Welfare: An Analysis of the Probability of Welfare Exits for New York City Public Housing Residents*. New York: New York City Housing Authority, Department of Research and Policy Development.

Bratt, Rachel G. 1996. *Housing Policy and Family Self-Sufficiency*. Background briefing report for the Family Impact Seminar. Washington, DC.

Bratt, Rachel G., and Langley C. Keyes. 1997. *New Perspectives on Self-Sufficiency: Strategies of Nonprofit Housing Organizations*. Medford, MA: Tufts University, Department of Urban and Environmental Policy.

Brooklyn Thrift Stores Provide Welfare-to-Work Training for Public Housing Residents. 1997. *Housing and Development Reporter*, September 8, pp. 276–77.

Brown, Prudence. 1996. Comprehensive Neighborhood-Based Initiatives. *Cityscape* 2(2):161–76.

Caftel, Brad, and Arthur Haywood. 1994. Making Section 3 Work: Employment Training and Job Opportunities for Low-Income People. *Clearinghouse Review* 27:1336–41.

Carter, Ron. 1998. Building on the Basics. *NHC News* 6(1):32–33.

Center for Community Change. 1999. *Comprehensive Services in Public Housing: Lessons from the Field*. Washington, DC.

CHA Promotes Resident Businesses, Job Training. 1997. *Housing and Development Reporter*, November 17, pp. 424–25.

Cohen, Carol S., Michael H. Phillips, Manuel A. Mendez, and Rosemary Ordonez. 2001. Sustaining Strong Communities in a World of Devolution: Empowerment-Based Social Services in Housing Settings. In *Social Work in the Era of Devolution: Toward a Just Practice*, ed. Rosa Perez-Koenig and Barry D. Rock, 286–304. New York: Fordham University Press.

CommonBond. 1998. *CommonBond Communities: 1997 Annual Report*. St. Paul, MN.

Connell, Terrence L., Deborah Devine, and Lester Rubin. 1998. *Welfare Reform Impacts on the Public Housing Program: A Preliminary Forecast*. Washington, DC: U.S. Department of Housing and Urban Development.

Corcoran, Mary, and Colleen Heflin. 2002. Barriers to Work among Housing Assistance Recipients. *Cityscape*, forthcoming.

Coulton, Claudia, Laura Leete, and Neil Bania. 1999. Housing, Transportation, and Access to Suburban Jobs by Welfare Recipients in the Cleveland Area. In *The Home Front: Implications of Welfare Reform for Housing Policy*, ed. Sandra J. Newman, 123–48. Washington, DC: Urban Institute Press.

Council of Large Public Housing Authorities. 2000. News from Congress. *CLPHA News* 17(16):1.

Diaz, Ricardo. 1997. Milwaukee's Application of the Community Building Strategy in the Coordination of Housing and Welfare Reform Initiatives. Paper read at the Urban Institute conference, Washington, DC, September 9.

Ebb, Nancy. 1997. *Lemon-Aid? Making the New Welfare Law Work for Children and Families*. Washington, DC: Children's Defense Fund.

Ellen, Ingrid Gould, and Margery Austin Turner. 1997. Does Neighborhood Matter? Assessing Recent Evidence. *Housing Policy Debate* 8(4):833–66.

Fleischer, Wendy, and Kay E. Sherwood. 2000. *The Next Wave: Employing People with Multiple Barriers to Work. Policy Lessons from the Next Step: Jobs Initiative*. New York: Corporation for Supportive Housing.

Franco, Rubin. 1995. From Welfare to Work in New York City Public Housing. *Fordham Urban Law Journal* 22(4):1197–1206.

Gallagher, L. Jerome, Megan Gallagher, Kevin Perese, Susan Schreiber, and Keith Watson. 1998. *One Year after Federal Welfare Reform: A Description of State Temporary Assistance for Needy Families (TANF) Decisions as of October 1997*. Washington, DC: Urban Institute.

Goldberg, Heidi, and Liz Schott. 2000. *A Compliance-Oriented Approach to Sanctions in State and County TANF Programs*. Washington, DC: Center on Budget and Policy Priorities. Also available at <http://www.cbpp.org/10-1-00TANFcover.htm>.

Golden, Olivia. 1998. Testimony before the House Ways and Means Committee, Subcommittee on Human Resources, March 19. World Wide Web page <http://waysandmeans.house.gov/105hear.htm> (accessed January 2002).

Gramlich, Ed. 1998. *CDBG: An Action Guide to the Community Development Block Grant Program*. Washington, DC: Center for Community Change.

Hecht, Bennett L. 1996. Housing-Led Economic Development. *Shelterforce* 89.

Herr, Toby, Suzanne L. Wagner, and Robert Halpern. 1996. *Making the Shoe Fit: Creating a Work-Prep System for a Large and Diverse Welfare Population*. Chicago: Project Match.

High-Rise Project Rehabilitated with Property Disposition Grant. 1998. *Housing and Development Reporter*, September 7, pp. 263–64.

Hughes, Mark Alan. 1995. A Mobility Strategy for Improving Opportunity. *Housing Policy Debate* 6(1):271–97.

Job Readiness, Upgraded Skills Emphasized in Danbury Program. 1999. *Housing and Development Reporter*, January 11, p. 569.

Johnson, Clifford M. 1998. *Washington State's Community Jobs Initiative*. Washington, DC: Center on Budget and Policy Priorities.

Kato, Linda Y., and James A. Riccio. 2001. *Building New Partnerships for Employment: Collaboration among Agencies and Public Housing Residents in the Jobs-Plus Demonstration*. New York: Manpower Demonstration Research Corporation.

Khadduri, Jill, Mark Shroder, and Barry Steffen. 2003. Can Housing Assistance Support Welfare Reform? In *A Place to Live, a Means to Work: How Housing Assistance Can Strengthen Welfare Policy*, ed. Barbara Sard and Amy S. Bogdon, 23–62. Washington, DC: Fannie Mae Foundation.

Kingsley, G. Thomas, Joseph B. McNeely, and James O. Gibson. 1997. *Community Building: Coming of Age*. Washington, DC: Development Training Institute, Inc., and Urban Institute.

Knox, Virginia, Cynthia Miller, and Lisa A. Gennetian. 2000. *Reforming Welfare and Rewarding Work: A Summary of the Final Report on the Minnesota Family Investment Program*. New York: Manpower Demonstration Research Program. Also available at <http://www.mdrc.org/Reports2000/MFIP/MFIPSummary.htm>.

Kramer, Frederica D. 2000. Designing a Family-Centered, Housing-Based Employment Program. *Welfare Information Network Design Brief* 1(1). World Wide Web page <http://www.welfareinfo.org/krameraprildesign.htm> (accessed February 9, 2002).

Lazere, Ed. 2000. *Welfare Balances after Three Years of TANF Block Grants: Unspent TANF Funds at the End of Fiscal Year 1999*. Washington, DC: Center on Budget and Policy Priorities. Also available at <http://www.cbpp.org/1-11-00wel.pdf>.

Lazere, Ed, and Jennifer Daskal. 2003. Will Changing the Rent Formula Encourage Moves from Welfare to Work? In *A Place to Live, a Means to Work: How Housing Assistance Can Strengthen Welfare Policy*, ed. Barbara Sard and Amy S. Bogdon, 181–210. Washington, DC: Fannie Mae Foundation.

Leavitt, Jacqueline, and Mary Ochs. 1997. Failing, But Not Fooling, Public Housing Residents: The Impact of Job Interventions. Unpublished paper. University of California at Los Angeles, School of Public Policy, Department of Urban Planning.

Lombardi, Joan. 1996. Remarks by the Department of Health and Human Services Director of Child Care at the Department of Housing and Urban Development Forum on Public Housing in the Era of Welfare Reform. Washington, DC, December 17.

Loprest, Pamela. 1999. Families Who Left Welfare: Who Are They and How Are They Doing? Assessing the New Federalism Discussion Paper 99–02. Washington, DC: Urban Institute.

Loprest, Pamela. 2001. *How Are Families That Left Welfare Doing? A Comparison of Early and Recent Welfare Leavers*. New Federalism National Survey of America's Families Paper B–36. Washington, DC: Urban Institute.

Lubell, Jeffrey M., Kathryn P. Nelson, and Barbara Sard. 2003. How Housing Programs' Admissions Policies Can Contribute to Welfare Reform. In *A Place to Live, a Means to Work: How Housing Assistance Can Strengthen Welfare Policy*, ed. Barbara Sard and Amy S. Bogdon, 211–67. Washington, DC: Fannie Mae Foundation.

Lubell, Jeffrey, M., and Barbara Sard. 1999. *Welfare-to-Work Housing Vouchers: An Innovative Approach to Welfare Reform*. Washington, DC: Center on Budget and Policy Priorities. Also available at <http://www.cbpp.org/12-2-98hous.htm>.

Ludwig, Jens, Greg J. Duncan, and Joshua C. Pinkston. 2000. Neighborhood Effects on Economic Self-Sufficiency: Evidence from a Randomized Housing-Mobility Experiment. Unpublished paper. Georgetown University.

Madison Park Development Corporation. 1998. Overview of the Customer Service Training Program, Robert A. Rapoza Associates. *Welfare to Work: Briefings for Community-Based Organizations*. Paper presented at the conference by Danette Jones, Newton, MA, January 26.

MAHN [Meeting America's Housing Needs] Conference/Dialogue. 1998. Housing Employing Tenants: Providing the Jobs Low-Income Residents Need. Remarks by C.J. Ross from the American Federation of State, County, and Municipal Employees. Washington, DC, May 21.

Manpower Demonstration Research Corporation. 1996. *Lessons from the Field on the Implementation of Section 3*. Washington, DC: U.S. Department of Housing and Urban Development, Office of Policy Development and Research.

McIntire, Claire. 1998. Testimony of the Commissioner of the Massachusetts Department of Transitional Assistance at the oversight hearing of the Joint Committee on Human Services. Boston, March.

McKay, Emily Gantz, and Cristina Lopez. 1997. *Linking Human Services and Economic Development*. Washington, DC: Center for Community Change.

Mendes, Dominic. 1998. Beyond the Barriers. *NHC News* 6(1):25–27.

Mobile Public Housing Effort Links Retail Store, Training. 1999. *Housing and Development Reporter*, September 6, pp. 271–72.

Moffitt, Robert, and Jennifer Roff. 2000. *The Diversity of Welfare Leavers*. Background paper. *Welfare, Children, and Families: A Three-City Study*. Working Paper 00–01. Also available at <http://www.jhu.edu/~welfare/leav1a_all.pdf>.

Nagle, Gloria. 2001. *Comparing Housing-Assisted and Unassisted Welfare Leavers in Massachusetts*. Boston: Massachusetts Department of Transitional Assistance.

Naparstek, Arthur J., Susan R. Freis, G. Thomas Kingsley, with Dennis Dooley and Howard E. Lewis. 2000. *HOPE VI: Community Building Makes a Difference*. Washington, DC: U.S. Department of Housing and Urban Development.

National Association of Housing and Redevelopment Officials. 1998. *1998 NAHRO Agency Awards of Merit in Housing and Community Development*. Washington, DC.

National Council of State Housing Agencies, Working Group on Welfare and Housing. 1998. Final Report. Washington, DC.

National Housing Conference. 1998. Neighborhood Networks: Computer Learning Centers Help Residents Map a New Path to a Brighter Future. *NHC News* 6(1):28–31.

National Housing Conference Panel. 1998. Putting the Pieces Together. *NHC News* 6(1):15–19, 34–35.

National Housing Law Project. 1993. Jobs for Residents of Assisted Housing and Low-Income Neighborhoods: Fulfilling the Promise—and the Law. *Housing Law Bulletin* 23 (November/December):93, 95

National Housing Law Project. 1994. *HUD Housing Programs: Tenants' Rights*. 2nd ed. Part 14.2.6.5. Oakland, CA.

National Housing Law Project. 1999. PHAs Surveyed on Program and Policy Responses to New Welfare Law. *Housing Law Bulletin* 29 (April):55, 65.

National Low-Income Housing Coalition. 1998. *NLIHC's Findings on Images of Low-Income Housing*. World Wide Web pages <http://www.nlihc.org/mediapr.htm> and <http://www.nlihc.org/pollresl.htm> (accessed May 1, 1998).

Newman, Sandra J., and Joseph Harkness. 1999. The Effects of Welfare Reform on Housing: A National Analysis. In *The Home Front: Implications of Welfare Reform for Housing Policy*, ed. Sandra J. Newman, 29–80. Washington, DC: Urban Institute Press.

Newman, Sandra J., and Ann B. Schnare. 1997. "…And a Suitable Living Environment": The Failure of Housing Programs to Deliver on Neighborhood Quality. *Housing Policy Debate* 8(4):703–41.

Nightingale, Demetra Smith, Terri Thompson, Nancy Pindus, Pamela Holcomb, Edgar Lee, Jesse Valente, and John Trutko. 2000. *Early Implementation of the Welfare-to-Work Grants Program: Findings from Exploratory Site Visits and Review of Program Plans*. Princeton, NJ: Mathematica Policy Research, Inc.

Nowak, Jeremy. 1998. Expanding the Scope of Community Development. *Shelterforce* 97:10–12.

Olson, Krista, and LaDonna Pavetti. 1996. *Personal and Family Challenges to the Successful Transition from Welfare to Work*. Washington, DC: Urban Institute.

Ong, Paul. 1998. Subsidized Housing and Work among Welfare Recipients. *Housing Policy Debate* 9(4):775–94.

Peterson, George E., and Kale Williams. 1995. Housing Mobility: What Has It Accomplished and What Is Its Promise? In *Housing Mobility: Promise or Illusion?* ed. Alexander Polikoff, 7–102. Washington, DC: Urban Institute.

Pitcoff, Winton. 1997. Redefining Community Development Comprehensive Community Initiatives, Part I. *Shelterforce* 96:CCI1–CCI15.

Pollack, Wendy, and Dina Schlossberg. 1999. Department of Housing and Urban Development and Section 3: Challenges and Opportunities. *Clearinghouse Review* 33:50–65.

Primus, Wendell, Lynette Rawlings, Kathy Larin, and Kathryn Porter. 1999. The *Initial Impacts of Welfare Reform on the Incomes of Single-Mother Families*. Washington, DC: Center on Budget and Policy Priorities.

Public Housing: Utah Ties Housing to Welfare Reform Program. 1997. *Housing and Development Reporter*, July 28, p. 167.

Riccio, James A. 1999a. Lessons from Welfare-to-Work Experiments and Their Implications for Housing-Based Self-Sufficiency Programs. In *The Home Front: Implications of Welfare Reform for Housing Policy*, ed. Sandra J. Newman, 175–200. Washington, DC: Urban Institute.

Riccio, James A. 1999b. *Mobilizing Public Housing Communities for Work: Origins and Early Accomplishments of the Jobs-Plus Demonstration*. New York: Manpower Demonstration Research Corporation.

Riccio, James A., and Alan Orenstein. 2003. Are Welfare Recipients in Public Housing Really Harder to Employ? In *A Place to Live, a Means to Work: How Housing Assistance Can Strengthen Welfare Policy*, ed. Barbara Sard and Amy S. Bogdon, 63–103. Washington, DC: Fannie Mae Foundation.

Richer, Elise, Steve Savner, and Mark Greenberg. 2001. *Frequently Asked Questions about Working Welfare Leavers*. Washington, DC: Center for Law and Social Policy.

Robins, Philip K. 1988. Child Care and Convenience: The Effects of Labor Market Entry Costs on Economic Self-Sufficiency among Public Housing Residents. *Social Science Quarterly* 69(1):122–36.

Rohe, William M., and Rachel Garshick Kleit. 1997. From Dependency to Self-Sufficiency: An Appraisal of the Gateway Transitional Families Program. *Housing Policy Debate* 8(1):75–108.

Rohe, William M., and Rachel Garshick Kleit. 1999. Housing, Welfare Reform, and Self-Sufficiency: An Assessment of the Family Self-Sufficiency Program. *Housing Policy Debate* 10(2):333–69.

Rojas, Diana. 1997. New Model Holds Promise of True Resident Self-Sufficiency in Assisted Housing Projects. *Multifamily Advisor*, Summer, pp. 1–2, 6–8.

Rosenbaum, James E. 1995. Changing the Geography of Opportunity by Expanding Residential Choice: Lessons from the Gautreaux Program. *Housing Policy Debate* 6(1):231–69.

Rosenbaum, James E., and Stefanie DeLuca. 2000. *Is Housing Mobility the Key to Welfare Reform? Lessons from Chicago's Gautreaux Program*. Washington, DC: Brookings Institution, Center on Urban and Metropolitan Policy.

Rosenbaum, James E., and Susan J. Popkin. 1991. Employment and Earnings of Low-Income Blacks Who Move to Middle-Class Suburbs. In *The Urban Underclass*, ed. Christopher Jencks and Paul E. Peterson, 342–56. Washington, DC: Brookings Institution.

Rosenbaum, James E., Linda K. Stroh, and Cathy A. Flynn. 1998. Lake Parc Place: A Study of Mixed-Income Housing. *Housing Policy Debate* 9(4):703–40.

Rothman, Iris, Dave Beckwith, and Rich Stolz. 1998. *Getting to Work: An Organizer's Guide to Transportation Equity*. Washington, DC: Center for Community Change.

Sard, Barbara. 1993. The Massachusetts Experience with Targeted Tenant-Based Rental Assistance for the Homeless: Lessons on Housing Policy for Socially Disfavored Groups. *Georgetown Journal on Fighting Poverty* 1(1):16–27.

Sard, Barbara. 2000. The Intersection of Housing and Welfare Reform. *Clearinghouse Review* 33:502–23. An updated version of this article is available at <http://www.equaljustice.org/substantive.htm>.

Sard, Barbara. 2001a. *The Family Self-Sufficiency Program: HUD's Best Kept Secret for Promoting Employment and Asset Growth*. Washington, DC: Center on Budget and Policy Priorities. Also available at <http://www.cbpp.org/4-12-01hous.htm>.

Sard, Barbara. 2001b. Housing Vouchers Should Be a Major Component of Future Housing Policy for the Lowest-Income Families. *Cityscape* 5(2):89–110.

Sard, Barbara. 2001c. Section 8 Renewal Rule: Use It or Lose It. *Journal of Housing and Community Development* 58(3):27–32.

Sard, Barbara. 2002. *Outline of How Federal Housing Programs Can Help Provide Employment and Training Opportunities and Support Services to Current and Former Welfare Recipients*. Washington, DC: Center on Budget and Policy Priorities. Also available at <http://www.cbpp.org/1-6-00hous.htm>.

Sard, Barbara, and Jeffrey M. Lubell. 1998. *How the Statutory Changes Made by the Quality Housing and Work Responsibility Act of 1998 May Affect Welfare Reform Efforts*. Washington, DC: Center on Budget and Policy Priorities. Revised in January 2000. The revised version is also available at <http://www.cbpp.org/12-17-98hous.htm>.

Sard, Barbara, and Patricia Sanders. 2001. *Promoting Work among Residents of Public Housing: The Role of Welfare Agencies in Implementing the Earned Income Disregard*. Washington, DC: Center on Budget and Policy Priorities. Also available at <http://www.cbpp.org/10-17-01hous.htm>.

Schwartz, Alex, and Kian Tajbakhsh. 1997. Mixed-Income Housing: Unanswered Questions. *Cityscape* 3(2):71–92.

Section 3 Employment Efforts Have Had Success, but Strong Economy May Require New Strategies. 1998. *Housing and Development Reporter*, June 1, pp. 30–40.

Sexton, Joe. 1997. In a Pocket of Brooklyn Sewn by Welfare, an Unraveling. *New York Times*, March 10, pp. A1, A18.

Sherman, Arloc, Cheryl Amey, Barbara Duffield, Nancy Ebb, and Deborah Weinstein. 1998. *Welfare to What? Early Findings on Family Hardship and Well-Being*. Washington, DC: Children's Defense Fund and National Coalition for the Homeless.

Shlay, Anne B. 1993. Family Self-Sufficiency and Housing. *Housing Policy Debate* 4(3):457–95.

Strawn, Julie. 1998. *Beyond Job Search or Basic Education: Rethinking the Role of Skills in Welfare Reform*. Washington, DC: Center on Law and Social Policy.

Sweeney, Eileen P. 2000. *Recent Studies Make Clear That Many Parents Who Are Current or Former Welfare Recipients Have Disabilities and Other Medical Conditions*. Washington, DC: Center on Budget and Policy Priorities.

Toloken, Lisa. 1997. Community College, Housing Authority Bridge Fear of Education. *Employment & Training Reporter*, September 3, pp. 6–7.

Tull, Tanya. 1996. Service-Enriched Housing: Breaking the Cycle of Poverty through Empowerment. *Shelterforce* 88.

Turner, Margery Austin. 1998. Moving Out of Poverty: Expanding Mobility and Choice through Tenant-Based Housing Assistance. *Housing Policy Debate* 9(2):373–94.

Turner, Margery Austin, and Kale Williams. 1998. *Housing Mobility: Realizing the Promise*. Washington, DC: Urban Institute.

U.S. Department of Health and Human Services, Office of the Assistant Secretary for Planning and Evaluation. 2000. *"Leavers" and Diversion Studies: Summary of Research on Welfare Outcomes Funded by ASPE*. World Wide Web page <http://aspe.os.dhhs.gov/hsp/leavers99/fy00.htm> (last modified April 8, 2002).

U.S. Departments of Health and Human Services, Labor, and Transportation. 2000. *Joint Guidance on Use of TANF, WtW, and Job Access Funds for Transportation*. World Wide Web page <http://www.acf.dhhs.gov/programs/ofa/pa002.htm> (last modified May 26).

U.S. Department of Housing and Urban Development. 1997a. *Occupancy Requirements of Subsidized Multifamily Housing Programs*. HUD Handbook 4350.3, CHG–28. Washington, DC.

U.S. Department of Housing and Urban Development. 1997b. *The State of the Cities*. Washington, DC.

U.S. Department of Housing and Urban Development. 1997c. *The HUD Management Agent Handbook*. HUD Handbook 4381.5, REV–2, CHG–2. Washington, DC.

U.S. Department of Housing and Urban Development. 2000a. *Congressional Justifications for 2001 Estimates*. World Wide Web pages <http://www.hud.gov/budget01/justif/pih/degflih.html> and <http://www.hud.gov/budget01/justif/hcf.html> (accessed December 9, 2001).

U.S. Department of Housing and Urban Development. 2000b. Funding Availability for the HOPE VI Program and for the Public Housing Resident Opportunities and Self Sufficiency (ROSS) Program. *Federal Register* 65:9599, 9697. February 24.

U.S. Department of Housing and Urban Development. 2001a. *Congressional Justifications for 2002 Estimates*. World Wide Web page <http://www.hud.gov/about/budget/fy02/cjs/toc1.cfm.> (accessed December 9, 2001).

U.S. Department of Housing and Urban Development. 2001b. Super Notice of Funding Availability. *Federal Register* 66:11638–12425. February 26.

U.S. Department of Housing and Urban Development. 2002a. *Neighborhood Networks*. World Wide Web page <http://www.hud.gov/nnw/nnwaboutnn.html> (accessed January 11, 2002).

U.S. Department of Housing and Urban Development. 2002b. Notice of Funding Availability (NOFA): Fair Shares Allocation of Incremental Voucher Funding, Fiscal Year 2002. *Federal Register* 67:8428–8440. February 22.

U.S. Department of Housing and Urban Development, Office of Fair Housing and Equal Opportunity. 1995. *Section 3: Job Training, Employment, and Contracting Opportunities for Low-Income Persons*. Washington, DC.

U.S. Department of Housing and Urban Development, Office of Fair Housing and Equal Opportunity. 2000. *Regional Opportunity Counseling (ROC) Program: 1999 Second-Year Report Summaries*. Washington, DC. April.

U.S. Department of Housing and Urban Development, Office of Policy Development and Research. 1998. Characteristics of Households in Public and Assisted Housing. *Recent Research Results*. Washington, D.C. March. World Wide Web page <http://www.huduser.org/periodicals/rrr/3_98pub.html> (accessed December 9, 2001).

U.S. Department of Housing and Urban Development, Office of Policy Development and Research. 1999. *Moving to Opportunity for Fair Housing Demonstration Program: Current Status and Initial Findings*. Washington DC.

U.S. Department of Housing and Urban Development, Office of Public and Indian Housing. 1997. *FY 1997 and 1998 Subsidies for Operation of Low-Income Housing Projects*. PIH Notice 97–61. Washington, DC. December 8.

U.S. Department of Housing and Urban Development, Office of Public and Indian Housing. 1999. *FY 1999 Subsidies for Operation of Low-Income Housing Projects*. PIH Notice 99–13. Washington, DC. February 23.

U.S. Department of Housing and Urban Development, Office of Public and Indian Housing. 2000a. *FY 2000 Subsidies for Operation of Low-Income Housing Projects and FY 2000 Performance Funding System Inflation Factor, Equation-Related Tables and Special Notes Related to Operating Subsidy Eligibility*. PIH Notices 2000–03 and 2000–04. Washington, DC. February 3.

U.S. Department of Housing and Urban Development, Office of Public and Indian Housing. 2000b. Public Housing Assessment System (PHAS): Technical Correction. *Federal Register* 65:36042. June 6.

U.S. Department of Housing and Urban Development, Office of Public and Indian Housing. 2000c. The Welfare-to-Work Program Evaluation. Conference materials (pp. 7–15) from the Welfare-to-Work Vouchers: Partnerships to Success National Conference, Washington, DC, February 24.

U.S. Department of Housing and Urban Development, Office of Public and Indian Housing. 2001. *Submission of Operating Subsidy Eligibility Requests for FY 2001, Proration Factor and Other Special Notes*. PIH Notice 2001–32. Washington, DC. August 24.

U.S. Department of Labor. 1992. *Coordination of Housing and Job Training Services: A Review of Best Practices in 12 Cities*. Research and Evaluation Report Series 92–D. Washington, DC.

U.S. Department of Labor. 1999. *Welfare-to-Work Grant Announcements*. World Wide Web page: <http://www.doleta.gov/competitive> (accessed December 9, 2001).

U.S. Department of Transportation, Federal Transit Administration. 2000. Notice of Availability of Funds for Job Access and Reverse Commute Competitive Grants. *Federal Register* 65:13210. March 10.

U.S. General Accounting Office. 1992. *Public and Assisted Housing: Linking Housing and Supportive Services to Promote Self-Sufficiency*. GAO/RCED–92–142BR. Washington, DC.

U.S. General Accounting Office. 1993. *Self-Sufficiency: Opportunities and Disincentives on the Road to Economic Independence*. GAO/HRD–93–23. Washington, DC.

U.S. General Accounting Office. 1996. *Public Housing: Partnerships Can Result in Cost Savings and Other Benefits*. GAO/RCED–97–11. Washington, DC.

U.S. General Accounting Office. 1997. *Welfare Reform: Issues and Possible Implications for HUD's Programs and Tenants*. GAO/RCED–97–148R. Washington, DC.

U.S. General Accounting Office. 1998a. *Welfare Reform: Changes Will Further Shape the Roles of Housing Agencies and HUD*. GAO/RCED–98–148. Washington, DC.

U.S. General Accounting Office. 1998b. *Welfare Reform: Transportation's Role in Moving from Welfare to Work*. GAO/RCED–98–161. Washington, DC.

U.S. General Accounting Office. 2000. *Welfare Reform: State Sanction Policies and Number of Families Affected*. GAO/HEHS–00–44. Washington, DC.

Vale, Lawrence J. 1998. Comment on James E. Rosenbaum, Linda K. Stroh, and Cathy A. Flynn's "Lake Parc Place: A Study of Mixed-Income Housing." *Housing Policy Debate* 9(4):749–56.

Watkins, Dan. 1993. *Creating Economic Lift: Job, Training, and Business Opportunities in Public and Indian Housing*. Washington, DC: U.S. Department of Housing and Urban Development, Office of Public and Indian Housing, Office of Resident Initiatives.

Weiss, Marcus, and Kevin Kelly. 2000. *Building Partnerships between State TANF Initiatives and CDCs*. Washington, DC: National Congress for Community Economic Development.

Welfare Information Network. 1999. Housing and Welfare Reform: Strategic Intersections in Place-Based Strategies, *Resources for Welfare Decisions* 3(4). World Wide Web page <http://www.welfareinfo.org/housingresource.htm> (accessed December 9, 2001).

Wood, Michelle, Gretchen P. Locke, B. Hannah Shulevitz, Diane M. Porcari, Sandra Nolden, and Jean Amedolia. 1999. *From Welfare to Work: Using HUD's Programs to Help Families in Transition*. Washington, DC: U.S. Department of Housing and Urban Development, Office of Policy Development and Research.

Wright, David J., Ingrid Gould Ellen, and Michael H. Schill. 2001. *Community Development Corporations and Welfare Reform: Linkages, Roles, and Impacts*. Albany, NY: Nelson A. Rockefeller Institute of Government.

Zdenek, Robert O. 1998. Connecting People to Jobs. *Shelterforce* 19(1):13–15.

CHAPTER 5

An Alternative View of the Role of Housing Providers in an Era of Welfare Reform

Sunia Zaterman
Council of Large Public Housing Authorities

Abstract

Housing authorities are responding to today's varied challenges with increasing creativity, innovation, and pragmatism. Despite limited resources, they are acting strategically and resourcefully through their core housing mission and beyond to promote the economic self-sufficiency of families in public housing. A thoughtful approach requires considering several key factors that shape the role of housing authorities under welfare reform: limited resources, regulatory constraints, barriers to self-sufficiency, competing demands for services, and limited understanding of what really works.

Housing authorities must have the flexibility to craft effective, locally determined self-sufficiency strategies but should not be viewed as substitutes for welfare and service agencies. The debate should focus on reducing poverty rather than on welfare caseloads. Until families' incomes rise above the poverty level, the need for housing assistance will far outstrip the supply. Decent, affordable housing can play a critical role in welfare-to-work transitions and underlies meaningful, effective, and appropriate partnerships.

Keywords: Low-income housing; Welfare

Introduction

Housing authorities are responding to today's varied challenges with increasing creativity, innovation, and pragmatism. A key challenge is to implement effective, locally determined self-sufficiency strategies with positive outcomes in the face of limited resources, inconsistent mandates, and competing priorities. Identifying effective economic self-sufficiency strategies that support, rather than undermine, the core mission to provide good-quality, safe, and affordable housing to those in need is critical.

Good economic times fueled welfare reform initiatives that resulted in a 59 percent reduction in welfare caseloads from July 1994 to July 2001, but poverty has not been significantly reduced. As the economy suffered a downturn, caseloads began to increase. From July 2001 to December 2001, national welfare caseloads increased by 2.3 percent (Besharov 2002). Even with a sustained period of economic prosperity, the Department of Housing and Urban Development (HUD) reports that 4.9 million renter households still have worst-case needs for rental assistance (2001). Employment without increased earnings gives families few options in the private unsubsidized housing market. Until families' incomes rise above the poverty level, the demand and need for housing assistance will far outstrip the supply. Further, if housing helps provide stability to families moving from welfare to work, then housing and welfare agencies can be valuable partners. Therein lies the basis for meaningful, effective, and appropriate partnerships.

While there is much to agree with in Chapter 4, a thoughtful approach requires adequate consideration of several key factors that shape the role of housing authorities[1] in the welfare reform era:

1. *Fiscal challenges*. The core mission of public housing agencies to provide decent and safe affordable housing is undermined by astoundingly large shortfalls in federal funding. In the past decade, shortfalls for operating subsidies to support basic property management and maintenance for public housing totaled more than $1.5 billion (Council of Large Public Housing Authorities [CLPHA] 2002). Over $22 billion in capital investment is needed to modernize and revitalize aging, outdated, and poorly designed public housing.

2. *Competing demands for services and resources*. While there are some specific sources for funding services for public housing residents, they are woefully inadequate to meet the competing needs of the elderly, those with disabilities, and children living in public housing. Further exacerbating the situation was the elimination of the Public Housing Drug Elimination Program (PHDEP) in fiscal year (FY) 2002. This program funded many crime prevention, security, and youth programs that must now search for other sources of funding.

3. *Regulatory challenges*. A history of burdensome and contradictory federal regulations created disincentives for self-sufficiency that are only now beginning to be addressed through the implementation of

---

[1] Housing authorities also administer the Section 8 housing voucher program, which serves a significant number of welfare recipients. The Section 8 program has a different set of fiscal and regulatory constraints in addressing the self-sufficiency needs of voucher holders and requires separate discussion. The focus of this chapter is primarily the public housing program.

the Quality Housing and Work Responsibility Act (QHWRA) of 1998.

4. *Self-sufficiency challenges.* Public housing residents who remain on welfare are more likely to experience multiple barriers to employment requiring higher levels of diverse services. Roller-coaster economic conditions will also have a significant impact on success.

5. *Limited knowledge of what really works.* There is little empirical research showing that housing-driven strategies have an effect on increasing wages. Moreover, even the experts disagree on which strategies work.

6. *Need for locally determined strategies.* Economic self-sufficiency strategies must be locally determined because public housing residents, their local economies, and job markets vary considerably across metropolitan areas.

7. *Housing providers versus social service providers.* There are inherent conflicts in having the housing provider act as a welfare agency because the provider's primary responsibility is to maintain and protect the public housing asset in order to serve the community as a whole and its residents.

Fiscal Challenges

The ability of public housing agencies (PHAs) to provide decent, safe, and affordable shelter to a tenant population consisting of low-income families, the elderly, and those with disabilities depends on adequate and continued federal funding for basic operations. Primarily because of the restrictions on rents established by Congress, PHAs have no other source of funds to cover their shortfalls when that body appropriates less than full funding for operating subsidies. This lack of adequate funding has an immediate effect on critical staffing levels needed for management, maintenance, security, and other functions. CLPHA estimates that the past decade has seen public housing developments endure operating fund shortfalls of over $1.5 billion (2002). Some of these cuts were used to pay for U.S. troops in Bosnia and other defense programs.

A further blow, delivered by Congress in FY 2002, was the administration's request to end the PHDEP, which funded security, crime prevention, and resident services for more than 10 years at roughly $300 million per year. The cut was justified by stating that more funds were available to cover security needs. Yet the FY 2002 operating fund proration rate (the percentage of the operating subsidy need met by appropriations) shows that the amount appropriated covers only operating costs, with no resources available for the security and crime prevention programs funded by PHDEP.

In addition, the continuous and severe lack of funding for modernizing public housing means that basic capital investment in aging properties is routinely thwarted. Funding levels that cover only annual wear and tear (accrual need) cannot effectively reduce the backlog of modernization needs. By HUD's own admission, past appropriations covered little more than annual accrual needs. Unmet capital needs of $22 billion beg for attention. As a result, physical depreciation of the public housing stock continues, creating a new need for large amounts of additional rehabilitation and redevelopment.

Competing Demands for Services and Resources

All services, activities, and functions have costs, either monetary costs or the costs of choosing one kind of service or activity over another. The historic underfunding of basic public housing operations and capital improvements makes all cost decisions a zero sum game. While self-sufficiency strategies for employable residents constitute one specific need, elderly and disabled households occupy almost 45 percent of public housing units, and the need for continuum of care services to facilitate and prolong independent living for those aging in place is increasing. In addition, there are over a million children living in public housing, and their need for educational, social, recreational, and crime prevention activities is also increasing. The competing demands on the woefully inadequate funds that are allotted for services create fierce competition for limited dollars. Even though some funds are available exclusively to housing agencies, they fall far short of what is needed to sustain effective initiatives over time.

Regulatory Challenges

Throughout the past decade, housing authorities have called for reform of a burdensome and counterproductive regulatory and funding system fraught with disincentives and unintended negative consequences for public housing residents. The years of debate preceding the passage of QHWRA in 1998 showed how rigid, overly bureaucratic, one-size-fits-all federal housing policies in fact stymied self-sufficiency efforts instead of facilitating them. The preamble of QHWRA (Section 502) identifies the regulatory challenges facing public housing:

> Congress finds that...the inventory of public housing units owned, assisted, or operated by public housing agencies, an asset in which the Federal Government has invested over $90 billion, has traditionally provided rental housing that is affordable to low-income persons; despite serving this critical function, the public housing system is plagued by a series of problems, including the concentration of very poor people in very poor neighborhoods and disincentives for economic self-sufficiency; the federal method of overseeing every aspect of public housing by detailed and complex statutes and regulations has aggravated the problem and has placed excessive administrative burdens on the public housing agencies....The purpose of this title is to promote homes that are affordable to low-income families in safe and healthy environments, and thereby contribute to the supply of affordable housing, by—...deregulating and decontrolling public housing agencies, thereby enabling them to perform as property and asset managers;...facilitating mixed income communities and decreasing concentrations of poverty in public housing;...[and] creating incentives and economic opportunities for residents of dwelling units assisted by public housing agencies to work, become self-sufficient, and transition out of public housing. (60–61)

While QHWRA does not always live up to the promise of deregulation laid out in the preamble, it does attempt to remove disincentives, create incentives, and promote healthier mixed-income communities that by their very nature promote work. The following provisions, which support the core housing mission, are powerful tools to promote economic self-sufficiency. These are examined elsewhere in this volume:

1. Greater flexibility in setting rents through mandatory and optional income disregards allows residents to work without having rent increases rob them of the benefits of increased income.

2. The ability to use site-based waiting lists allows public housing applicants the same choice that all other federal housing assistance recipients already enjoy, namely choosing housing in a location that best suits employment, education, or child care needs as determined by the applicant.

3. Flexibility in targeting permits greater income mixing in developments, thereby promoting social capital through networking and positive role models.

4. More flexible use of capital funds to leverage mixed-income, mixed-finance developments improves the quality and supply of housing as a foundation for work readiness.

These provisions, working in tandem and tailored to local circumstances, begin to address the historic disincentives to work inherent in the public housing system. Using rent incentives and disregards can make work pay for public housing residents. Site-based waiting lists can remove transportation and child care obstacles to employment by allowing applicants to choose developments that best meet their locational needs. Greater income mixing reduces concentrations of poverty and builds social networks for employment. Housing authorities now have greater flexibility to tailor these provisions to local circumstances.

Self-Sufficiency Challenges

Lack of consistent, reliable data from HUD makes demographic analysis difficult. Estimates from the most recent information indicate that anywhere from 14 percent to 20 percent of public housing households depend on public assistance as their main source of income.[2] The current percentage of welfare recipients in public housing has declined from 1993, when 26 percent of households depended on Aid to Families with Dependent Children. The average tenant income has risen from $5,850 in 1994 (CLPHA 1995) to $9,206 in 2002 (HUD 2002).[3] Average income increased 57.4 percent from 1994 to 2002, but only 1.2 percent from 1998 to 2002 (HUD 2002). Public housing residents who remain on welfare are likely to be those facing the greatest challenges to self-sufficiency.

The Jobs-Plus Demonstration, managed by the Manpower Demonstration Research Corporation (MDRC), is one of the few research endeavors that begin to rigorously evaluate the effectiveness of employment initiatives on public housing. The demonstration

> seeks to make dramatic improvements in a variety of employment outcomes for residents of public housing developments suffering from low rates of steady employment and high rates of welfare use. The initiative uses a three-pronged strategy that combines (1) *employment-related services* to help residents prepare for and find jobs; (2) *financial work incentives* to "make work pay" by reducing

---

[2] Estimates based on HUD Multifamily Tenant Characteristics System data from May 2001.

[3] Statistics are based on a reporting rate of only 41 percent.

the extent to which a family's rent rises with increased earnings; (3) a *community support for work* component to strengthen and develop social ties that support residents' work efforts. (Kato and Riccio 2001, ES–1)

MDRC suggests that special efforts may be required for public housing and Section 8 residents because they are most likely to have substantial barriers to employment, while those in unsubsidized private housing are the least likely to have such barriers. Public housing and Section 8 residents also fared worse than recipients living in unsubsidized housing in finding jobs and leaving welfare but not in every case. MDRC also suggests that these differences may have more to do with the characteristics of the residents than with the nature of subsidized housing (2001a).

Regarding self-sufficiency challenges and resident participation in the Jobs-Plus program, MDRC reports the following:

- All sites are striving to reach all working age residents in their Jobs-Plus developments. While substantial numbers have come forward, significant proportions remain reluctant to participate.

- Sites are attempting to address a wide assortment of employment barriers as part of their efforts to reach the "harder-to-employ," such as physical and mental health problems, substance abuse, criminal records, and domestic violence.

- High resident move-out rates in some developments have limited exposure to and participation in Jobs-Plus, and present a continuing challenge to program operations.

- Data collected prior to Jobs-Plus found that residents with better jobs and without serious health problems were more likely to move. (2001b, 8)

Self-sufficiency challenges include low levels of education; few skills, and weak employment histories; unstable family structures and a lack of knowledge about parenting and child development; drug and alcohol dependency; and exposure to racial discrimination. The range and depth of the services required are significant, as are the costs.

Limited Knowledge of What Really Works

There is little research that clearly identifies effective strategies PHAs can use to raise incomes. Sard (2003) acknowledges,

> Some people may question whether such activities will be effective. It is true that only limited data are available to show that work-promoting activities led by or based at housing agencies can be effective (Bogdon 1999; Riccio 1999) or, perhaps most important, that they are any more effective than similar activities undertaken by employment and training agencies. Moreover, few relevant research efforts are under way. (122)

Studies in Atlanta, Minnesota, and Columbus (OH) discussed in Riccio and Orenstein (2003) find that welfare-to-work efforts show greater earnings and employment effects for those in public or subsidized housing, yet what caused this differential effect is not known.

Historically, many PHAs created separate housing-driven services, in part to respond to inconsistent and multiplying federal mandates. Some large PHAs are moving away from a strategy that has exacerbated the disconnection and isolation of public housing residents. Instead they are turning to human service providers, the educational system, workforce development services, and other public and private sector partners to focus on their core services delivered in an integrated system.

The Chicago Housing Authority (CHA), an example of a very large PHA with a history of authority-delivered service programs, is now transitioning social service programs to existing city departments. Last year, CHA signed interagency agreements that were approved by the city council and are expected to provide needed resident services and reduce costs for the authority. As part of its long-term transformation plan, CHA will provide significant funds to the department of human services to pay for "service connectors"—personnel who will be responsible for ensuring that CHA residents have access to social services that can help them get jobs. "'With the city's Service Connectors programs in place, we'll be able to end the isolation of CHA residents in their own separate social service programs,' according to [Terry] Peterson [Chief Executive Officer], adding, 'Public housing residents should have access to the same services as everyone else'" (CHA 2001, 1).

As Sard (2003) asserts, in some communities, housing authorities may have strategic advantages over welfare agencies in implementing work-promoting strategies. Yet there are clear strategic disadvantages to housing-driven programs in many communities, among them isolation of services, duplication of effort, lack of effectiveness, and diversion from the core mission.

Even without Jobs-Plus rent incentives, MDRC reports that public housing residents engaged in low-wage work are better off today than they were in 1990, thanks in large part to expansion of the Earned

Income Tax Credit (EITC) and Temporary Assistance to Needy Families work incentives and QHWRA reforms. MDRC maintains that ensuring the use of the EITC and access to child care subsidies remains essential for making work pay (2001b). That is why building comprehensive strategies on the local level, responsive to local circumstances, is so important.

Need for Locally Determined Strategies

Local economies, housing markets, demographics, and community priorities vary widely across metropolitan areas. Strategies must be tailored to local circumstances that take these factors into account. CLPHA recently surveyed its members, which own and operate over 40 percent of the nation's public housing, primarily in large urban areas, on the implementation of QHWRA. Every PHA reported a wide array of policies, services, activities, and partnerships in support of economic self-sufficiency efforts. PHAs across the country are rising to the challenge by selecting strategies suitable to their circumstances. The strategies vary just as the communities they serve vary.

For example, the Cambridge, MA, Housing Authority Work Force Program focuses on increasing employment opportunities for youth through academics, mentoring, and job internships. Program participants have a significantly higher college attendance rate than students in the public school system. The City of Los Angeles Housing Authority has focused on supporting resident-owned businesses that provide relocation, moving, and construction services. The Milwaukee Housing Authority created public housing "communities that work" to support Wisconsin's welfare reform initiatives, providing an array of supportive services to facilitate employment and thereby significantly increasing residents' employment rates and earned income.

The key role of affordable housing in welfare-to-work strategies is now being recognized in Congress, as reflected in the Welfare Reform and Housing Act (S. 2116) introduced in 2002 by Senator John Kerry (D-MA). The bill calls for states to address housing needs in their welfare plans and to enter into cooperative agreements with housing authorities for economic self-sufficiency activities and also authorizes an interagency housing demonstration.

Some of the factors and obstacles shaping local partnerships are examined in recent Jobs-Plus findings:

- Endurance of the partnerships has been impressive, but sustaining partner commitment has required ongoing attention.

- Welfare and workforce systems have contributed significant resources, but mostly in kind (e.g., staff).

- Many partners did not want a broad governance role and found efforts at collective decision-making unproductive. (MDRC 2001b, 6)

Housing Providers versus Social Service Providers

Kato and Riccio (2001) also point out that there are inherent conflicts in having the housing provider act as a welfare agency: "Social welfare and property management, however, represent different organizational and professional priorities that call for the housing authority to assume a dual 'good cop/bad cop' role" (68). The need to ensure fiscal solvency and the safety of the premises requires the enforcement of specific rules and regulations that may chafe against social welfare goals. The PHA has a responsibility to maintain and protect the public housing asset in order to serve the community as a whole and its residents. The service provider is often in the role of advocate for an individual resident seeking an accommodation that may conflict with the housing authority's responsibility to protect and manage for the entire community.

Conclusion

Implementing effective, locally determined self-sufficiency strategies with positive outcomes is complicated by limited resources, inconsistent mandates, and competing priorities. Self-sufficiency strategies should support, rather than undermine, the core mission to provide good-quality, safe, and affordable housing to those in need. Developing these strategies must be considered in light of the fiscal and regulatory challenges facing housing authorities and the self-sufficiency challenges facing public housing residents. We need more flexibility, more resources, more collaboration, more knowledge about achieving success, and more commonly agreed on goals and principles.

Furthermore, we should not miss the opportunity presented by the reauthorization of the welfare program and by changes to housing programs to shift the central focus of welfare reform from reducing welfare caseloads to reducing poverty. Until families can lift themselves out of poverty through employment, the need for housing assistance will far outstrip the supply. Decent, affordable housing can play a critical role in welfare-to-work transitions and therein lies the basis for meaningful, effective, and appropriate partnerships.

Author

Sunia Zaterman is Executive Director at the Council of Large Public Housing Authorities.

References

Besharov, Douglas J. 2002. Welfare Rolls: On the Rise Again. *Washington Post*, July 16, p. A17.

Bogdon, Amy S. 1999. What Can We Learn from Previous Housing-Based Self-Sufficiency Programs? In *The Home Front: Implications of Welfare Reform for Housing Policy*, ed. Sandra J. Newman, 149–74. Washington, DC: Urban Institute Press.

Chicago Housing Authority. 2001. News Release: City Approves Cost-Cutting Agreement between Chicago Housing Authority, Dept. of Human Services, Fleet Management. February 8.

Council of Large Public Housing Authorities. 1995. *Demographic Characteristics of Public and Indian Housing Residents*. Washington, DC.

Council of Large Public Housing Authorities. 2002. Funding History: Public Housing Operating Fund. Unpublished report. World Wide Web page <http://www.clpha.org> (accessed August 7).

Kato, Linda Y., and James A. Riccio. 2001. *Building New Partnerships for Employment: Collaboration among Agencies and Public Housing Residents in the Jobs-Plus Demonstration*. Manpower Demonstration Research Corporation. Also available at <http://www.mdrc.org>.

Manpower Demonstration Research Corporation. 2001a. *Welfare, Housing, and Employment: Learning from the Jobs-Plus Demonstration*. Policy Brief. New York.

Manpower Demonstration Research Corporation. 2001b. Where Are We in the Demonstration and What Are We Learning? Unpublished briefing paper.

Riccio, James A. 1999. Lessons from Welfare-to-Work Experiments and Their Implications for Housing-Based Self-Sufficiency Programs. In *The Home Front: Implications of Welfare Reform for Housing Policy*, ed. Sandra J. Newman, 175–200. Washington, DC: Urban Institute.

Riccio, James A., and Alan Orenstein. 2003. Are Welfare Recipients in Public Housing Really Harder to Employ? In *A Place to Live, a Means to Work: How Housing Assistance Can Strengthen Welfare Policy*, ed. Barbara Sard and Amy S. Bogdon, 63–103. Washington, DC: Fannie Mae Foundation.

Sard, Barbara. 2003. The Role of Housing Providers in an Era of Welfare Reform. In *A Place to Live, a Means to Work: How Housing Assistance Can Strengthen Welfare Policy*, ed. Barbara Sard and Amy S. Bogdon, 107–65. Washington, DC: Fannie Mae Foundation.

U.S. Department of Housing and Urban Development. 2002. *Resident Characteristics Report*. Washington, DC. February.

U.S. Department of Housing and Urban Development, Office of Policy Development and Research. 2001. *A Report on Worst-Case Needs in 1999: New Opportunity amid Continuing Challenges*. Washington, DC.

Part IV—Admissions and Rent Policies

CHAPTER 6

Will Changing the Rent Formula Encourage Moves from Welfare to Work?

Ed Lazere and Jennifer Daskal
Center on Budget and Policy Priorities

Abstract

This chapter addresses the question of whether rent rules in federally subsidized housing reduce the degree to which welfare recipients receiving rental assistance seek employment. When such families go to work, their increased earnings are partially offset by benefit reductions in several programs. In most states, the loss of welfare benefits is greater than the amount lost due to increased rents. Changes in welfare disregards are thus more likely to affect monetary gain from work than changes in rent policies. Research suggests that substantially expanding earnings disregards in the Temporary Assistance to Needy Families program encourages work, including work among those in subsidized housing.

Revising the basic rent policy for subsidized housing could also encourage work. Because work incentives have public costs, such revisions should be narrowly targeted. Finally, an earned income disregard for public housing residents should not include Section 8 recipients until its impacts have been evaluated.

Keywords: Employment issues; Rental housing; Welfare

Introduction

In recent years, promoting employment among residents of subsidized housing has become a serious concern in federal low-income housing policy. As one example, the Quality Housing and Work Responsibility Act (QHWRA) of 1998 altered admission rules, particularly in public housing, in ways that allow public housing agencies (PHAs) to admit more working families. The new law also includes a provision to limit rent increases in public housing when unemployed families or families that receive welfare-related assistance increase their earnings. In part, the new policies stem from a long-term concern that subsidized housing projects may create a climate that discourages work. But these new policies also reflect an increasingly dominant trend in U.S. social welfare policy generally, a trend led by federal and state efforts to reform welfare.

In fact, the enhanced focus on work in low-income housing policy may be partly a result of welfare reform efforts. Most states have altered welfare programs to include strict work requirements, time limits, and sanctions for failing to comply with program rules. The outcome of these policies for subsidized housing is important, because roughly one-quarter of all subsidized housing tenants receive welfare.[1] If these families lose income as a result of welfare reform, it could adversely affect the environment in subsidized developments; it would also put financial pressure on the Department of Housing and Urban Development (HUD) and PHAs. Under most circumstances, rental payments decline when a tenant's income falls.[2] PHAs thus could face a reduction in public housing rental income, which helps meet operational and administrative costs, and HUD could face an increase in per unit subsidy costs within the Section 8 program (Connell, Devine, and Rubin 1998). Maintaining resident incomes by encouraging employment may thus be an important goal to those administering low-income housing programs.

The concern over whether welfare recipients living in subsidized housing will successfully navigate the transition to employment has focused greater attention on a long-standing question: Do the basic rent rules in subsidized housing programs—under which an increase in income from increased earnings means an increase in rent as well—reduce the degree to which families living in subsidized housing seek employment? Some research (for example, Painter 2001) finds that housing subsidies modestly reduce employment. There is little empirical research that isolates the effect of the rent formula on employment. Nevertheless, anecdotal and research data indicate that many tenants of subsidized housing believe that the rent policy is a disincentive to work (Riccio 1999).

This chapter explores the potential work disincentive effect of the subsidized housing rent formula. In particular, it compares the increase in rent that families experience when they go to work with the loss of cash assistance and other means-tested benefits they face in such circumstances. The analysis also focuses on rent increases for families that are not eligible for the new public housing earned income disregard, such as families that receive a Section 8 housing subsidy. Roughly three-fourths

---

[1] This number is based on 1996 Aid to Families with Dependent Children quality control data (Sard and Daskal 1998). The proportion of the current Temporary Assistance to Needy Families caseload that also receives housing assistance may be somewhat higher.

[2] Under the 1998 federal housing law, some subsidized housing rents do not decline when families face a reduction in welfare cash assistance as a sanction for not complying with a work requirement (Sard and Lubell 2000a).

of the welfare recipients in subsidized housing are Section 8 recipients and thus do not qualify for this earned income disregard.

This chapter provides a context for assessing the potential disincentive of the rent policy, as well as the impact of any changes in the rent formula, including the changes enacted in QHWRA for certain public housing residents. Given the fact that current federal welfare rules offer states discretion over benefit rules, the analysis also explores the impact of changing a state's welfare benefit formula to encourage work and compares the merits of altering the welfare benefit formula with altering the subsidized housing rent formula.

What Happens to a Family's Net Income When a Parent Goes from Welfare to Work?

For a family receiving welfare benefits, an increase in earnings triggers a complex change in taxes and government benefits. For families living in subsidized housing, this may include an increase in their rent payment. In most cases, welfare recipients who move to work or increase their earnings experience a decline in total government assistance, since benefits in most programs phase out as income rises. The combined loss of benefits thus lowers the net gain from the additional earnings. This is the context in which the potential work disincentive effect of subsidized housing rent policies should be examined.

The following describes the benefit formulas—in a somewhat simplified fashion—for subsidized housing and other programs providing cash or near-cash benefits that welfare recipients are most likely to receive: that is, cash assistance under Temporary Assistance for Needy Families (TANF), food stamps, subsidized housing, the federal Earned Income Tax Credit (EITC), and other federal taxes related to earnings. The descriptions focus on the effect of additional earnings on benefits.

Cash Assistance under the TANF Block Grant

The primary cash assistance program for needy families with children is funded in each state under the TANF block grant, using federal TANF funds and/or the maintenance-of-effort (MOE) funds states are required to spend as a condition of receiving these federal funds. Under the 1996 federal welfare law that established TANF, states have broad flexibility to design their welfare program, including the benefit formula. In all states except Arkansas and Connecticut, a family's TANF benefit is based on the difference between countable income—income after various deductions—and either the state's maximum benefit or its standard of need.[3] In every state except Wisconsin, a portion of earned income is deducted from gross income before the TANF grant amount is determined, although these earned income disregards vary substantially from state to state.

In every state except Colorado, Delaware, and Georgia, the benefit formula under TANF cash assistance, including the earned income disregard, is more generous for some or all working families than it was under the Aid to Families with Dependent Children (AFDC) program that preceded it. (See table 6A.1.[4]) These enhanced earned income disregards are intended to allow families to keep a share of their welfare benefits when they begin working and to phase out benefits gradually as earnings rise, thereby helping families make the transition from welfare to work.

Table 6A.1 describes each state's earned income disregard policy. Nine states disregard a substantial portion of family earnings for a brief period and then reduce the disregard substantially. For example, in Kentucky, all earnings are disregarded for two months, which means that families going to work experience no reduction in cash assistance benefits. After two months of work, Kentucky welfare recipients are subject to the former AFDC earned income disregards.

In most other states, the earned income disregard is a fixed dollar amount (e.g., $200 in Wyoming), a percentage of earnings (e.g., 50 percent in Oregon), or a combination of the two (e.g., $200 and 20 percent of remaining earnings in Michigan).

Because the earned income disregards vary from state to state and sometimes by categories of families within the state, it is not possible to provide a single measure of the effect of additional earnings on welfare

---

[3] Fourteen states determine TANF benefits using "fill-the-gap" rules, under which a family's countable income is subtracted from a standard higher than the maximum benefit. The family's benefit level equals the difference between countable income and the standard—or a percentage of the difference—but the benefit can be no greater than the maximum benefit.

In Arkansas, families are eligible either for the maximum benefit or 50 percent of the maximum payment, depending on gross income. There is no other variation in benefits based on nonwelfare income. In Connecticut, families subject to the state's 21-month time limit receive the maximum benefit as long as earnings are below the federal poverty guideline. Once earnings exceed the poverty line, families become ineligible for benefits.

[4] Earnings disregards, benefit calculations, and earnings eligibility levels for a family of three are found in appendix A (tables 6A.1, 6A.2, and 6A.3).

benefits. These calculations must be made on a state-by-state basis, as in the following examples.

Food Stamps

Unlike TANF, food stamp policy is set nationally, and the program structure is largely uniform across states. Families are expected to contribute 30 percent of their countable income toward food, which means that an increase in countable income leads to a decline in food stamp benefits equal to 30 percent of the increase in countable income. In measuring countable income, 20 percent of gross earnings is disregarded. If a family's countable income increases as a result of new earnings, the decline in food stamp benefits thus equals 24 percent of the increase in earnings. For example, an increase of $100 in a family's gross earnings would result in an $80 increase in countable income for food stamp purposes. The reduction in benefits in this example would be 30 percent of the additional $80 of countable income, or $24.[5]

Subsidized Housing

Families receiving "deep" rental subsidies from the federal government—those living in public housing or Section 8 project-based housing or receiving a Section 8 certificate or voucher—generally pay 30 percent of their countable income for rent. Some families pay a flat rent that does not vary with income (and is often higher than 30 percent of income), or they may be paying an amount that differs from 30 percent of their countable income in rent for other reasons.[6]

For most families living in public housing or receiving Section 8 assistance, an increase in earnings increases the rent they are required to pay by an amount equal to 30 percent of their additional gross earnings.

---

[5] For many families *not* in subsidized housing, the phase-out rate resulting from increased earnings in food stamps is somewhat higher. Families that pay more than half of their income for rent receive an "excess shelter deduction," which has the effect of raising their food stamp benefit amount. As families' earnings increase, this excess shelter deduction generally decreases. The result is a phase-out rate of up to 36 percent of increased earnings for families that pay more than half of their income for rent, with variations depending on the circumstances.

[6] For example, families that have a voucher and rent a unit costing more than the PHA-determined "payment standard" pay 30 percent of their income *plus* the difference between the unit's actual cost and the payment standard. Families that are paying a "ceiling rent" in public housing may pay less than 30 percent of their adjusted income for rent.

Housing agencies have the discretion to delay a rent increase when a family receives additional income from working. Such a delay is equivalent to a 100 percent earnings disregard for the period in question. Agencies that exercise this option may delay the rent increase until a tenant's regularly scheduled annual recertification to reduce administrative costs and burdens. They can also establish a shorter, fixed period following an increase in earnings during which tenants are not required to report it. Such delayed recertification policies are optional for PHAs (for public housing tenants and Section 8 participants) and for private owners with project-based Section 8 units. About 40 percent of PHAs have adopted a variant of the delayed rent recertification option, at times explicitly to promote the transition from welfare to work (HUD 1998).

In addition, QHWRA included a provision to limit rent increases for some families that increase their earnings. Under this provision and implementing regulations issued in March 2000 for determining rent, eligible families living in public housing receive a 100 percent disregard for new income from earnings for 12 months, after which the disregard drops to 50 percent of additional income for another 12 months. Eligible families are those that have received cash assistance or at least $500 in other services during the previous six months from a program supported by TANF, state MOE, or Welfare-to-Work block grant funds; families that experience an increase in earnings after participating in a training or self-sufficiency program; and families in which an adult has been unemployed for at least a year. TANF and MOE funds can be used to support a variety of programs, such as cash assistance, child care, or transportation. Receiving the threshold level of assistance from any such program establishes eligibility for the disregard.

This policy means that welfare recipients who live in public housing and go to work or increase their earnings—except for families receiving Section 8 assistance—experience no increase in rent for a year and a relatively modest increase for the following year. While this policy has been in effect since October 1999, it is not clear at this time when all PHAs will have implemented it. The history of prior earned income disregards for subsidized housing residents indicates that they were not implemented broadly.

EITC

The EITC is a refundable tax credit for low-income workers, primarily those with children. Families that owe little or no income tax receive the EITC in the form of a refund check that is indistinguishable from other tax refund checks. For low-income workers, the EITC thus provides not only tax relief, but also acts to supplement income. EITC benefits are not counted as income in federal housing programs, in the food stamp program, or in nearly all state TANF programs.

For families with low earnings, the EITC benefit is equal to a percentage of earnings. This means that families with no earnings are not eligible for it. It also means that EITC benefits *increase* as earnings rise for some families, unlike the case for the other means-tested programs described here. In 2000, the EITC equaled 40 percent of the first $9,720 of earnings for families with two or more children, for a maximum credit of $3,888. It equaled 34 percent of the first $6,920 of earnings for families with one child, resulting in a maximum credit of $2,353. For individuals or couples with no children, the EITC equaled 7.65 percent of the first $4,610 of earnings, with a maximum credit of $353.

Families with children remain eligible to receive the maximum EITC until their income reaches a specified level ($12,690 in 2000). The EITC then phases out gradually as incomes rise above this level—at a rate of roughly 16 percent for families with one child and about 21 percent for families with two or more children.

For most families moving from welfare to work, an increase in earnings leads to a larger EITC benefit. For welfare recipients with earnings in the maximum-benefit range, an increase in earnings results in no change in the EITC benefit. Few families with earnings in the EITC phase-out range are eligible for welfare benefits (State Policy Documentation Project 1999).

Taxes

The most significant tax that low-wage workers face is the payroll tax, which is paid to the Social Security and Medicare trust funds. (Most workers who qualify for welfare assistance do not pay federal income tax, since the structure of the income tax exempts nearly all families with incomes below the poverty line.) A number of states impose state income taxes on working poor families, but because these amounts vary and are relatively small in most cases, we will not discuss them here.

Some 7.65 percent of workers' earnings are deducted from their paychecks for the payroll tax. (Employers also contribute an amount equal to 7.65 percent of every employee's wages.) If a parent's earnings increase by $100, net income after payroll taxes would be $92.35.

How Does It All Add Up? Michigan as an Example

To understand the combined effect of tax and benefit changes on welfare recipients who live in subsidized housing and increase their earnings, consider the example of a single parent with two children living in a Section 8–subsidized apartment in Michigan. The maximum welfare benefit for a family of three in Detroit is $459 a month. In calculating cash benefit levels, the state's TANF program disregards the first $200 of earnings, plus 20 percent of remaining earnings.

In 2000, a mother and two children who lived in Detroit and had no other income except government benefits received $459 in welfare plus $237 in food stamps, for a total monthly income of $696.

If such a parent found a half-time, year-round job that paid minimum wage—$5.15 an hour for 20 hours per week, or $446 in gross monthly earnings—the family's income and benefits would change as follows. (See figure 6.1.)

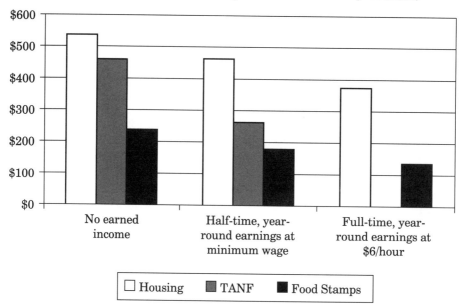

Figure 6.1. **Monthly Housing, TANF, and Food Stamp Assistance by Earnings Levels for a Family of Three in Detroit, MI (2000)**

1. After payroll taxes, the family's take-home pay would be $412 a month.

2. The family's welfare benefit would be reduced by $197.

3. The family's food stamp benefits would be reduced by $58 a month.

4. The family's rent would increase by $75. (If the family lived in public housing and qualified for the new earned income disregard, there would be no increase in rent for the first 12 months and a $38 increase for the next 12 months.)

5. If the parent worked 20 hours a week throughout the year, after filing a tax return, the family would receive a lump-sum EITC of $2,141, equivalent to $178 a month.

Before the EITC is taken into account, the family would experience a net increase in income of $92 a month, the equivalent of a little more than $1 per hour worked. If the family had even a modest amount of work-related expenses, such as transportation, the increase would be still lower. When the EITC is taken into account, the family's monthly income gain is $270, the equivalent of about $3 for each hour of work. (These examples assume that the family has no out-of-pocket work-related expenses, because they are difficult to estimate. To the extent that families have such expenses, the net income gained is even less.)

If the family lived in public housing and qualified for the new earned income disregard, its rent would not increase during the first 12 months of employment. During that period, its monthly income gain would be $167 without considering the EITC, or about $2 per hour of work, and $345, almost $4 per hour of work, when the EITC is taken into account.

It is worth noting that if the family is not living in subsidized housing, the net income increase would be $321. This is somewhat larger than the income gain that a family living in Section 8 housing would receive and somewhat less than the gain for families that live in public housing and receive the disregard. Families living in private housing would not face a rent increase, but they would generally experience a greater loss of food stamps than a family with a Section 8 subsidy.[7]

---

[7] As noted, families with high housing costs (which includes most low-income families in private housing) receive more food stamps than families with the same income but lower housing costs. At the same time, the families with high housing costs experience a faster phase-out of food stamp benefits when their earnings rise.

Impact on a Family Moving to Full-Time Work

Suppose that the same parent in Michigan moved from being unemployed and receiving TANF to having a full-time job paying $6 an hour. In this case, the mother's take-home pay is $924 a month after payroll tax deductions.[8] At this level of earnings, the family loses its entire $459 TANF benefit and $102 in food stamps, and its rent would rise by $162. At the same time, it would qualify for an EITC benefit of $3,888 a year, equal to $324 a month. The family's net increase in income would be $201 a month without the EITC—the equivalent of $1.20 an hour. With the EITC, the net gain is $525 per month, the equivalent of $3.15 per hour of work. If the family lived in public housing and qualified for the 100 percent earned income disregard, the income gain for the first year of work would be $363 without the EITC, or the equivalent of $2.18 per hour of work. With the EITC, the family's income gain would be $687 per month, or $4.12 per hour. These are roughly equivalent to the hourly gains of families moving to part-time work.

It is also worth noting that in 38 states, the rise in earnings would make the mother—but generally not her children—ineligible for Medicaid after one year of work (Guyer and Mann 1999). If such a mother is not offered affordable health coverage by her employer, it is likely that she would lack health insurance. Research from some states shows that half to two-thirds of parents who leave cash assistance lack health insurance (Abt Associates 1997; South Carolina Department of Social Services 1998).

These calculations show that families on welfare experience a net income gain when they go to work (assuming no unreimbursed work-related expenses), although much of the gross increase in earnings is lost to benefit reductions. This is true even for families not living in subsidized housing. For families that live in subsidized housing and do not qualify for the public housing earned income disregard, however, the net income gain from working is even more modest. Beyond these basic assessments, these calculations also show the following:

The biggest decline in benefit income comes from the loss of welfare benefits. With half-time, minimum-wage work, the loss of welfare benefits for the family in Detroit is $197, compared with a $48 reduction in food stamps and a $75 rent increase.

The decline in welfare benefit is the largest for two reasons. First, the earnings disregard in Michigan's welfare program phases out benefits

---

[8] This is based on average monthly earnings of $6 an hour for 40 hours a week, 50 weeks a year (assuming two weeks of unpaid leave).

at a rate of 80 percent of earnings above $200 a month, which is much faster than the 24 percent phase-out rate used in the food stamp program and the 30 percent phase-out rate for rent subsidies. The loss of welfare benefits for the Detroit parent with a half-time, minimum-wage job equals 48 percent of her take-home pay.

Second, because food stamp benefits and subsidized housing rents are based on income *after* welfare benefit reductions are considered, the benefit reductions in these programs are, in fact, much smaller than 24 percent and 30 percent, respectively, of incremental earnings. In the examples above, the food stamp reduction equals less than 11 percent of gross earnings, while the rent increase equals less than 17 percent of earnings.

The EITC makes a substantial difference. Without the EITC, families that move from welfare to work see very modest increases in net income. The substantial EITC benefit offsets much of the loss of other benefits such families face. By providing a larger benefit as earnings increase, the EITC also provides a clear reward for greater effort. In light of these figures, it is not surprising that the EITC has been a major factor behind a substantial increase in labor force participation among single parents since the mid-1980s (Meyer and Rosenbaum 1999) and that the EITC lifts more working families with children out of poverty than any other program (Porter et al. 1998).

Earnings Increases and the Impact on Families

In most states, when a family's earnings increase, the loss of welfare benefits is greater than the income lost to rent increases. Table 6.1 focuses on changes solely in welfare benefits and in subsidized housing rent that a family would face if it moves from welfare to work. The table highlights the changes in benefits for families moving from unemployment to half-time, minimum-wage work—$446 in gross monthly earnings—and from unemployment to roughly the average earnings for families that leave welfare—$850 in gross monthly earnings. The latter amount is slightly less than the equivalent of full-time work at the federal minimum wage. The decline in welfare benefits is based on state rules that apply to families that have been working six months, which means that it does not reflect the very large earned income disregards some states allow for the first few months of work. The rent changes identified in the table are those that would be faced by a family that does not receive the new public housing earned income disregard, such as a family with a Section 8 housing subsidy.

Table 6.1. **Changes in Welfare Benefits and Subsidized Housing Rents for Families Moving from Welfare to Work**

	Monthly Earnings of $446		Monthly Earnings of $850	
	Reduction in Cash Assistance	Increase in Rent	Reduction in Cash Assistance	Increase in Rent
Alabama	$164	$85	$164	$206
Alaska	$131	$94	$363	$146
Arizona	$249	$59	$347	$151
Arkansas	$0	$134	$204	$194
California	$111	$101	$313	$161
Colorado	$325	$36	$356	$148
Connecticut	$0	$134	$0	$255
Delaware	$44	$121	$246	$181
District of Columbia	$94	$105	$228	$187
Florida	$123	$97	$303	$164
Georgia	$182	$79	$280	$171
Hawaii	$100	$104	$307	$163
Idaho	$186	$78	$293	$167
Illinois	$149	$89	$283	$170
Indiana	$0	$134	$0	$255
Iowa	$178	$80	$340	$153
Kansas	$214	$70	$403	$134
Kentucky	$152	$88	$262	$176
Louisiana	$240	$62	$240	$183
Maine	$77	$111	$279	$171
Maryland	$290	$47	$439	$123
Massachusetts	$163	$85	$365	$146
Michigan	$197	$75	$459	$117
Minnesota	$277	$51	$527	$97
Mississippi	$163	$85	$170	$204
Missouri	$59	$116	$193	$197
Montana	$185	$78	$488	$109
Nebraska	$186	$78	$364	$146
Nevada	$223	$67	$348	$151
New Hampshire	$223	$67	$425	$128
New Jersey	$223	$67	$424	$128
New Mexico	$148	$89	$350	$150
New York	$192	$76	$410	$132
North Carolina	$162	$85	$272	$173
North Dakota	$138	$92	$262	$176
Ohio	$98	$104	$300	$165
Oklahoma	$163	$85	$292	$167
Oregon	$223	$67	$460	$117
Pennsylvania	$223	$67	$403	$134
Rhode Island	$138	$92	$340	$153
South Carolina	$109	$101	$203	$194
South Dakota	$285	$48	$430	$126
Tennessee	$0	$134	$86	$229

Table 6.1. **Changes in Welfare Benefits and Subsidized Housing Rents for Families Moving from Welfare to Work** *(continued)*

	Monthly Earnings of $446		Monthly Earnings of $850	
	Reduction in Cash Assistance	Increase in Rent	Reduction in Cash Assistance	Increase in Rent
Texas	$207	$72	$207	$193
Utah	$173	$82	$375	$143
Vermont	$222	$67	$525	$98
Virginia	$0	$134	$0	$255
Washington	$223	$67	$425	$128
West Virginia	$268	$54	$453	$119
Wisconsin	$446	$0	$673	$53
Wyoming	$246	$60	$340	$153
Median	$173	$82	$340	$153

Note: This assumes a parent has worked at least six months. The $446 monthly earnings figure is equivalent to half-time work at the minimum wage. The $850 monthly earnings figure is roughly equivalent to the typical earnings of families that have left welfare for work in recent years.

The table shows that in nearly every state, families that move from welfare to work, whether part-time or close to full-time, lose more in welfare benefits than they lose to increased rents. In the typical state, families that find work with earnings of $446 per month lose nearly 40 percent of their gross earnings or $173 in welfare benefits, while the typical rent increase is $82, or 18 percent of gross earnings. Similarly, the typical loss of welfare benefits for families finding work that pays $850 in gross monthly earnings—$340—is more than twice as large as the rent increase of $153.

Table 6.1 shows that in 38 states, welfare benefit declines exceed rent increases at both earnings levels. The 12 states plus the District of Columbia where rent increases are larger than welfare benefit declines fall into two groups: Alabama, Arkansas, and Mississippi are states with benefits that are well below average and that phase out fairly quickly when families go to work. For example, the maximum benefit for a family of three in Alabama is $164, and families that have worked for more than six months lose all assistance when earnings reach $205 per month. In all three states, families that move to work do not lose much in cash assistance because they were not receiving much in the first place. Thus, much of their earnings gain translates into a net income gain.

In the rest—Connecticut, Delaware, District of Columbia, Hawaii, Indiana, Maine, Missouri, Ohio, Tennessee, and Virginia—the modest declines in welfare benefits for families that move to work reflect relatively generous welfare benefit formulas. In Connecticut, Indiana, and Virginia, for example, families are able to keep the full benefit until earnings reach or exceed the poverty threshold. For families in these states, substantial new earnings also translate largely into net income gains, and thus subsidized housing rents increase significantly.

It is important to note that while rent increases are more substantial in the latter group, the net increase in income when families go to work is higher than in states with less generous earned income disregards. For example, Kansas disregards $90 and 40 percent of remaining earnings. A Kansas family moving from no earnings to $850 per month would lose $620 to declines in cash and food stamps and to rent increases. By contrast, in Connecticut, where all earnings up to the poverty level are disregarded and thus there is no loss of cash assistance, declines in the rent subsidy and in food stamps consume $459 of the earnings gain.

While most states have more generous earned income disregards in their TANF cash assistance program than they did under AFDC, welfare benefits still phase out fairly sharply in many states when families move to low-paying work, as table 6.1 shows. The table also shows that when welfare benefits decline sharply as earnings rise, rent increases are modest. By contrast, rent increases for families that live in subsidized housing and are not eligible for the public housing earned income disregard are largest when welfare benefits are reduced little as a family's earnings rise, since such families experience significant net income gains from their employment.

Housing Assistance Is Often the Largest Subsidy for Families Moving to Work

Another way to assess the phase-out of benefits is to examine the amount of the subsidy received by families at different earnings levels.

Figure 6.1 shows the subsidy amount from cash, food stamps, and federal housing assistance that a family in Detroit would receive at various earnings levels. The housing subsidy is determined as the difference between the tenant contribution and the fair market rent for a two-bedroom unit in Detroit ($650 per month in 2000), assuming that the family is using a Section 8 voucher and renting a unit at or below the housing agency's payment standard.[9]

---

[9] The housing subsidy amount, that is, the difference between the tenant's rental payment and the payment standard, is not necessarily the same as the income benefit

At all income levels, the housing subsidy is the most generous of the benefits delivered on a monthly basis. When a family finds full-time work at $6 per hour, for example, it no longer is eligible for any welfare benefit and receives only a modest food stamp benefit. But its housing subsidy remains fairly large.

Figure 6.1 also reflects the fact that families can benefit from housing assistance at income levels well above the point at which eligibility for TANF ends. A family of three in Detroit would continue to be eligible for some Section 8 assistance until its income reached $2,250 per month.[10] By contrast, the family would lose all cash assistance when monthly earnings reach $774. As a result, housing assistance can play a critical role in helping families not only while they make the transition from welfare to work, but also after they are no longer eligible for TANF. This may be important in providing stability for low-wage workers and helping such families remain off welfare. (See Lubell, Nelson, and Sard [2003] for a discussion of the stabilizing role of housing assistance for working families.)

Financial Incentives in Means-Tested Programs Can Increase Work, but Are Likely to Have Costs

The limited information available on the impact of subsidized housing rent policy on employment, particularly in a period when welfare recipients generally face work requirements as a condition of receiving welfare assistance, makes it difficult to predict the marginal impact of changes in rent policies designed to encourage work. There is considerable research on other efforts to make work pay, however, particularly from welfare reform efforts and the federal EITC.

---

received by the family. In the absence of a housing subsidy, the family likely would have made other housing choices and probably would have lived in cheaper housing. Thus, the income benefit to the family is the difference between what the family would have paid out-of-pocket for housing with and without the subsidy. This amount is generally lower than the subsidy amount, which is the government cost of providing the subsidy.

[10] This assumes that the family lives in an apartment that costs the fair market rent for a two-bedroom apartment in the Detroit metropolitan area, or $650 per month in 2000. The family would benefit from a Section 8 subsidy as long as its rental payment—30 percent of adjusted income—is less than $650 a month.

Financial Incentives Boost Employment

Recent research generally shows that making work pay better for families that move from welfare to work has a positive impact on labor force participation. Evaluations of the EITC find that it has contributed to a substantial increase in workforce participation among single women with children (Liebman 1998). One study found that the expansion in the EITC since the mid-1980s explains more than half of the increase in employment among single mothers over the 1984–96 period (Meyer and Rosenbaum 1999). Another leading study, which examined a shorter time period (from 1992 to 1996) found that both welfare policy changes and EITC expansions had large effects in increasing the employment of single mothers during this period, with welfare changes being the larger factor (Ellwood 1999).

In addition, several analyses of state welfare programs have shown that increasing welfare earnings disregards can have positive effects on employment rates. An evaluation of Michigan's welfare reform program, for example, found that three years after an expanded earnings disregard was put into place, average earnings among welfare recipients receiving the disregard were 13 percent higher than among the group of welfare recipients that did not (Werner and Kornfeld 1996).

A 2000 evaluation of Minnesota's welfare reform program, known as the Minnesota Family Investment Program (MFIP), provides even more promising findings. While the MFIP design was fairly complex, its central features included increasing the earnings disregard substantially in combination with requiring recipients to participate in work activities. The evaluation of MFIP at three years found that employment among long-term welfare recipients who lived in urban areas and participated in the program was 35 percent higher than among similar recipients in the control group. Earnings were 23 percent higher, and the proportion of families with incomes that exceeded the poverty line rose by two-thirds. The evaluation also found that the program decreased the incidence of domestic abuse, improved children's behavior and performance in school, and increased marriage rates (Knox, Miller, and Gennetian 2000). Of special note, the MFIP evaluation gathered information on the housing status of participants. Findings indicate that most of the success was due to the substantial increases in employment and earnings MFIP generated among families receiving housing assistance. Employment and earnings gains for families that did not live in subsidized housing were much more modest (Sard and Lubell 2000b).

In a recent publication, the Manpower Demonstration Research Corporation (MDRC) (Berlin 2000) summarized the promising results of welfare research in Minnesota and other sites by concluding that

> [m]ake-work-pay programs increased employment, earnings, and income; lowered the fraction of families with below-poverty-level incomes; and improved the well-being of children. Preliminary analysis of three-year follow-up data...suggests that the findings reported here have held up over time. (v)

An interesting element of the MDRC analysis is that financial incentives in isolation may not have significant impacts. Instead, MDRC concludes that such incentives work best when paired with a requirement that families work or participate in work activities and when the incentives are "marketed" to affected families, that is, when the relevant agency makes a concerted effort to explain to welfare recipients the financial benefits of going to work.

Financial Incentives Have Net Public Costs

Efforts to encourage work among welfare recipients by offering financial incentives are likely to lead to public savings with respect to some families and public costs with respect to others. The net effect will probably be added costs. When financial incentives in a welfare program encourage some families that otherwise would not have worked to do so, those families are likely to experience some reduction in cash assistance as a result of their earnings, even with a relatively slow phase-out of benefits. For these families, work incentives yield public savings. However, work incentives are likely to benefit some families that would have gone to work without any incentives. These families receive higher benefits and remain eligible for assistance longer as a result of a more gradual phase-out of assistance. Thus, the cost of serving these families rises.

The MDRC summary of welfare evaluations finds that the net effect of these offsetting factors is typically a modest increase in government costs. This does not mean that work incentives are inefficient. MDRC found that in the programs it studied, a dollar spent as a result of more work incentives resulted in more than a dollar of increased earnings. Not surprisingly, the MDRC report noted that the costs of such efforts can be minimized by targeting financial incentives to long-term welfare recipients, the families least likely to work in the absence of such incentives.

Increasing Financial Incentives in Welfare Programs May Be More Advantageous Than Changing Rules on Subsidized Housing Rents

The findings highlighted in this analysis indicate primarily that a change in subsidized housing rent policies may not be critical to encouraging work among welfare recipients if other measures are adopted. In particular, greater financial incentives offered through state welfare programs may have a significant impact on employment among assisted tenants.

When families go to work, the reduction in welfare benefits is much larger than the loss of other forms of assistance. Because these families often lose a large share of their new earnings to reductions in welfare benefits, they often experience relatively modest gains in net cash income and thus only modest increases in rental payments. As a result, the loss of welfare benefits in many states may discourage work more than the rent increase that families face. On a practical level, in states where welfare benefits phase out quickly, easing rent increases for families that go from welfare to work is likely to have little effect on employment, since rent increases are not steep. In addition, the research highlighted here shows that offering financial incentives within welfare programs promotes work and that the employment effect on welfare recipients who live in subsidized housing is as high or higher than the effect on welfare recipients who do not live in subsidized housing. This result is somewhat surprising, since the rent formula in subsidized housing results in smaller income gains for families that live in assisted housing and go to work than for other families. These findings suggest that subsidized housing provides recipients with certain advantages, such as a greater sense of housing security, that better enable them to succeed in their employment efforts.

Changes in Rent Policy May Be Appropriate in Certain Circumstances

While it may be advantageous to enhance the earnings disregard within a state's welfare program, PHAs may have limited ability to influence welfare policy. To the extent that PHA officials and federal policy makers responsible for housing programs wish to promote work, altering the rent formula is one way to do so. Moreover, the data presented in this analysis indicate that rent increases for families that live in subsidized housing and move from welfare to work can be significant, particularly in states that have generous earned income disregards in their welfare benefit formula. In these states, rent increases may negate some of the intent of the welfare policy to make work pay. Finally, while the research cited earlier indicates that housing assistance does not appear to discourage work in a meaningful way, it may be that revising the subsidized housing rent policy to encourage work may lead to higher rates of employment.

More generally, there is some indication that certain subsidized housing tenants feel that rent increases may discourage them from working. For example, families participating in the Jobs-Plus demonstration program were asked whether rent increases would present a problem if they were to begin working full-time. Nearly half replied that the rent increase would present a serious problem (Riccio 1999).

For these reasons, some modification of rent policies may be appropriate. This analysis suggests several factors that should guide such changes:

1. Rent changes should be made in the context of a state's welfare program. This includes understanding the welfare benefit formula and how cash assistance benefits phase out when families move to work, as well as other financial incentives or disincentives welfare recipients face.

2. Changes in rent policy should be targeted in ways that limit costs and that affect the families most likely to respond.

3. Housing agencies must take aggressive action to publicize any preferential rent policy if it is to have a meaningful effect.

In addition, because housing agencies now are required to provide an earned income disregard to some tenants and have the option to provide disregards to others in public housing, understanding the likely impact of these policies on employment is important. The new public housing earned income disregard provides an opportunity to conduct empirical research. Evidence of the effects of this policy could ultimately inform PHA decisions about optional disregards, as well as future federal housing policy.

Assessing the New Public Housing Earned Income Disregard for TANF Recipients

Under final regulations issued in March 2000, eligible public housing residents who experience an increase in earnings have 100 percent of their additional income disregarded for rent purposes for 12 months, which means that families will experience no increase in rent as a result of their new earnings. After 12 months, half of the increased income is disregarded for purposes of setting rent. After two years, a PHA's basic rent rules apply, which generally means that families will pay 30 percent of their countable income for rent.

The new disregard is limited to three groups of public housing residents: tenants with a family member who has been unemployed for a year or longer, tenants with a family member whose earned income increases after participating in a family self-sufficiency or other job-training program, and tenants who are or were receiving TANF or Welfare-to-Work block grant–funded assistance within the previous six months. Disabled persons with vouchers who meet one of the above three criteria are also eligible.

This new policy meets the first two guidelines highlighted earlier because it is limited in duration and limited to a targeted group of public housing residents. The significant initial disregard is consistent with the welfare policies in a number of states that disregard all or nearly all of a family's earnings when a member first goes to work. Restricting the disregard to families receiving TANF or Welfare-to-Work benefits is likely to limit benefits primarily to families that have not worked significantly, another important form of targeting. The Clinton administration's budget proposal for fiscal year 2001 projected that the new disregard would reduce rental payments by $65 million in 2001. This amount is relatively modest in comparison to federal operating funds, the major source of funds for public housing, which totaled nearly $3 billion in 2000. The cost of the public housing earned income disregard will equal about 2 percent of federal operating assistance for public housing.

Should the New Disregard Apply to Families in Section 8 Housing as Well?

The rationale for enacting a significant earned income disregard for public housing tenants applies to families in Section 8 projects and families with Section 8 tenant-based subsidies. As noted elsewhere, a substantial majority of welfare recipients in federally subsidized housing are Section 8 recipients, not public housing residents. Given that the new disregard is targeted toward TANF and Welfare-to-Work recipients, with the goal of supporting the efforts of such families to move to work, a policy limited to public housing residents will provide limited benefit to welfare recipients in subsidized housing.

However, some research cited here suggests that the Section 8 subsidy, particularly tenant-based certificates or vouchers, may help families find work by allowing them to move closer to job opportunities. The need for financial work incentives for recipients of Section 8 tenant-based subsidies thus may be less than for public housing residents.

Most important, expanding the new disregard to Section 8 recipients could increase costs significantly and limit the expansion of housing assistance to additional needy families. It thus may make sense to continue to limit the new disregard to public housing residents while its impact on work and its costs are studied. A rigorous evaluation of the public housing earned income disregard should be conducted expeditiously.

Other Rent Policy Options

Under the new law, PHAs are obliged to set flat rents for each public housing unit, which a family may choose on an annual basis as an alternative to paying 30 percent of countable income. PHAs are also given the authority to administer ceiling rents, escrow accounts, and optional earnings disregards. Assessing the potential impact of these policies on work effort among welfare recipients is important.

Ceiling rents and flat rents. Ceiling rents are caps on the amount of rent paid by families for a unit of a certain size. Housing agencies can now set ceiling rents as low as 75 percent of operating costs, or about $300 a month. Such a policy generally benefits only families that would pay more than the ceiling rent if payments were based on 30 percent of adjusted income (i.e., families with at least $12,000 in annual income). While ceiling rents thus may help retain in public housing families that are working full-time, they generally do not have an effect on families making the transition from welfare to work.

The 1998 housing law allows families to choose to pay a flat rent that a PHA establishes on the basis of the market value of the unit. Tenants who choose this flat rent, rather than an income-based one, would not lose any share of earned income increases to higher rents. Conversely, tenants whose income declines could lose the benefit of a rent reduction, although the law allows a family to switch to an income-based rent if it cannot pay the flat rent due to financial hardship. A family that expects its earnings to rise significantly may choose the flat rent, even though that amount exceeds 30 percent of its current adjusted income, in the hope of paying less than 30 percent when its income climbs. Because families usually cannot predict changes in their income, selecting a flat rent carries an element of risk. Subsidized housing is generally intended to mitigate such risks. There is no indication that the number of families that will benefit from a flat rent is greater than the number that would be hurt. As such, this does not seem to be an appropriate way to increase work incentives for subsidized housing residents.

Beyond that, flat rents in most public housing developments are likely to be set at levels that exceed 30 percent of adjusted income for most unemployed welfare recipients; this suggests that the benefits of a flat rent would accrue primarily to families that are already working and thus have somewhat higher incomes.

Escrow accounts. These allow tenants who increase their earnings to place some or all of their rent increase in a savings account. Under the 1998 housing law, families eligible for the mandatory public housing earnings disregard may choose to place rent they would have paid if the earnings disregard were not in place in a savings account administered by the PHA, if it chooses to provide this option. Similarly, under the Family Self-Sufficiency program, which was authorized and in effect before the 1998 law, the additional rent families pay when their earnings rise is placed in an escrow account for them (Sard 2001). These policies do not provide additional income to families when a parent goes to work; instead they help tenants build assets and accumulate a tangible benefit from working. Further study of the impact of such policies is warranted.

Optional earnings disregards. PHAs have the discretion to establish earned income disregards for public housing residents beyond those required under the 1998 law. Because the new earned income disregard for tenants who receive TANF or Welfare-to-Work services or benefits is relatively well targeted to public housing families that might respond to financial incentives, it seems likely that further disregards would have only modest effects on employment and may have substantial costs, and thus may not be warranted. PHAs that wish to experiment with changes in rent policies through optional earned income disregards should design such policies carefully to limit costs and target families most likely to respond to the disregard by increasing their earnings.

Conclusion

This chapter explored whether the rent rules in federally subsidized housing programs reduce the degree to which welfare recipients who also receive rental assistance seek employment. Among the key findings are the following:

1. When subsidized housing residents go from welfare to work, a substantial share of their new earnings are offset by reductions in cash

assistance and food stamps and by an increase in rent. Even with the EITC, which offers an income boost for families that move to work, increases in earnings often translate into only modest increases in income.

2. The increase in subsidized housing rent that families face when they begin working can be sizable, but in most states the loss of welfare benefits is much greater. Moreover, changes in rents are directly linked to a state's welfare benefit formula, because rents in subsidized housing are generally based on cash income—earnings plus welfare benefits. Because welfare benefits typically decline as earnings increase, a family's rent increase, which is equal to 30 percent of additional *income*, is typically less than 30 percent of additional *earnings*. For example, if a single mother in Detroit moves from being unemployed and on TANF to full-time work at $6 an hour, her rent increase would equal 16 percent of her gross earnings. In states where welfare benefits are reduced sharply as earnings rise, families that go to work experience limited increases in total cash income and even more modest increases in their rental payment. In states with more generous welfare benefit formulas, families that go to work retain a larger share of their new earnings and thus face more significant rent increases. Similarly, for families that have left welfare, rent increases can be substantial, since earnings increases are not offset by a reduction in cash assistance benefits.

3. Making work pay better results in higher employment. Research on the impact of earned income disregards in welfare programs, under which benefits phase out gradually as earnings rise, show that financial incentives do encourage very low income adults to increase their work effort, particularly when the incentives are substantial and coupled with work requirements. Aggressive efforts to "market" financial incentives in order to ensure that recipients understand the financial benefits of working appear to be critical to the success of these incentives.

4. Financial incentives typically have a cost. They may lead some unemployed families to move to work, thus reducing benefit costs and generating public savings. Yet financial incentives also benefit some families that would have gone to work without such incentives, thus adding to program costs. Assessments of welfare earned income disregards indicate that the net effect of these offsetting factors is a modest increase in government spending. PHAs may derive other fiscal benefits from increased employment, such as reduced security or maintenance costs within public housing projects, although these savings are speculative and cannot be quantified.

5. Research indicates that expanded financial incentives in welfare programs, when combined with required participation in work activities, lead to increased employment among recipients who live in subsidized housing without any change in rent policy (Lubell, Nelson, and Sard 2003; Sard and Lubell 2000b). This may reflect the fact that subsidized housing provides benefits that support work, such as housing stability, which may mask a rent disincentive effect to the extent that it exists. This research does not address the question of whether employment rates would increase even more if policies were modified to limit rent increases when earnings rise.

These findings lead to the following conclusions:

1. Efforts to use TANF funds to make work pay better in state welfare programs are likely to have a greater effect on promoting work than changes in rent rules for subsidized housing. In states where benefits phase out sharply as earnings rise, changes in rent policies are likely to have a limited effect on welfare recipients, since they do not face steep rent increases. Changes in the welfare benefit formula would also help the large majority of welfare recipients who have earnings but do not live in subsidized housing. Changes in the subsidized housing rent formula may be appropriate for families that face the largest rent increases. This includes welfare recipients in states with the most generous earned income disregards, as well as families that have left welfare but still have low incomes.

2. A change in the subsidized housing rent policy to encourage work should not be expected to pay for itself. To the extent that PHAs pursue changes in rent policies, they should be based on the broad benefits of increasing employment among subsidized housing residents, not as an effort to bolster rental revenue.

3. Limiting the costs of changes in rent policies is important. Many needy families are not entitled to federal housing assistance, and only about one-quarter of eligible families receive it. Changes in rent policies that carry substantial costs would limit the ability to expand assistance to more families. To limit costs, changes in rent policies should be targeted as much as possible to families that are most likely to respond to the incentive. The earned income disregard in the 1998 federal housing law is an example of a targeted disregard. It is available only to families in public housing that either currently or recently received welfare-related benefits, that participate in job training, or that have been unemployed for at least a year. As of April 20, 2001, disabled persons with housing vouchers who meet one of the above three criteria are eligible as

well. Even among these families, the disregard is limited to two years of increased earnings.

4. The employment effect and costs of the new public housing earned income should be studied. If the new disregard shows promising results, it may make sense to extend it to Section 8 tenants as well, since most welfare recipients with federal housing subsidies are in Section 8 projects or have tenant-based Section 8 vouchers or certificates.

5. Because families in most states continue to benefit from housing assistance even when their incomes exceed the level at which they are eligible for TANF benefits, housing assistance may play an important role in helping families achieve self-sufficiency.

Appendix 6A

Supplementary Tables

Table 6A.1. **Earnings Disregards for Recipients of TANF Cash Assistance, 2000**

Alabama	100 percent for 3 months
	20 percent in subsequent months
Alaska	$150 and one-third of the remainder for 12 months
	$150 and 25 percent of the remainder for the next 12 months
	$150 and 20 percent of the remainder for the next 12 months
	$150 and 15 percent of the remainder for the next 12 months
	$150 and 10 percent of the remainder for the next 12 months
Arizona	$90 and 30 percent of the remainder
Arkansas	20 percent and 60 percent of the remainder
California	$225 and 50 percent of the remainder
Colorado	[a]
Connecticut	100 percent until earnings exceed the poverty level[b]
Delaware	[a]
District of Columbia	$160 and 67 percent of the remainder
Florida	$200 and 50 percent of the remainder
Georgia	[a]
Hawaii	20 percent, then $200, then 36 percent of the remainder
Idaho	40 percent
Illinois	67 percent
Indiana	100 percent until earnings exceed the poverty level
Iowa	20 percent and 50 percent of the remainder
Kansas	$90 and 40 percent of the remainder
Kentucky	100 percent for 2 months
	[a] in subsequent months
Louisiana	$1,020 for 6 months
	$120 in subsequent months
Maine	$108 and 50 percent of the remainder
Maryland	35 percent

Table 6A.1. **Earnings Disregards for Recipients of TANF Cash Assistance, 2000** *(continued)*

Massachusetts	$120 and 50 percent of the remainder
Michigan	$200 and 20 percent of the remainder
Minnesota	38 percent
Mississippi	100 percent for 6 months
	$90 in subsequent months
Missouri	67 percent and $90 of the remainder for 12 months
	$90 in subsequent months
Montana	$200 and 25 percent of the remainder for 24 months
	$200 in subsequent months
Nebraska	20 percent
Nevada	100 percent for 3 months
	50 percent for the next 9 months
	Greater of $90 or 20 percent in subsequent months
New Hampshire	50 percent
New Jersey	50 percent
New Mexico	$150 and 50 percent of the remainder
New York	$90 and 46 percent of the remainder
North Carolina	27.5 percent
North Dakota	Greater of $90 or 27 percent, and 50 percent of the "employment incentive limit" for 8 months
	Greater of $90 or 27 percent, and 30 percent of the "employment incentive limit" for the next 2 months
	Greater of $90 or 27 percent, and 10 percent of the "employment incentive limit" for the next 2 months
	Greater of $90 or 27 percent in subsequent months
Ohio	$250 and 50 percent of the remainder
Oklahoma	$120 and 50 percent of the remainder
Oregon	50 percent
Pennsylvania	50 percent
Rhode Island	$170 and 50 percent of the remainder
South Carolina	50 percent for 4 months
	$100 in subsequent months
South Dakota	$90 and 20 percent of the remainder
Tennessee	$150
Texas	$120 and 90 percent of the remainder for 4 months
	$120 in subsequent months
Utah	$100 and 50 percent of the remainder
Vermont	$150 and 25 percent of the remainder
Virginia	100 percent until earnings reach the poverty level[b]
Washington	50 percent
West Virginia	40 percent
Wisconsin	none
Wyoming	$200 for single parents
	$400 for two-parent families

Source: State Policy Documentation Project 1999.

[a] These states follow former AFDC policy, under which $120 and one-third of the remainder were disregarded for 4 months, $120 was disregarded for the next 8 months, and $90 was disregarded in subsequent months.

[b] In Connecticut and Indiana, families lose all benefits when earnings exceed the poverty level. In Virginia, combined earnings and benefits cannot exceed the poverty level, so benefits begin to phase out as earnings approach the poverty level.

Table 6A.2. **Monthly Cash Assistance Benefits for a Single-Parent Family of Three with No Earnings, 2001**

Alabama	$164	Montana	$493
Alaska	$923	Nebraska	$364
Arizona	$347	Nevada	$348
Arkansas	$204	New Hampshire	$600
California[a]	$645	New Jersey	$424
Colorado	$356	New Mexico	$439
Connecticut[a]	$543	New York[a]	$577
Delaware	$338	North Carolina	$272
District of Columbia	$379	North Dakota	$457
Florida	$303	Ohio	$373
Georgia	$280	Oklahoma	$292
Hawaii	$570	Oregon	$460
Idaho	$293	Pennsylvania[a]	$403
Illinois	$377	Rhode Island	$554
Indiana	$288	South Carolina	$203
Iowa	$426	South Dakota	$430
Kansas[a]	$403	Tennessee	$185
Kentucky	$262	Texas	$207
Louisiana	$240	Utah	$451
Maine	$461	Vermont[a]	$631
Maryland	$439	Virginia[a]	$320
Massachusetts[a]	$633	Washington	$546
Michigan[a]	$459	West Virginia	$453
Minnesota[b]	$801	Wisconsin[a]	$673
Mississippi	$170	Wyoming	$340
Missouri	$292		

[a] Benefits vary by region or by category of recipient. The benefit level shown is for the region or category with largest number of recipients in the state.

[b] TANF and food stamps are issued as a combined benefit.

Table 6A.3. **Earnings Eligibility Level for a Family of Three Beyond Which It Becomes Ineligible for Cash Assistance**

	13th Month of Earnings		13th Month of Earnings
Alabama	$205	Montana	$857
Alaska	$1,641	Nebraska	$669
Arizona	$586	Nevada	$438
Arkansas	$697	New Hampshire	$1,200
California*	$1,515	New Jersey	$848
Colorado	$511	New Mexico	$1,028
Connecticut*	$1,219	New York*	$1,157
Delaware	$1,004	North Carolina	$750
District of Columbia	$1,307	North Dakota	$1,014
Florida	$806	Ohio	$996
Georgia	$514	Oklahoma	$704
Hawaii	$1,363	Oregon	$616
Idaho	$625	Pennsylvania*	$806
Illinois	$1,131	Rhode Island	$1,278
Indiana	$1,219	South Carolina	$709
Iowa	$1,065	South Dakota	$628
Kansas*	$762	Tennessee	$949
Kentucky	$646	Texas	$327
Louisiana	$360	Utah	$1,002
Maine	$1,214	Vermont*	$991
Maryland	$675	Virginia*	$1,219
Massachusetts*	$1,386	Washington	$1,092
Michigan*	$774	West Virginia	$755
Minnesota	$1,421	Wisconsin*	$673
Mississippi	$458	Wyoming	$540
Missouri	$382		

*Benefit rules vary by region or by category of recipient. These figures reflect benefit rules that affect the largest number of recipients in the state.

Authors

Ed Lazere is a Senior Research Analyst at the Center on Budget and Policy Priorities. Jennifer Daskal is a Staff Attorney at the D.C. Public Defender Service.

The opinions expressed in this chapter are those of the authors and do not necessarily reflect the position of the Fannie Mae Foundation, its officers, or any of the other organizations that convened or cooperated in the research roundtable.

References

Abt Associates. 1997. *The Indiana Welfare Reform Evaluation: Who Is On and Who Is Off? Comparing Characteristics and Outcomes for Current and Former TANF Recipients.* Cambridge, MA.

Berlin, Gordon L. 2000. *Encouraging Work and Reducing Poverty: The Impact of Work Incentive Programs*. New York: Manpower Demonstration Research Project.

Connell, Terrence L., Deborah Devine, and Lester Rubin. 1998. *Welfare Reform Impacts on the Public Housing Program: A Preliminary Forecast*. Washington, DC: U.S. Department of Housing and Urban Development.

Ellwood, David T. 1999. *The Impact of the Earned Income Tax Credit and Social Policy Reforms on Work, Marriage, and Living Arrangements*. Cambridge, MA: Harvard University, John F. Kennedy School of Government.

Guyer, Jocelyn, and Cindy Mann. 1999. *Employed but Not Insured: A State-by-State Analysis of the Number of Low-Income Working Parents Who Lack Health Insurance*. Washington, DC: Center on Budget and Policy Priorities.

Knox, Virginia, Cynthia Miller, and Lisa Gennetian. 2000. *Reforming Welfare and Rewarding Work: A Summary of the Final Report on the Minnesota Family Investment Program*. New York: Manpower Development Research Corporation.

Lazere, Ed. 2000. *Welfare Balances after Three Years under the TANF Block Grant: Unspent TANF Funds at the End of Fiscal Year 1999*. Washington, DC: Center on Budget and Policy Priorities.

Liebman, Jeffrey. 1998. The Impact of the Earned Income Tax Credit on Incentives and Income Distribution. In *Tax Policy and the Economy*, Vol. 12, ed. James M. Poterba, 83–119. Cambridge, MA: MIT Press.

Lubell, Jeffrey M., Kathryn P. Nelson, and Barbara Sard. 2003. How Housing Programs' Admissions Policies Can Contribute to Welfare Reform. In *A Place to Live, a Means to Work: How Housing Assistance Can Strengthen Welfare Policy*, ed. Barbara Sard and Amy S. Bogdon, 211–67. Washington, DC: Fannie Mae Foundation.

Meyer, Bruce, and Dan Rosenbaum. 1999. *Welfare, the Earned Income Tax Credit, and the Labor Supply of Single Mothers*. NBER Working Paper 7363. Cambridge, MA: National Bureau of Economic Research.

Painter, Gary. 2001. Low-Income Housing Assistance: Its Impact on Labor Force and Housing Program Participation. *Journal of Housing Research* 12(1):1–26.

Porter, Kathryn, Wendell Primus, Lynette Rawlings, and Esther Rosenbaum, 1998. *Strengths of the Safety Net: How the EITC, Social Security, and Other Government Programs Affect Poverty*. Washington, DC: Center on Budget and Policy Priorities.

Riccio, James. 1999. *Jobs-Plus Baseline Survey Data Resources Book*, Vol. II. New York: Manpower Development Research Corporation.

Sard, Barbara. 2001. *The Family Self-Sufficiency Program: HUD's Best Kept Secret for Promoting Employment and Asset Growth*. Washington, DC: Center on Budget and Policy Priorities.

Sard, Barbara, and Jennifer Daskal. 1998. *Housing and Welfare Reform: Some Background Information*. Washington, DC: Center on Budget and Policy Priorities.

Sard, Barbara, and Jeffrey M. Lubell. 2000a. *How the Statutory Changes Made by the Quality Housing and Work Responsibility Act of 2000 May Affect Welfare Reform Efforts*. Washington, DC: Center on Budget and Policy Priorities.

Sard, Barbara, and Jeffrey M. Lubell. 2000b. *The Value of Housing Subsidies to Welfare Reform*. Washington, DC: Center on Budget and Policy Priorities.

South Carolina Department of Social Services. 1998. *Survey of Former Family Independence Program Clients: Cases Closed during January through March 1997*. Columbia, SC.

State Policy Documentation Project. 1999. *Selected Data from the Joint Project of the Center for Law and Social Policy and the Center on Budget and Policy Priorities*. World Wide Web page <http://www.spdp.org> (accessed June 2001).

U.S. Department of Housing and Urban Development, Office of Policy Development and Research. 1998. *Welfare Reform Impacts on the Public Housing Program: A Preliminary Forecast*. Washington, DC.

Werner, Alan, and Robert Kornfeld. 1996. *The Evaluation of "To Strengthen Michigan Families": Fourth Annual Report: Third-Year Impacts*. Abt Associates. Cambridge, MA.

CHAPTER 7

How Housing Programs' Admissions Policies Can Contribute to Welfare Reform

Jeffrey M. Lubell and Kathryn P. Nelson
U.S. Department of Housing and Urban Development

Barbara Sard
Center on Budget and Policy Priorities

Abstract

Recent research suggests that, under certain circumstances, housing subsidies may help families obtain and/or retain employment. Particularly when combined with welfare reform interventions that reward work effort and provide work-promoting services, housing subsidies appear to be helpful in promoting employment among welfare recipients.

Our review of available research leads us to question the popular view that the best way for housing providers to promote welfare reform is to adopt an admissions preference for households with a full-time worker. Such a preference fails to cover many of the households most likely to benefit from the work-promoting aspects of housing subsidies—especially households attempting to make the transition from welfare to work—while including some households with relatively higher incomes that are less likely to have a severe housing problem. This chapter provides recommendations for alternative admissions preferences that are better targeted to families trying to move from welfare to work.

Keywords: Admissions policy; Employment issues; Low-income housing; Welfare

Introduction

Most people would agree that the primary goal of low-income housing programs is to provide shelter to those who need it. Consistent with this objective, debates within the housing policy world tend to focus on such issues as how to expand the supply of affordable housing, whether to use tenant-based solutions like vouchers or project-based solutions like new construction, and how to prioritize applicants for the limited number of housing subsidies.

The advent of welfare reform has raised an additional set of questions: What is the role of housing assistance in this era of welfare reform? Is housing assistance likely to help or hinder welfare reform? Are there steps housing agencies could take to promote welfare reform? If so, what are they? Elsewhere in this volume, Barbara Sard (2003) examines the issue of the shifting role of housing agencies, exploring the reasons why they should care about the extent to which their tenants succeed in moving from welfare to work and the types of activities they can undertake to help their tenants succeed.

This chapter has a related but distinct focus. Here, we examine two questions:

1. Can housing assistance help families make the transition from welfare to work and, if so, under what circumstances?

2. What are the implications of our findings for public housing agencies (PHAs) and private owners as they decide who will receive preference for the limited supply of housing subsidies?

This inquiry has separate welfare and housing contexts. The welfare side is fairly well known. In 1996, Congress enacted comprehensive welfare reform legislation that included work participation requirements and a five-year lifetime limit on receiving federal welfare assistance. The new legislation also gave states substantial discretion to decide how to use federal welfare funds and state matching funds. Although welfare caseloads were already declining relative to their peak levels when the legislation was enacted, the decline has accelerated since 1996. As of 2001, welfare caseloads stood at approximately 2.1 million families, less than half of their peak levels in 1994, with most of the decline occurring between 1996 and 1999 (U.S. Department of Health and Human Services 2002).

Although opinions on the relative importance of each factor differ, it appears likely that some of the decline was due to changes in welfare policy and some was due to the strong economy. (See Council of Economic Advisers 1999 and Schoeni and Blank 2000.) Some of the decline may also be due to policy changes unrelated to the welfare reform law, such as an increase in the Earned Income Tax Credit (EITC), an increase in the minimum wage, and changes in Medicaid eligibility that allow families to take certain low-paying jobs without losing their health coverage (Schott, Greenstein, and Primus 1999). Regardless of one's interpretation of the caseload decline data and the wisdom of time limits,[1] there seems to be agreement that the flexible nature of the

---

[1] The full effects of welfare reform will not be visible until more families hit time limits. Nevertheless, there are some early indications that welfare reform will lead to more people becoming destitute (Primus et al. 1999).

new welfare block grant has led to an increased focus on providing low-income families with the supports they need to increase their earnings. One question this chapter seeks to address is whether housing assistance can, under certain circumstances, serve as one of those supports.

The housing context is less familiar to a general audience. Attempts to turn federal housing assistance into a block grant, as was done with federal welfare assistance, have not succeeded. In the Quality Housing and Work Responsibility Act of 1998 (QHWRA), however, Congress did increase the flexibility of state and local PHAs and private owners of subsidized housing to determine which groups should receive preference for the limited supply of federal housing assistance.[2] A key question addressed in this chapter is whether there is a way for PHAs to use this newly expanded discretion to promote welfare reform.

Although the research base is still fairly small, it suggests that, under certain circumstances, housing subsidies may help families obtain or retain employment. Such subsidies appear to be particularly helpful in promoting employment among welfare recipients when combined with welfare reform interventions that reward work effort and provide work-promoting services. This conclusion is based in part on research indicating that welfare reform interventions have a greater impact among residents of public and subsidized housing than among residents of private-market housing. (One such study by Riccio and Orenstein [2003], which reports on the results of the Job Opportunities and Basic Skills [JOBS] program in Atlanta, is published elsewhere in this volume.)

We hypothesize that certain attributes of housing subsidies—such as increased residential stability and the potential to move to neighborhoods offering better job opportunities—can have a positive impact on employment rates of welfare recipients in subsidized housing, provided that subsidies are accompanied by welfare reform interventions that support and reinforce work participation. Such interventions may include improved access to supportive services, partial or complete disregard of increased earnings in computing benefit levels, and/or work requirements.

This analysis has a number of implications for PHAs and private owners interested in adopting admissions preferences that promote welfare reform. The most direct one is that agencies and owners should adopt preferences favoring households enrolled in welfare-to-work programs. This could be accomplished either by reserving a specific proportion

---

[2] Congress also gave PHAs greater flexibility to determine how public housing rents are set and to vary the level of the payment standard used to compute the subsidy amount for the Section 8 voucher program (Sard and Lubell 1998).

of new admissions for households in welfare-to-work programs or by expanding an existing preference for working households to include them.

If housing subsidies can help promote work among households currently enrolled in welfare-to-work programs, one would expect that they can also help promote work among households that have graduated from such programs (or chosen to bypass the welfare system altogether) yet are stuck in low-wage jobs. To reach these households, PHAs and private owners should consider instituting a preference for extremely low income households with some income from work.[3] If such a preference were substituted for a broader working preference, it would help increase the likelihood that families with severe housing problems get housing assistance.[4]

Our final recommendation is that PHAs and private owners consider using the housing subsidies generated through turnover or incremental voucher allocations as barter to obtain work-promoting services for their tenants. Households with housing subsidies appear to be well positioned to benefit from such services.

This chapter is structured as follows: We first discuss the expanded discretion of PHAs and private owners to set admissions preferences. Because housing subsidies appear to be correlated with lower employment rates, we next inquire whether these subsidies are the cause of this correlation. We conclude that most if not all of the variation appears to be due to differences in the characteristics of households with and without housing assistance.

We then discuss studies that have analyzed the different impacts of welfare reform initiatives on households with and without housing assistance. These studies indicate that households that received housing assistance benefited much more from the initiatives than households that did not. One interpretation of these results is that housing subsidies can be helpful in promoting employment when they are combined with welfare interventions that reward and support work.

---

[3] Under Department of Housing and Urban Development rules, "extremely low income" households are those with incomes below 30 percent of the area median family income, as adjusted for family size and other factors. The area median family income varies greatly by region.

[4] We also recommend that PHAs and private owners that choose to serve households with incomes between 31 and 50 percent of the area median income limit such assistance to households with severe housing problems.

In the final section, we consider the policy implications of these studies for PHAs and private owners interested in adopting admissions preferences that promote welfare reform. We discuss various preferences that could be adopted to help target those attempting to move from welfare to work and discuss how our proposed admissions preferences would serve the additional objective of targeting households with severe housing problems.

Expanded Discretion of Public Housing Agencies and Private Owners to Set Admissions Policies

Unlike federal entitlements such as Medicaid and food stamps, federal rental housing subsidies are not made available to all households that qualify for and need such assistance. Approximately 4.1 million households currently receive "deep" federal rental subsidies[5] (Khadduri, Shroder, and Steffen 2003). Despite this level of assistance, in 1999 an estimated 4.9 million very low income renter households spent more than half of their income on housing or lived in severely substandard housing but received no government housing assistance (Department of Housing and Urban Development [HUD] 2001).[6] This suggests that federal housing subsidies are provided to less than half of the renter households most in need of them. Sard and Lubell (2000) have estimated that only one in four qualifying households eligible for and in need of federal rental assistance actually receives it.

Considerable attention is paid each year to the number of new subsidies (if any) funded by Congress. While important, they are not the only game in town. For fiscal years (FY) 1999 and 2000, Congress appropriated funds for 50,000 and 60,000 new housing vouchers, respectively. However, as table 7.1 shows, due to turnover among

---

[5] Our discussion of federal rental subsidies is limited to those federal programs that provide "deep" subsidies, that is, subsidies sufficient to cover the expected costs for rent and utilities above a fixed fraction (usually 30 percent) of tenants' incomes. These include subsidies provided through the public housing, tenant-based Section 8, and project-based Section 8 programs. Since the source of our data is the chapter by Khadduri, Shroder, and Steffen (2003), printed elsewhere in this volume, we follow them in excluding Indian housing, which serves approximately 75,000 additional households. Some 300,000 more households receive "shallow" rent subsidies from the Department of Housing and Urban Development (HUD) that are less generous than the deep subsidy programs. Finally, some number of additional households benefit from HUD's HOME block grant program and the Low-Income Housing Tax Credit program administered by the Internal Revenue Service; in most cases, the benefits provided by these programs are similar to a shallow rent subsidy.

[6] HUD defines "very low income" households as those with incomes below 50 percent of the area median family income, as adjusted for family size and other factors. As noted earlier, the area median family income varies greatly by region.

existing participants, approximately 500,000 federal housing subsidies become available every year for use by new households. (The number of subsidies newly available each year to families with children is roughly 242,000.) Assuming that new voucher appropriations continue at about this level, the total number of rental subsidies available for use by new households in any given year is about 550,000. This is clearly a significant resource, even though it represents only about 10 percent of the 4.9 million households with worst-case housing needs in 1999.

Table 7.1. **Estimated Annual Availability of Federally Assisted Housing Units to New Households as a Result of Turnover**

	Total Occupied Units	Estimated Annual Turnover Rate	Estimated Yearly Turnover Units	Number of Units Occupied by Families with Children	Estimated Yearly Turnover Units Available to Families with Children
Certificates and vouchers	1,500,000	11%	165,000	980,000	107,800
Project-based Section 8 units	1,400,000	13%	182,000	480,000	62,400
Public housing	1,200,000	13%	156,000	550,000	71,500
Totals	4,100,000		503,000	2,010,000	241,700

Source: Adapted from Khadduri, Shroder, and Steffen (2003).

The Federal Framework for State and Local Admissions Preferences

Given the limited supply of federal rental assistance, the policies used to select which households will receive preference for newly available assistance are of considerable importance. For many years, federal law required that most newly available housing subsidies be awarded to households with certain "priority" housing problems, defined as paying more than 50 percent of income for rent, involuntary displacement, residence in severely substandard housing, or homelessness.

There was considerable opposition to these federal preference rules from state and local PHAs that wanted to set their own admission preferences. Their opposition led to the temporary suspension of federal admissions preferences in the FY 1996, 1997, and 1998 appropriations acts and their eventual elimination in the QHWRA.

In place of the federal preference system, QHWRA created a system in which each PHA is free to set its own admissions preferences, so long as they result in a certain proportion of available housing subsidies being provided to "extremely low income" households.[7] (Admissions preferences must also be consistent with fair housing requirements and public housing deconcentration requirements.) As discussed later, extremely low income households are much more likely to have severe housing problems than households with higher incomes. The targeting of assistance on such households thus appears to be consistent with the goal of serving households with greater needs.

QHWRA requires that at least 40 percent of the public housing units that become available and are filled each year at each PHA be provided to extremely low income households. To similar effect, private owners of Section 8 project-based housing are required to reserve at least 40 percent of available subsidized units for such households. The balance of public housing units may be provided to households with incomes as high as 80 percent of the area median income (AMI).[8]

The stated justification for permitting up to 60 percent of newly available public housing units to go to households with incomes as high as 80 percent of AMI is that PHAs should be permitted to use their admissions policies to reduce the concentration of poverty and achieve a diversity of incomes in their developments.[9] Since tenant-based vouchers and certificates help subsidize the rents of apartments that families locate on the private market, they disperse rather than concentrate poor families.[10] The factors motivating the relaxation of targeting in public housing—that is, deconcentration of poverty and income mixing—thus do not apply to the tenant-based program. Accordingly, the law requires PHAs to use at least three-fourths of the Section 8 vouchers that become available each year to assist extremely low income

---

[7] Under certain limited circumstances, PHAs that exceed their minimum targeting requirements in the tenant-based program may provide less than 40 percent of newly available public housing units to extremely low income families. See 24 C.F.R. 960.202(b)(2).

[8] QHWRA did not change existing law, which requires that 75 to 85 percent of newly available units in project-based Section 8 developments be provided to very low income households (i.e., households with incomes below 50 percent of AMI). See 24 C.F.R. 5.653.

[9] See, for example, pages 15–16 of Senate Report 105–21, The Public Housing Reform and Responsibility Act of 1997 (May 23, 1997) on S.462, the Senate version of the bill that became QHWRA.

[10] As Khadduri, Shroder, and Steffen (2003) and Newman and Schnare (1997) show, tenant-based subsidy recipients are less likely to live in high-poverty areas than residents of either public housing or project-based Section 8 housing.

households—a level roughly comparable to pre-QHWRA practice.[11] The balance may be provided to households with incomes up to 80 percent of AMI.[12]

Although housing agencies have the discretion to serve households with incomes as high as 80 percent of AMI, there appears to be little justification for PHAs to serve households with incomes above 50 percent of AMI. As discussed later, serious housing problems are rare among households with incomes between 50 and 80 percent of AMI. Moreover, in most areas, the 50 percent threshold is high enough that it does not seriously limit the ability of PHAs and private owners to choose those whom they want to serve. Table 7.2 shows HUD's FY 2000 eligibility and income-targeting thresholds for three-person households in the 10 largest metropolitan (or primary metropolitan) statistical areas. As the table indicates, in 9 out of 10 of the areas listed, the 50 percent of AMI threshold for a family of three exceeds $25,000.[13]

While the 30 percent of AMI limit does constitute a meaningful constraint on PHA and private owner discretion, it is not an onerous one. As table 7.2 shows, 30 percent of AMI (as adjusted for a family of three) ranges from $14,050 to $21,750 in the 10 largest metropolitan areas. The category of households with incomes below 30 percent of AMI thus embraces far more than the poorest of the poor. In most areas, this category includes a large number of working households, including many with severe housing problems. In 1997, more than 2 million households with incomes below 30 percent of AMI and earnings as their primary source of income either spent more than half of their income on housing or lived in severely substandard housing but received no government housing assistance (HUD 2000a).[14]

---

[11] In the years leading up to the enactment of QHWRA, approximately 81 percent of all vouchers and certificates were provided to households with incomes below 30 percent of AMI (Lubell and Sard 1998). QHWRA merged the certificate and voucher programs into a new voucher program. Since October 1, 1999, all families receiving new Section 8 tenant-based subsidies have received vouchers (Sard and Lubell 1998).

[12] In the Section 8 voucher program, PHAs may provide newly available assistance to households with incomes between 50 and 80 percent of AMI only if those households meet some additional eligibility criterion consistent with the needs identified in the PHA plan and the jurisdiction's consolidated plan. 24 C.F.R. 982.201(b)(1)(iii).

[13] We use HUD income limits for a family of three because that is the most common size of households with welfare income. Income limits are higher for larger households and lower for smaller ones.

[14] A later section provides greater detail on the extent to which the 30 percent of AMI threshold includes households making the transition from welfare to work and other working households.

Table 7.2. **HUD's FY 2000 Income Limits for Three-Person Households in the 10 Largest Metropolitan Areas**

Metropolitan Statistical Area	30% of AMI (As Adjusted)	50% of AMI (As Adjusted)	80% of AMI (As Adjusted)
Los Angeles	$14,050	$23,450	$37,500
New York	15,150	25,300	40,450
Chicago	18,350	30,550	45,200
Philadelphia	15,600	26,000	41,600
Washington, DC	21,750	36,250	45,200
Detroit	16,850	28,100	44,950
Houston	15,300	25,500	40,800
Atlanta	17,050	28,400	45,200
Boston	17,700	29,500	45,200
Dallas	16,400	27,350	43,800

Source: HUD 2002.
Note: Income limits in this table reflect a number of statutory adjustments, including one for a family size of three (0.9).

In sum, while ensuring that a minimum proportion of newly available housing subsidies is targeted for households with incomes below 30 percent of AMI—a group with a high incidence of severe housing problems—the new system gives PHAs and private owners great latitude to determine which groups of households receive the limited supply of available rental assistance.

Admissions Preferences That Advance Welfare Reform

Most PHAs and private owners that have considered welfare reform objectives in setting their admissions policies have chosen to adopt a preference for working households. In this model, housing assistance is assumed to promote work by rewarding those who comply with the employment preference. In this respect, housing assistance plays a role similar to that of Temporary Assistance for Needy Families (TANF) cash assistance, which is generally given only to those who comply with applicable work requirements.

But what if housing assistance can contribute more to welfare reform than simply a reward for good behavior? What if housing assistance itself—like child care and transportation—can help families move successfully from welfare to work? If so, perhaps admissions preferences should be crafted to target those in the process of moving from welfare to work, rather than those who have already managed the transition.

In the next two sections, we review research bearing on the question of whether housing subsidies can be helpful in achieving the objectives of welfare reform. On the basis of the available research, we conclude that when combined with welfare reform interventions that emphasize the importance of working and provide work supports, housing assistance can be helpful in promoting employment and other welfare reform goals.

Do Housing Subsidies Depress Work Activity?

Any examination of the effect of subsidized housing on work participation must begin with the simple fact that housing subsidy receipt tends to be correlated with low rates of employment. Based on 1994 Aid to Families with Dependent Children (AFDC) quality control data, Newman and Harkness (1999a) estimate that 6.8 percent of the heads of households with both welfare income and rental housing assistance were employed, compared with 9.1 percent of the renter households with AFDC income but no housing assistance. Although the AFDC quality control data do not provide information on the proportion of AFDC households that were employed the previous year, this information has been collected by researchers for a number of specific areas. For example, an Atlanta survey found that only 18.4 percent and 24.1 percent of AFDC recipients in public housing and Section 8 housing, respectively, had been employed in the previous year, compared with 37.4 percent of recipients in private-market housing (Riccio and Orenstein 2003). Similarly, a Columbus survey found that only 22 percent and 20 percent of AFDC recipients in public housing and Section 8 housing, respectively, had been employed in the previous year, compared with 34 percent of recipients in private-market housing (Riccio and Orenstein 2003).[15]

---

[15] A survey of welfare recipients in four counties in California found results that were similar in certain respects and different in others (Ong 1998). Among the welfare recipients who reported working in the past month, the average number of hours was highest for those in private-market housing (75.2 hours) and lowest for those in public housing (36 hours), with Section 8 recipients falling in between (66 hours). This suggests a pattern similar to Atlanta's. Because the proportion of Section 8 recipients who reported working in the past month was higher than that for households in private-market housing (29 percent versus 16 percent), however, the average number of hours worked for all Section 8 recipients (including those with zero hours) was higher than for all households in private-market housing (19.3 hours versus 12.3 hours). The proportion of public housing residents who reported working in the past month was comparable to that of households in private-market housing (18 percent versus 16 percent); however, the average number of hours worked among all public housing residents (including those with zero hours) was lower than for all households in private-market housing (6.5 hours versus 12.3 hours).

There are two main potential explanations for this correlation: The housing subsidies themselves may be depressing work effort, or the different outcomes may be attributable to differences in the characteristics of the populations of welfare households with and without housing assistance. We begin our analysis by exploring some of the theoretical reasons why each of these might be the case. We then consider the results of studies that have examined the relationship between housing assistance and employment rates.

Competing Explanations for the Correlation of Housing Subsidy Receipt and Low Employment Rates

There are a number of reasons why housing assistance could lead to reduced employment rates. First, households with housing assistance do not need to earn as much as other households to achieve an equivalent standard of living. Economic theory suggests that this "income effect" would lead to reduced labor market participation among those receiving assistance.[16] Second, households with federal housing assistance are generally required to contribute 30 percent of their adjusted income for rent and utilities.[17] As their incomes increase from work, their required rent contributions increase as well, reducing their take-home pay substantially. Since they receive less benefit from each additional dollar of earnings, subsidized housing residents may have less incentive to work or increase their earnings. (As discussed elsewhere in this volume by Lazere and Daskal [2003], the tax on the marginal earnings of housing subsidy recipients increases significantly if they also receive food stamps and welfare benefits.)

Third, Section 8 households may be less willing to increase their earnings beyond the point where they lose their subsidy—generally, where

---

[16] Of course, the point of providing government benefits such as subsidized housing is to increase the standard of living for participating families. To the extent that benefit transfers result in work disincentives, as suggested in some experiments with guaranteed incomes—see, for example, SRI International (1983)—it may make sense to combine benefit transfers with work-promoting strategies, such as a partial disregard of increased earnings from work, case management services, and so on. For more information on such strategies in the welfare context, see Berlin (2000). For a discussion of how housing agencies could implement such strategies, see Sard (2003).

[17] Not all households with deep federal rental subsidies pay this amount. Households with vouchers are allowed to contribute more to rent above the maximum subsidy paid by the PHA, and households in public housing have the option of choosing a flat rent that does not vary based on their income. In addition, housing agencies may set "ceiling rents" for public housing developments, in which rents are based on tenants' income up to a set maximum or "ceiling." For more information on these alternative rent formulas, see Sard and Lubell (1998).

the subsidy remains at zero for more than six months—since it protects them against any future declines in income they might experience and since waiting lists for housing assistance are lengthy in most places. (By contrast, those in public housing cannot lose their units as a result of increased income.) A fourth reason to expect that housing subsidies may lead to lower employment rates is that residence in certain public housing projects may depress work activity by exposing people to an entrenched culture of poverty and joblessness. (This applies mainly to public housing, as opposed to other federal housing programs.) Finally, the poor location of many public housing projects and some Section 8 developments may isolate residents from jobs.

However, there are a number of reasons to expect that the differences in employment rates could be predominantly if not entirely due to differences in the characteristics of households with and without housing assistance.[18] It is not easy to obtain a housing subsidy. Applicants must go out of their way to apply for assistance, endure waiting periods that can last for years,[19] and provide a great deal of information to the housing agency to prove that they qualify for assistance under whatever preferences the agency has adopted. One would expect that households with fewer barriers to work would be less willing to undergo this process and less likely to qualify for any preferences based on severe housing needs when their names finally do come to the top of the list.[20]

There is also some reason to believe that self-selection occurs *after* entry into subsidized housing, particularly public housing. Much has been written about the problems of inner-city public housing developments. (See, for example, Vale 1993.) In light of these issues, one would expect that households with fewer barriers to work would be more

---

[18] The characteristics of households with federal housing assistance appear to vary by program type (Newman and Schnare 1993). It is possible that such differences are also relevant to labor market participation.

[19] According to *A Picture of Subsidized Households in 1998: United States Summaries* (HUD 1998), households with Section 8 certificates or vouchers in 1998 had waited an average of 28 months to obtain their subsidies, while households residing in public housing in 1998 had waited an average of 11 months to get in. In some areas, the reported waiting times were considerably longer. In Houston, for example, the average wait for a Section 8 certificate or voucher was 93 months.

[20] As noted earlier, under the old system, households with severe housing needs were given preference for the limited supply of newly available federal housing subsidies. Most households that received federal housing subsidies between 1988 and 1996, therefore, had severe housing needs. Although the federal preference rules are no longer in effect, many housing authorities continue to give preference to households with severe housing needs. For a thoughtful discussion of some of the different ways in which the housing subsidy selection process can influence the characteristics of households with housing subsidies, see Newman and Harkness 1999b.

likely to choose to leave public housing. Since households with a Section 8 certificate or voucher can choose to move and keep their subsidy, one would not expect this principle to apply to them. However, the hassle factor associated with periodic income recertifications and the need to convince landlords to accept the subsidy may lead work-motivated households to give up their Section 8 tenant-based subsidies as well.

Finally, relative to all welfare recipients, those with housing assistance may be concentrated in cities (and within cities, within neighborhoods) that have high concentrations of poor families with multiple barriers to work. As Khadduri, Shroder, and Steffen (2003) and Newman and Schnare (1997) show, both welfare and nonwelfare households residing in public housing are much more likely to reside in high-poverty census tracts than welfare recipients generally are. This disparity is likely to be due partly to where public housing developments are sited *within* metropolitan areas and partly to the concentration of these developments in metropolitan areas with high poverty rates.[21]

The AFDC quality control data compiled by Newman and Harkness (1999a) point to a number of significant differences between households with and without housing assistance. A key difference is race. Whereas 48.3 percent of households that received both AFDC and federal rental assistance in 1994 were African-American, non-Hispanic households, only 32.7 percent of AFDC renters who did not receive federal rental assistance were African-American, non-Hispanic households. (This phenomenon appears to be specific to African-American households, rather than to minority households generally.[22])

AFDC recipients with federal rental assistance were also much more likely to be long-term welfare recipients than renter households receiving only AFDC. Newman and Harkness (1999a) estimate that 30.2 percent of AFDC recipients with housing assistance (as opposed

---

[21] As Kingsley and Tatian (1999) show, public housing developments are not distributed evenly across the country. They tend to be concentrated in the older cities of the Northeast, Midwest, and Southeast, "since they demonstrated the greatest needs in the 1950s, 1960s, and early 1970s, when that program was growing rapidly" (Kingsley and Tatian 1999, 87). Although an analysis comparing the distribution of public housing units by metropolitan area with 1990 census variables used to characterize metropolitan characteristics did not find any "strong patterns or relationships," it did find modest correlations between public housing location and the following metropolitan-wide variables: "percentages of the population that had not graduated from high school (+0.49) or had moved over the preceding five years (–0.48) and the household poverty rate (+0.33)" (Kingsley and Tatian 1999, 95).

[22] AFDC renters without federal housing assistance were somewhat more likely to be Hispanic than AFDC renters with federal housing assistance (21.9 percent versus 16.1 percent) (Newman and Harkness 1999a).

to 19.5 percent of AFDC renters without it) had current spells of AFDC receipt that lasted longer than 60 months. The same trend is evident in the statistics on the number of months of cumulative life-time welfare receipt. Some 47.5 percent of AFDC recipients with housing assistance had cumulative spells longer than 60 months, as opposed to 33.2 percent of AFDC renters without housing assistance.

Of course, one cannot rule out the possibility that the greater incidence of long-term welfare receipt among AFDC households with housing subsidies is due to subsidized housing itself. In light of the other evidence we discuss, however, we think the more plausible explanation is that AFDC households with subsidized housing are more likely than other AFDC households to have multiple barriers to work.

Studies of the Relationship between Housing Subsidies and Employment Rates

A number of attempts have been made to construct an income-leisure model that predicts the likely impact of the availability of housing subsidies on labor market participation. The complexity of the delivery mechanism for housing subsidies poses a number of challenges for such a project,[23] and there appears to be no consensus on how housing subsidy receipt should be modeled. Most of the studies of this nature predict that the availability of housing benefits has a small but significant negative effect on labor market participation, on the order of a few

---

[23] One challenge in developing such a model is that housing assistance is not an entitlement. Not only are housing subsidies limited in number, but the choice of which groups to prioritize varies from area to area (see also Painter 2001). This makes it difficult to construct an accurate model of who has access. A related challenge is demonstrating that eligible households are aware of the varying rules that determine their eligibility or preference for subsidies or even of the amount of assistance to which they are entitled. If they are not aware of these rules, it is hard to see how they could have a causal effect on behavior.

A third challenge is that the housing subsidy amount and formal eligibility levels vary by metropolitan area (or by nonmetropolitan county). To the extent that a correlation is observed between employment rates and housing eligibility or benefit levels, it may be attributable to differences among metropolitan areas (or nonmetropolitan counties), rather than housing benefit or eligibility levels. A fourth challenge is that a housing subsidy does not provide merely a monetary transfer; it also provides a stable, affordable living environment. The latter set of benefits may have an independent effect on employment rates of recipients that may be difficult to capture through a standard income-leisure model.

Finally, and perhaps most important, there is the challenge of incorporating into future models the effects of welfare work requirements and time limits. One would expect that these policy changes would have a significant impact on calculating work incentives. Per Khadduri, Shroder, and Steffen (2003), approximately half of the households with children in subsidized housing in late 1996 had welfare income.

percentage points,[24] although Keane and Moffitt (1998) were unable to discern any statistically significant effect.

In contrast to these theoretical attempts to predict the possible effects of receiving a housing subsidy, a number of studies have examined whether *actual* receipt leads to reductions in labor market participation. We will discuss four such studies.[25] All four found that, after controlling for other variables, residence in a public housing development had little or no negative impact on employment rates. Indeed, two of the studies concluded that housing subsidies may have *positive* effects on employment rates: one concluded that Section 8 assistance had a positive, sizable, and significant effect on employment rates; another found that public housing may have had a positive impact on the adult employment rates of youth who resided in public housing sometime between 1968 and 1982.

Public Housing Residents in Chicago. Using data from the Urban Poverty and Family Life Survey, a stratified random sample of parents aged 14 to 47 who lived in poverty areas in Chicago in 1986, David Reingold (1997) examined the effect of public housing residence on the employment rates of non-Hispanic black female heads of household who received AFDC and lived in census tracts where 40 percent or more of the residents were below the poverty line. After controlling for age and education levels, Reingold (1997) found no statistically significant effect of public housing residence on four different measures of employment.[26]

---

[24] For example, Houser and Dickert-Conlin (1998) conclude that "[a] 10 percent increase in expected housing benefits decreases the typical single parent's probability of labor market participation by just over 1 percentage point and has essentially no effect on primary earners" (23). Similarly, Painter (2001) estimates that "[a]n increase of one hundred dollars in the housing programs decreases [labor market] participation probabilities by 1.6 percentage points" (17). Currie and Yelowitz (1998) estimate that increasing housing benefits by $184 per month would reduce labor force participation by 4.6 percentage points. Murray (1980) estimates that residence in public housing reduces work effort by 1.4 to 1.7 hours per week, "or about 4 percent of presubsidy work effort" (80).

[25] Three of these studies examined the impact of public housing on current adult residents; the fourth examined whether growing up in a public housing development affects youths' labor market participation as adults. The only other published studies of this nature of which we are aware are those that examine the differential effects of welfare reform interventions (or welfare exit) on families with and without housing assistance. These studies are discussed in the next section.

[26] As Reingold (1997) observes, by focusing only on respondents living in high-poverty areas, he does not test whether the siting of public housing developments in high-poverty areas inhibits resident employment. In a more recent article, Reingold, Van Ryzin, and Ronda (2001) use data from the Multi-City Study of Urban Inequality to analyze the relative effects of public housing and neighborhood disadvantage on households' labor force activity and social capital development. They conclude that "neighborhood disadvantage, not public housing, is the more important determinant of social

Public Housing Residents in Atlanta. Elsewhere in this volume, Riccio and Orenstein (2003) examined the employment and welfare rates over time of households on AFDC in Atlanta. Like Newman and Harkness (1999a), Riccio and Orenstein (2003) found that public housing residents on AFDC had significantly lower employment rates than residents of private market housing.[27] They also found that this difference narrowed considerably once one accounted for a small set of demographic characteristics, with the difference narrowing to the point of insignificance once a broader range of variables was considered. They concluded that current housing status had little or no residual effect on welfare recipients' subsequent earnings in the three-year period examined.[28]

Public Housing Residents and Section 8 Participants in California. A study by Paul Ong (1998) similarly found that public housing had no statistically significant independent effect on the number of hours worked. His study examined a sample of 1,111 single-parent renter households on AFDC with a female head of household who was between the ages of 18 and 54; their sample was drawn from a survey of four California counties (Alameda, Los Angeles, San Bernardino, and San Joaquin) by the Survey Research Center, University of California, Berkeley, between October 1993 and September 1994 (Ong 1998).

By contrast, Ong (1998) found that participation in the tenant-based Section 8 program had a positive and significant effect ($p < 0.01$) on the number of hours worked.[29] According to Ong, "The Section 8

---

capital and labor force activity among Boston's low-income households" (499). They also note that the "contextual factors in the model—neighborhood disadvantage and especially public housing—appear to be relatively limited influences on social capital and labor force activity when compared with the background characteristics and other resources of residents" (499).

[27] This discussion relates to Riccio and Orenstein's (2003) analysis of the "control group" of households that were not targeted to receive special services under the JOBS program. We discuss the somewhat different results for the treatment group later.

[28] As Riccio and Orenstein (2003) caution, it is possible that some of the variables used to control for background differences among households, such as prior welfare receipt, may themselves have been influenced by residence in public housing. They thus indicate that their study does not assess the cumulative effects of housing subsidy receipt over time.

[29] Ong (1998) compared the employment rates of families in three groups: unsubsidized housing, public housing, and subsidized housing other than public housing. He notes that the vast majority of families in the third group participated in the Section 8 certificate and voucher programs.

variable is positive, sizable, and highly statistically significant, indicating that those in this housing program worked 60 hours [per month] more than those in the private rental market, *ceteris paribus*"[30] (1998, 786). He writes, "One interpretation [of these findings] is that a well-designed housing program can help welfare recipients form a greater attachment to the labor market" (775). While Ong (1998) considers a number of possible reasons for these findings, he concludes that the most "plausible explanation is that Section 8 housing offers recipients residential choice and mobility, improving opportunities for employment" (775).

Unlike Ong, Riccio and Orenstein (2003) did not find a causal connection between Section 8 receipt and employment rates among AFDC households.[31] There are a number of possible explanations for this difference. One is that the proportion of Section 8 households in Riccio and Orenstein's Atlanta sample who had *tenant-based* (as opposed to project-based) Section 8 subsidies may have been different from Ong's California sample. Another possibility is that, due to differences in the local housing markets, California households with Section 8 tenant-based assistance may have been better able to take advantage of the "mobility" potential of these subsidies to allow them to move to areas with better access to jobs.

A third possibility is that some portion of Ong's (1998) sample may have received supportive services through the JOBS program then in effect in California. As noted in the next section, some evidence suggests that JOBS and other welfare reform initiatives have a greater impact on households in subsidized housing. Riccio and Orenstein (2003) conducted their analysis on an Atlanta sample that specifically *excluded* persons targeted to receive JOBS services.[32]

---

[30] This analysis was based on a Tobit regression that accounts for all families—whether working or not working—but estimates the value of the coefficient over the part of the sample that is working. A separate Tobit regression limited to long-term welfare recipients indicates a positive and significant ($p < 0.01$) impact for Section 8 receipt of 62 hours per month. While an ordinary least squares (OLS) regression also yields a positive and significant ($p < 0.01$) impact of Section 8 receipt, it suggests a smaller impact of approximately 11 hours a month. Ong (1998) attributes this difference to the fact that the OLS model estimates the value of the coefficient over the entire sample, most of whom reported no hours of work.

[31] Once again, we are discussing Riccio and Orenstein's (2003) analysis of the control group of households that were not targeted to receive special services under the JOBS program.

[32] We note these possibilities simply as potential theories. Further research would be required to determine the extent to which they explain the varying results.

Children of Public Housing Residents. Using a unique database that identifies the housing subsidy status of households in the Panel Study of Income Dynamics, Newman and Harkness (1999b) examined the long-term self-sufficiency outcomes of children who spent some time in public housing or privately owned assisted housing between 1968 and 1982, when they were 10 to 16 years old. While the youth who had lived in public housing had adult earnings (at ages 25 to 27) that were 20 percent lower than youth who had not lived in public housing or privately owned assisted housing did, these differences "vanish...[o]nce measured family background characteristics are taken into account" (Newman and Harkness 1999b, 31).

The adult employment rates of public housing youth did not differ significantly from those of youth who had not lived in public housing or privately owned assisted housing. Under an instrumental variable approach, however, which accounts for unmeasured differences between families of different housing statuses, "public housing residence is estimated to raise the average sample member's probability of work by 23 percentage points, which is a very large increase. While the statistical significance is fairly modest ($p = .06$), it seems likely that public housing may have a positive effect on employment" (Newman and Harkness 1999b, 32).

In sum, these studies suggest that most, if not all, of the correlation between housing subsidy receipt and low employment rates can be explained by differences between the populations of households with and without housing subsidies. This conclusion does not necessarily mean that *no* aspect of housing subsidy receipt has a negative impact on labor market participation. Negative effects may well be associated with some or all of the factors that are presumed to depress labor market participation but are offset by other positive aspects of housing subsidy receipt. Housing subsidies could have a positive effect on labor market participation by helping to stabilize families' living situations, thus better enabling them to focus on obtaining or retaining employment. In addition, Section 8 tenant-based subsidies (and certain project-based subsidies) may be able to help families move to neighborhoods with better access to jobs.

If there were indeed aspects of housing subsidy receipt that affected labor market participation in opposite and offsetting ways, the challenge for policy makers would seem to be to discover how to counteract any work-depressing aspects while allowing the work-promoting aspects to continue. The data suggest that this challenge can be met by combining housing subsidy receipt with the welfare reform interventions already under way across the country. The simplest way to accomplish this would be to target newly available housing subsidies on households actively engaged in moving from welfare to work.

The Potential Contribution of Housing Subsidies to Welfare Reform

We do not know of any studies designed to test the hypothesis that various attributes of housing subsidy receipt have positive effects on labor market participation, while others have negative effects. This hypothesis appears to be consistent, however, with data collected as part of the evaluations of several recent welfare reform initiatives. In general, these data show that housing subsidy recipients benefited much more from welfare reform initiatives than nonrecipients. A potential explanation is that the welfare reform initiatives successfully countered the aspects of subsidized housing policy that have the potential to depress labor market participation, allowing the positive attributes to dominate.[33]

Another potential explanation for these results is that welfare reform interventions supply one or more missing ingredients (such as services to improve skills or provide child care or transportation) that are necessary to enable welfare households to take advantage of the work-promoting benefits of subsidized housing. This hypothesis does not require postulating that aspects of housing subsidy receipt have a negative impact on work participation. Rather, the hypothesis is that a substantial number of those in subsidized housing lack the skills, services, or confidence necessary to increase their work effort and that this deficiency cannot be remedied simply by giving them housing subsidies. Once the skills/confidence/child-care/transportation barrier is addressed through welfare reform, however, these households may be able to take advantage of the work-promoting aspects of housing subsidies.[34]

Under each of these hypotheses, research results suggest that housing subsidies can play an important role in the success of welfare reform and provide support for admissions policies that target households actively engaged in making the transition from welfare to work for

---

[33] The first half of this hypothesis—that a welfare reform initiative can help offset aspects of subsidized housing policy believed to depress work participation—was proposed by Miller (1998) and Knox, Miller, and Gennetian (2000).

[34] A third possibility is that households in assisted housing may have been more likely than households in private-market housing to use the services and incentives to which they were entitled. This could occur, for example, if households living in project-based housing shared information on the incentives to go to work (and/or the services provided) by the welfare reform initiatives.

newly available housing subsidies. As discussed elsewhere in this volume by Barbara Sard (2003), another implication of these data is that PHAs should consider providing additional work-promoting services to their tenants. Finally, these data provide support for using state-controlled funds (such as TANF and state matching funds) for new rental subsidies to families enrolled in state or local welfare-to-work programs. For more information on such programs, see Sard and Harrison (2001) and Sard and Lubell (2000).

Recent Research Results on the Extent to Which Residents of Subsidized Housing Benefit from Welfare Reform

Minnesota Family Investment Program (MFIP). An evaluation of Minnesota's welfare reform initiative by the Manpower Demonstration Research Corporation (MDRC) found that public and subsidized housing residents benefited more from that initiative than other poor families (Knox, Miller, and Gennetian 2000; Miller 1998; Riccio 1999; Riccio and Orenstein 2003). The central features of MFIP were a substantial increase in the amount of earned income that was disregarded in determining the family's eligibility for, and benefit level under, the state's cash assistance program; increases in welfare benefit levels for working households; and a requirement that recipients participate in work activities.[35] The evaluation found that among single-parent long-term welfare recipients in urban counties subject to both the work participation requirements and the earnings disregard, employment and earnings increases were significantly greater for families living in public or subsidized housing than for those in private housing.

Table 7.3 summarizes the differences in the impact of MFIP services on single-parent long-term welfare recipients in urban counties who were residents and nonresidents of public or subsidized housing.[36] Whereas eligibility for full MFIP services (i.e., both the earnings disregard and the work participation requirement) raised the proportion of residents of public and subsidized housing employed in any quarter in year 3 by 17.9 percentage points, it raised the corresponding employment rates of nonresidents by only 7.9 percentage points. That is, the employment impact of the full welfare reform initiative on residents of public and subsidized housing was more than double the impact of the same treatments on other families. Similarly, whereas eligibility for full MFIP

---

[35] Although most state welfare programs require work and offer some form of earned income disregard, MFIP is unusual in offering increased welfare benefit levels to working households (Berlin 2000).

[36] These data are based on tables 4.8 and 4.9 in Knox, Miller, and Gennetian (2000).

Table 7.3. **Impact of Full MFIP Services on Single-Parent Long-Term Welfare Recipients in Urban Counties: Quarterly Averages in Year Three**

Population	Extent to Which the Employment Rate of Families Eligible to Receive Full MFIP Services Exceeded That of AFDC Families Not Receiving MFIP Services in Year 3	Extent to Which the Average Quarterly Earnings of Families Eligible to Receive Full MFIP Services Exceeded Those of AFDC Families Not Receiving MFIP Services in Year 3
Nonresidents of public or subsidized housing	7.9 percentage points	$23* (an increase of 1.8%)
Residents of public or subsidized housing	17.9 percentage points	$333 (an increase of 25.2%)

Source: Knox, Miller, and Gennetian 2000, tables 4.8 and 4.9.
*Not statistically significant.

services raised the average quarterly earnings of public and subsidized housing residents in the third year by $333 (an increase of 25.2 percent), it raised the average earnings of nonresidents over the same time period by an insignificant $23 (2 percent). MDRC reports that the greater impact of MFIP on residents of public and subsidized housing compared with nonresidents cannot be explained by differences in observable demographic characteristics (Miller 1998; Riccio 1999; Riccio and Orenstein 2003).

In addition, among those eligible to receive full MFIP benefits and services (i.e., the treatment group), residents of public or subsidized housing appear to have outperformed residents of private housing. The average third-year quarterly earnings for single-parent long-term welfare recipients in urban counties who were eligible for full MFIP benefits and lived in public or subsidized housing ($1,657) were higher than the average quarterly earnings of eligible nonresidents ($1,305). A similar disparity was evident in employment rates in the third year (61.2 percent versus 53.2 percent).

It is important to note that a similar comparison within the control group (i.e., long-term welfare recipients in urban counties who were not eligible for any MFIP services) does not show that households with housing subsidies performed substantially better than those in private-market housing. This suggests that housing assistance may have a net positive effect on the labor market participation of welfare households only if they are also benefiting from a well-designed welfare reform intervention.

Another interesting finding is that the MFIP financial incentives alone—without the mandatory services and reinforced incentives message in the full MFIP intervention—had little effect on those who did not receive housing assistance, but a significant effect on those who did.[37] One potential explanation for this finding is that the financial incentives helped compensate for a perceived disincentive to work in the subsidized housing rent rules.

MDRC's discussion of these data (Knox, Miller, and Gennetian 2000), as well as an analysis of the similar 18-month MFIP data by Cynthia Miller (1998), reach no definitive conclusions. Both analyses point out that the MFIP initiative may have helped offset disincentives to work caused by the rent policy (and income effect) of subsidized housing. This may account for the greater impact of MFIP on those in subsidized housing, compared with those in private-market housing. It does not, however, explain why the portion of the MFIP treatment group residing in public or subsidized housing had greater earnings and higher employment rates than the portion in private-market housing. One possible explanation is that subsidized housing offers certain benefits that tend to promote employment, such as greater stability and the potential to move to neighborhoods with better access to jobs, and that MFIP allowed those benefits to dominate by offsetting those aspects of subsidized housing policy that may depress work participation.

Unfortunately, one cannot tell from the MFIP data which types of housing subsidies participants received. More than 80 percent of the families that identified themselves as residing in public or subsidized housing in the MFIP study indicated that they lived in subsidized (Section 8) housing; however, it is not possible to tell whether they received project-based or tenant-based subsidies (Miller 1998). Although there are difficulties involved in using surveys to collect accurate information on families' housing subsidy status (see Shroder and Martin 1996), this information is necessary to better understand the reasons for any impact of housing subsidies on labor market participation.

---

[37] Receipt of MFIP financial incentives (without the other components of the full intervention) increased quarterly employment rates in the third year of the demonstration for households in public or subsidized housing by a highly significant 9.8 percent compared with the control group, while financial incentives alone increased employment rates for nonresidents by an insignificant 0.1 percent. Households in public or subsidized housing receiving the MFIP financial incentives alone increased their average quarterly earnings in the third year by $90 compared with the control group, while those without housing assistance experienced an average quarterly earnings *loss* of $147. The earnings impacts of financial incentives alone, however, were not statistically significant. The positive earnings impact of the full MFIP intervention on households in public or subsidized housing was significant at the 5 percent level (Knox, Miller, and Gennetian 2000).

JOBS in Atlanta and Columbus. Studies of two different JOBS interventions among welfare recipients in Atlanta and Columbus similarly indicate that the programs' effects over a three-year period were concentrated among families in public or subsidized housing. Reviewing these results together with those of the MFIP program in Minnesota, MDRC researchers James Riccio and Alan Orenstein conclude:

> Taken together, the findings from the Atlanta, Columbus, and Minnesota studies point to an important and consistent result: All three mainstream welfare-to-work programs had their largest, most consistent employment and earnings impacts on welfare recipients who lived in public or Section 8 housing. The impact was smallest—and sometimes almost entirely absent—for recipients in unsubsidized private housing. (2003, 87).

Riccio and Orenstein's analysis of the baseline characteristics of the three housing groups in the Atlanta study indicates that the households living in public housing had substantially greater barriers to work than those in private market housing, with Section 8 recipients falling in between.[38] Despite their greater barriers, members of the treatment group that resided in public or Section 8 housing achieved final-quarter employment rates that were similar to (or even higher than) the employment rates of other members of the treatment groups. These data are again consistent with the hypothesis that housing subsidies can help promote work among households also receiving welfare reform services.[39]

Welfare Leavers in Massachusetts. A recent study of persons leaving welfare in Massachusetts in early 1999 found that, 6 to 15 months after the close of their welfare cases, those who had housing subsidies had a higher employment rate (74.2 percent) than those who did not (67.7 percent) (Nagle 2001). Welfare leavers in subsidized housing had this higher employment rate despite being more likely than those in unsubsidized housing to be long-term welfare recipients and to have

---

[38] Among other differences, the AFDC recipients in public or Section 8 housing were significantly more likely to have received AFDC for five or more years, to have been unemployed throughout the previous year, and to have low reading test scores and significantly less likely to be in their first spell of AFDC. In addition, the public housing residents were significantly more likely to lack a high school diploma or General Equivalency Diploma (GED) and to have three or more children (Riccio and Orenstein 2003).

[39] The Atlanta and Columbus results are part of the larger National Evaluation of Welfare-to-Work Strategies (NEWWS), which evaluates the effectiveness of 11 mandatory welfare-to-work programs in seven locales. Based on data from all 11 of the NEWWS component studies, Karin Martinson concluded that of those families that worked at all after random assignment, "those who were most successful in sustaining employment were somewhat more likely to live in [public and] subsidized housing" (Martinson 2000, 26).

two or more children and substantially more likely (59.2 percent versus 26.0 percent) to be black or Hispanic—factors normally correlated with less successful employment outcomes (Nagle 2001).

While both groups worked an average of 33 hours a week at their main job, unassisted leavers with earnings had somewhat higher hourly wages than assisted leavers (median of $8.50 versus $8.15). In addition, unassisted leavers were substantially more likely to have another adult in the household than assisted leavers (59.5 percent versus 31.0 percent) (Nagle 2001).[40] As additional wage earners play an important role in determining overall household income, the differences in household composition between assisted and unassisted households merits additional study.

National Job Training Partnership Act (JTPA). A study of JTPA sites suggests that some public housing residents may have fared less well under that program than nonresidents (Bloom et al. 1993).[41] This study, however, compares public housing residents with everyone else, including participants in other subsidized housing programs such as Section 8. It thus provides no basis for determining the relative success of the intervention for participants in project-based or tenant-based Section 8 programs or for households receiving no housing assistance.[42]

---

[40] Differences in employment rates and hourly earnings were statistically significant at the 10 percent level. There was no statistically significant difference in average weekly wages.

[41] The results are actually somewhat mixed. For adult women and adult men, the JTPA study reports a modest earnings gain among nonresidents of public housing and a modest earnings loss among residents. Both groups of male youth experienced a moderate decline in earnings, with male youths in public housing experiencing a slightly greater decline. Finally, female youths in public housing reported a slight *increase* in earnings, while female nonresident youths reported a slight *decline* (Bloom et al. 1993). The only one of the four groups studied for which the difference between residents and nonresidents of public housing was statistically significant was adult women ($p = 0.10$).

[42] Another limitation on this element of the JTPA study is the absence of any controls for differences in personal characteristics among residents and nonresidents of public housing. As noted earlier, AFDC recipients of public housing are generally (though not always) more likely to have multiple barriers to employment than AFDC recipients who are nonresidents. The comparability problem is magnified significantly in the case of the JTPA program, where only one-third of the persons who completed the program were on AFDC (Nudelman 2000). The JTPA study does not indicate whether public housing residents would fare better or worse than a control group having similar demographic characteristics. Another problem with the JTPA data is that "31 percent of adult AFDC women in the treatment group never enrolled in JTPA and generally did not receive any JTPA services" (Nudelman 2000, 125). In addition, some proportion of families in the control group likely received some training services from sources other than JTPA.

Upcoming Evaluation of the Welfare-to-Work Housing Voucher Program.
A HUD-funded evaluation now under way should provide additional
data that will enable one to test some of the hypotheses advanced in this
chapter. In FY 1999, Congress appropriated $283 million for 50,000 new
housing vouchers for households attempting to move from welfare to
work. Congress set aside up to 1 percent of the funds for an evaluation
of the impact of the program. HUD has contracted with Abt Associates
to conduct a randomized evaluation at 7 of the 22 PHAs that both
received funding under the program and volunteered to participate in
the evaluation. The experiment will examine whether households that
receive both housing vouchers and any work-promoting services provided under the program are more likely to obtain and/or retain employment (and to move to neighborhoods with better job access) than a
control group of households. Members of both the control and treatment
groups will be chosen from among eligible families on the PHA's Section
8 waiting list (HUD 2000b).

Impact of Subsidized Housing Receipt on Welfare Participation Rates

Since public and subsidized housing residents who receive welfare
income are more likely to be long-term welfare recipients than their
counterparts who reside elsewhere, it is not surprising that at the end
of the period the studies of the MFIP and Atlanta JOBS initiatives
found higher welfare participation rates among public or subsidized
housing residents than among nonresidents.[43]

Nevertheless, the data contain some small encouraging signs. While the
JOBS initiative in Atlanta appears to have led to lower welfare rates
in the final quarter of the study among residents of each of the three
housing groups (public housing, Section 8 housing, and private-market
housing), the only group for whom this reduction was statistically significant was the public housing group. Similarly, the initiative appears
to have resulted in larger reductions in the average value of welfare
receipt over a three-year period among public housing residents than
among private-market housing residents. These patterns hold for both
the labor force attachment (LFA) and human capital development
(HCD) approaches.[44]

---

[43] Boushey and Ding (2000) present a thoughtful analysis of some of the different factors affecting welfare caseload exits of residents of public housing run by the New York
City Housing Authority.

[44] The results for Section 8 recipients appear to vary by treatment approach. The magnitude of the reductions in the average amount of welfare received by Section 8 recipients over three years was comparable to that of public housing recipients (i.e., very

In the MFIP program, the treatment group had *higher* welfare participation rates and benefits than the control group, a result that does not
appear to vary significantly by housing subsidy status. The higher welfare levels were apparently due to the enhanced financial incentives
MFIP provided, which allowed participants to earn more without losing
their welfare benefits (Miller et al. 1997; Riccio and Orenstein 2003).

Some evidence suggests that welfare receipt among households living
in public housing can be reduced by helping them move to low-poverty
census tracts. As Ludwig, Duncan, and Pinkston (2000) show, public
housing households targeted to receive both housing vouchers and
counseling to help them move to low-poverty census tracts (mobility
counseling) in the Baltimore site of the randomized Moving to Opportunity (MTO) demonstration were significantly more likely to leave
welfare than either of two control groups: (a) public housing residents
targeted to receive vouchers but not mobility counseling and (b) public
housing residents not targeted to receive vouchers or mobility counseling.[45] On average, the proportion of families that were assigned to the
experimental group and received welfare assistance during any quarter
in the three-year follow-up period was 15 percent (6 percentage points)
lower than the average rate of quarterly welfare use by the families in
the second control group not given the opportunity to move out of public housing. Looking only at the families that actually moved to low-
poverty neighborhoods, however, shows a more substantial reduction in
welfare receipt. The share of families that received welfare benefits in
year 3 after moving to low-poverty neighborhoods was over one-third
less than for families assigned to the public housing control group. The

---

substantial) in the LFA approach, but closer to that of residents of private-market
housing (i.e., significant, but smaller) in the HCD approach. This may be due to the
fact that the initial emphasis on HCD delays any reductions in welfare receipt.

[45] In 1994, HUD began the MTO research demonstration program. Families living in
public housing or project-based Section 8 developments in high-poverty neighborhoods
in five cities (Baltimore, Boston, Chicago, Los Angeles, and New York) were given the
opportunity to volunteer for the program. Eligible volunteers were randomly assigned
to one of three groups: the MTO experimental or treatment group, which received tenant-based assistance (Section 8 vouchers or certificates) usable only in neighborhoods
with less than 10 percent poverty, along with counseling and assistance to locate a private rental unit; the Section 8 comparison group, which was provided with tenant-
based assistance without geographic restriction and whatever minimal assistance the
housing agency usually provided to families receiving housing vouchers; and an in-
place control group. Of the 1,820 families across the five sites originally assigned to the
experimental or treatment group, 860 moved to low-poverty neighborhoods. The outcomes for these families will be tested against the two control groups (Goering et al.
1999). The MTO design calls for follow-up studies periodically over a 10-year period.
Preliminary data from the initial follow-up surveys are now available for each of the
five sites (Del Conte and Kling 2001).

reduction in the rate of welfare receipt appeared to be largely due to increases in employment and earnings. Ludwig, Duncan, and Pinkston (2000) found no significant difference in welfare receipt between the two control groups.

Similarly, an analysis of data from the quasi-experimental Gautreaux program by Rosenbaum and DeLuca (2000) found that helping public housing residents and families on the waiting list for public housing move to neighborhoods with more educated residents substantially reduced the incidence of welfare receipt.[46]

The findings from other MTO sites, however, on the effects of moving to low-poverty neighborhoods have differed from the Baltimore and Gautreaux studies. Families offered the opportunity to move out of New York public housing using Section 8 vouchers also experienced a significantly larger decline in welfare use than families assigned to the public housing control group (Leventhal and Brooks-Gunn 2001). But in New York, the decline in welfare use was greater for the families receiving vouchers that were not restricted to lower-poverty neighborhoods than for the other families receiving vouchers. Two years after random assignment, the Boston site did not show any statistically significant difference in the rate of decline in welfare receipt among the three MTO groups (Katz, Kling, and Liebman 2001).

Three Ways in Which Housing Subsidies May Help Families Obtain and Retain Employment

The results of the MFIP and Atlanta JOBS initiatives are consistent with the hypothesis that when combined with welfare reform interventions, housing subsidies may help promote employment among welfare recipients. As noted earlier, one potential explanation is that welfare interventions offset aspects of housing subsidy receipt that tend to depress labor market participation, allowing the work-promoting aspects to dominate. An alternative explanation is that welfare reform interventions supply services or benefits needed to help households with multiple barriers to work take advantage of the work-promoting aspects of subsidized housing.

Both of these explanations assume that certain aspects of housing subsidy receipt may promote work. In this section, we explore what those aspects might be. We hypothesize that housing subsidies can help promote employment in three ways:

---

[46] A more thorough discussion of the Gautreaux program is provided later.

1. By making housing more affordable, housing subsidies may help
    stabilize the lives of low-income families and thereby improve their
    ability to secure and retain jobs.

2. By reducing housing costs, housing subsidies can free up funds
    within the budgets of low-income families for work-related
    expenses, such as child care, work clothes, and transportation.

3. Housing subsidies can help families move to areas with greater job
    opportunities.

Stability. Many housing and welfare professionals believe that poor
families need a stable housing situation to focus more on finding and
retaining employment. Reflecting on site visits to 21 nonprofit organizations involved in self-sufficiency efforts in 13 states, Bratt and Keyes
noted that their "field work underscored the importance of housing
being secured first, before people could pay serious attention to nonhousing issues....Housing is at the core of family stability" (1997, 77;
see also Bratt and Keyes 1998).

Similar comments were reported to Sandra Newman and Ann Schnare
during their visits to sites participating in Project Self-Sufficiency, an
early HUD-sponsored demonstration that combined tenant-based Section 8 assistance with job training and other supportive services (Newman and Schnare 1989) and in a study of HUD's Operation Bootstrap
program by Abt Associates, Inc. (Frees et al. 1994).[47]

The recognition that subsidized housing can contribute to self-
sufficiency by helping to stabilize families' living situations undergirds
the Family Self-Sufficiency (FSS) program, a more recent attempt by
Congress to encourage employment through a combination of subsidized housing and supportive services. As HUD observed in 1993 in
introducing FSS regulations in the *Federal Register*: "[T]he availability
of affordable housing is critical to the success of the program. A stable
housing environment frees FSS families from worrying about one of
the basic essentials of life—adequate shelter—and, thus, allows them to
focus better on education, training, and job search" (58 FR 30,863).

---

[47] The Abt report found that Section 8 certificates could serve as a facilitator: providing
additional security and stability on the path toward economic independence. Consider
the case of Bootstrap participants in Seattle, all of whom were homeless prior to being
selected and had been required to move from shelter to shelter every three weeks
because most city shelters place strict limits on the amount of time individuals may
remain there. By liberating participants from the stress of continually adjusting to new
environments, schools, and even case workers, the Bootstrap program allowed them to
spend their energy and attention pursuing training or employment opportunities. In its
role as a facilitator, a Section 8 certificate may also permit low-income individuals to
relocate closer to job opportunities. (Frees et al. 1994, 28–29)

The importance of stable, affordable housing to self-sufficiency efforts has also been recognized by human services practitioners and policy makers outside the housing field. The Human Services Integration of the Seattle Jobs Initiative (SJI), for instance, recognizes that housing is a "frequent and persistent barrier facing many clients" (SJI n.d., 5). The City of Seattle has thus incorporated housing assistance into SJI in an effort "to maintain stable housing conditions" (SJI, 5) for current SJI participants and "secure stable housing" for new ones (SJI, 5). On a similar note, Elaine M. Ryan, Director of the Government Affairs Department of the American Public Human Services Association, a national organization of welfare and other human services providers, writes, "Safe and affordable housing provides the stability families need to exit welfare for work" (Ryan 1998, 11).[48]

All of these accounts use some variant of the term "stability" to describe one of the benefits of housing subsidies. Yet it is difficult to define with any precision what the term means in this context. On the one hand, stability may be related to fewer physical moves. Some families with housing affordability problems may be evicted or otherwise forced to move frequently from the home of one friend or relative to another (or if no other options are available, to a homeless shelter). Housing subsidies can enable such families to stay in the same physical location for longer periods.[49]

---

[48] *Ancillary Services to Support Welfare to Work*, notes,
> Housing instability can cause a continued reliance or return to public assistance. Welfare agencies have begun to address several issues related to housing instability that can impede a successful transition from welfare to work: the financial burden of meeting the cost of housing and limited housing options in areas near job opportunities or served by local transit systems. Left unaddressed, welfare clients' successful transition to economic self-sufficiency is jeopardized by these issues. Self-sufficiency, if attained, is often temporary in the face of such obstacles. If agencies are to successfully support clients, they must consider approaches to dealing with a range of housing barriers to employment caused by unstable housing conditions. (Johnson and Meckstroth 1998, 113).

For more information on the housing-related activities of state and local welfare agencies, see Sard and Lubell (2000).

[49] A study of a sample of families in Cuyohoga County, OH (the Cleveland area), that had left welfare between October 1, 1998, and September 30, 1999, quantified the physical instability that may result from excessive rent burdens (Coulton et al. 2001). The study found that 42 percent of the families that paid more than half their income for housing moved in the six-month period after they left welfare. (Roughly 8 percent of the general population moves in any given six-month period.) Families did not generally move to neighborhoods with better access to jobs. In addition, families with such severe rent burdens were three to four times more likely to be evicted or have their utilities cut off than families paying less than 30 percent of their income for housing.

On the other hand, we suspect that many housing and human services practitioners use the term stability to mean much more than simply staying in the same physical abode for a length of time. Someone paying three-fourths of her income for housing does not have housing "stability" even if she somehow manages to come up with the rent for several years. Neither does someone regularly subject to domestic violence who stays in her current residence because she cannot afford to move. In neither case is the person likely to feel safe and secure in her continued tenancy. Conversely, someone who moves across town to be closer to a new job does not lack stability simply because she moves, as long as the move is planned and the new housing is affordable. Indeed, moving may enhance a household's stability if the household moves to a more affordable or secure dwelling.

The latter example suggests that stability is undermined not by moving per se, but by moves that are unplanned or that result in less secure or less affordable housing. The former examples suggest that stability also has psychological and emotional aspects. Housing subsidies can help enhance stability in both respects: by reducing or eliminating the need for unplanned moves and by reducing or eliminating the ongoing stress of worrying about how to pay the rent. To the extent that families have a finite amount of energy and attention to devote to all of their various responsibilities, this can free up energy and attention for work-related activities.

Because the three major federal housing subsidy programs generally base families' contributions toward rent and utilities on their income, housing subsidies also provide some protection against the adverse consequences of losing a job. For a poor working household without a subsidy, job loss may lead to eviction or foreclosure, since housing costs are not reduced to compensate for the loss of income. If that household has a housing subsidy, however, loss of income would lead to a rent reduction. This may help prevent the household from being evicted, having to move, or becoming homeless, thus minimizing the extent to which job loss disrupts the household's living situation.

The latter point highlights the fact that the housing subsidy structure may have an independent effect on labor market participation. (This effect may or may not be a net positive; as noted earlier, economic theory suggests that income-based rents may be a *disincentive* to work.) Nevertheless, this raises an important consideration for future research. Is it *affordable housing* that lends work-promoting stability in the context of welfare reform interventions, or *housing subsidies*? Although very low income renter households can generally secure decent, affordable housing only through a subsidy, some obtain such housing without it.[50]

One measure of the extent to which housing instability may undermine families' ability to focus on securing and retaining work comes from the Postemployment Services Demonstration (PESD), a project of the Administration for Children and Families of the U.S. Department of Health and Human Services. Between 1994 and 1996, the PESD provided case management and other services to newly employed welfare recipients who were participants in JOBS programs in Chicago; Portland, OR; Riverside, CA; and San Antonio. When asked in surveys what problems outside of work made it difficult for them to retain a job, nearly 20 percent of the 1,200 PESD participants surveyed cited housing problems (Rangarajan 1998).[51]

Increased Funds. Data from the American Housing Survey show that in 1999, some 65 percent of extremely low income families that had children and earnings as their primary source of income (but no government housing assistance) spent more than half their income on housing or lived in severely substandard housing (HUD 2001). Such high housing costs can leave families without enough money for basic necessities or to pay for child care, work clothing, transportation, and other expenses that must be met if families are to successfully make the transition from welfare to work. By reducing housing costs, housing subsidies can free up funds within the budgets of low-income families for these work-related expenses.

A study by Kathryn Edin and Laura Lein (1997) found that mothers in low-wage jobs (less than $8 per hour) have significantly higher total expenses (an average of $1,243 per month) than mothers relying primarily on welfare (an average of $876 per month). Among other

---

[50] A little less than 10 percent of very low income renter households with children pay 30 percent of their income or less for decent housing without a housing subsidy. Two-thirds of these households have incomes between 31 and 50 percent of AMI (HUD 2000a).

[51] Recent surveys in New Jersey and Ramsey County, MN, found similar results. Nearly half of the Work First New Jersey (WFNJ) families surveyed in 1999 reported experiencing one or more housing problems in the past year, and about one in five cited housing problems as a barrier to work (Rangarajan and Wood 1999). Tellingly, the proportion of employed and unemployed WFNJ clients who identified housing as a problem affecting work (19 percent versus 22 percent) did not differ substantially. This suggests that the lack of affordable housing continues to be a significant problem for many families after they have secured low-wage employment. Similarly, 18.2 percent of survey respondents in one of the counties that was part of the MFIP demonstration identified the inability to find adequate housing as a reason they were having difficulty finding or keeping a job (Auspos, Miller, and Hunter 2000).

items, wage-reliant mothers had higher expenses than welfare-reliant mothers for transportation, child care, medical care, and clothing. It is likely that wage-reliant mothers with housing subsidies would be in a better position to meet these additional expenses than wage-reliant mothers without them. Edin and Lein (1997) found that monthly housing costs for wage-reliant mothers with housing subsidies were $150 to $200 less than those of other wage-reliant mothers.

Increased Mobility. Families receiving tenant-based subsidies use them to rent housing in the private market. There are few formal restrictions on where subsidy holders can live; generally, they can rent wherever they find an agreeable landlord. By helping recipients rent apartments they could not otherwise afford, tenant-based subsidies can enable poor families to move to areas where access to jobs is better or where parents feel safe enough to go to work and leave older children unattended or return from work at night on public transportation. As several authors have observed (Coulton et al. 2001; Turner, Popkin, and Cunningham 2000; Turner and Williams 1998), however, families with vouchers may need additional services to overcome practical obstacles to mobility.

The Gautreaux program in Chicago provides evidence of the employment benefits that may result from helping families move to neighborhoods with better employment and educational opportunities. This program, which began in the mid-1970s as a result of a litigation consent decree and ended in 1998, provided Section 8 tenant-based assistance, along with housing search assistance, to African-American residents of (or families on the waiting list for) inner-city public housing developments in Chicago. As participating families came to the top of the list, they were offered housing either in city neighborhoods or in suburban neighborhoods outside of Chicago, depending on what was available. Although families had the right to reject the housing offered to them, few did so. As a result, researchers at Northwestern described the program as having a "quasi-experimental" design: a single group of participants that was divided, more or less randomly, into two subgroups—one that moved to low-income black neighborhoods within the city ("city movers") and one that moved to white middle-income suburban neighborhoods ("suburban movers") (Rosenbaum 1995; see also Rosenbaum and Popkin 1991).[52] An analysis of the attributes of families in the two subgroups shows that they were highly similar (Rosenbaum 1995).

---

[52] For the purposes of the Northwestern study, Gautreaux families that moved within the city, but not to neighborhoods the researchers considered to be "low-income black neighborhoods" were excluded from the "city mover" sample (Rosenbaum 1995).

To gauge the effects of the Gautreaux program, the Northwestern researchers have followed participating families over time and found higher employment rates among suburban movers than among city movers. Although the groups had similar employment rates before they moved, several years later, the suburban movers had an employment rate of 64 percent, compared with 51 percent for city movers. These results appear to have been achieved without any benefits or services other than mobility counseling.[53]

However, because Gautreaux was created by litigation rather than as a controlled experiment, the findings may be affected by selection bias. Families self-selected into the program and in at least some years were screened for suitability for specific neighborhoods or communities. Further, due to data limitations, some assessments of the effects of mobility were made based on nonrepresentative samples of participants.

It is not yet clear whether the apparent employment impact of Gautreaux will be replicated in the MTO demonstration. Preliminary evidence on this question is mixed. An early study in Los Angeles found no significant differences in employment rates among the three MTO groups but modestly higher numbers of hours worked and earnings among both treatment groups compared with the control group (Hanratty, McLanahan, and Pettit 1998). Researchers in Boston, by contrast, found no differences among the different MTO groups in terms of earnings or employment (Katz, Kling, and Liebman 2001). Researchers in New York found higher employment rates among members of the treatment groups that had been unemployed at baseline, compared with similarly situated members of the control group (Leventhal and Brooks-Gunn 2001); small sample sizes, however, mean that this subgroup analysis should be interpreted with caution. Researchers in Baltimore observed a decline in welfare receipt among the experimental group that may have been attributable to increases in employment, but this increase was not captured by Unemployment Insurance data.[54] Many of the strongest findings from the early rounds of analysis involve outcomes for younger children, some of which are discussed later in this chapter.

---

[53] For additional discussion of the effects of neighborhood moves, see Briggs (1997a) and Ellen and Turner (1997).

[54] Analysis of state welfare records by researchers for the Baltimore MTO site indicates that the greater decline in the rate of welfare use for the experimental group may be due to the higher rate at which such families left welfare for work. Data from the Unemployment Insurance system, however, did not demonstrate any significant difference among the groups in employment or earnings. Ludwig, Duncan, and Pinkston (2000) suggest that the differences between the two administrative data systems may be explained by the limitations of the jobs and earnings captured by these data.

While there is not yet a definite answer to the question of whether the MTO intervention has had a significant impact on families' employment and earnings, early focus groups have found that, as in Gautreaux, "moves to low-poverty neighborhoods have significantly reduced the fear of crime that plagued virtually all of the families before they moved out of public housing" (Goering et al. 1999, 44). Similarly, Harvard and Princeton researchers found that MTO participants in Boston experienced dramatic improvements in safety as measured by reductions in the presence of gunfire and drugs (Katz, Kling, and Liebman 2001). Given the role that families in the Gautreaux program attributed to perceived safety in supporting work, these early results are encouraging.

Although both Gautreaux and MTO used tenant-based assistance to help families move to lower-poverty neighborhoods, such moves may also be accomplished through well-located project-based assistance, including some public housing developments. The desirability of the neighborhoods in which public housing and project-based Section 8 housing developments are located varies considerably from place to place.[55] Where such developments are well located, they may serve as useful resources in helping families move from welfare to work. A study of minority families that moved from inner-city Yonkers neighborhoods to scattered-site public housing in predominantly white sections of the city found strong employment-related benefits from the move 3 to 36 months afterward. The study reported that being a "mover" to scattered-site public housing "makes full-time job holding twice as likely, all else held constant" (Briggs 1997b, 53).[56]

Additional Potential Social Benefits of Housing Subsidies

In addition to the potential role of housing subsidies in promoting employment among welfare recipients actively engaged in moving from

---

[55] While public housing and project-based subsidies are not mobile and generally are more likely than tenant-based subsidies to be located in census tracts with high concentrations of poverty, a sizable number of public housing and project-based units are situated in less poor areas. Somewhere between 17 percent and 24 percent of families with children in public housing, and between 32 percent and 50 percent of families with children in project-based Section 8 housing, reside in census tracts with a poverty concentration of less than 20 percent (Khadduri, Shroder, and Steffen 2003).

[56] As Shlay (1993) notes, there are two ways to improve the characteristics of a particular family's neighborhood: help the family relocate or help improve the quality of life provided by the current neighborhood. Although our discussion focuses on the former, the latter could also help promote work. See Sard (2003) for a discussion of different steps that housing agencies and private owners can take to promote employment among their existing tenants.

welfare to work, some preliminary evidence suggests that housing subsidies can help advance other important social objectives. Here, too, additional research is needed to confirm the validity of these suggestions.

We include a brief discussion of these additional potential benefits for two reasons. First, to the extent that housing subsidies can play a role in helping to achieve some of the objectives of welfare and other social programs for poor families, there is additional justification for targeting them on poor families. Second, some of these additional potential benefits may have a positive impact on the ability of low-income workers to retain employment. Particularly in low-wage positions, the need to leave work to attend to a family emergency can lead to loss of employment. To the extent that subsidies reduce the number of disruptions attributable to child health, child criminal activity, and domestic violence, they may further contribute to job stability and retention.

Education. Housing subsidies may help improve children's educational prospects in two ways. First, some studies have shown that the children of families that move frequently tend to do less well in school. By enabling poor families to find and keep affordable housing, subsidies may help children maintain attendance and remain in a stable school setting, thus improving their educational prospects.[57] Second, some evidence suggests that school performance is closely correlated with certain neighborhood characteristics, such as concentration of poverty. By enabling families to access neighborhoods with better educational opportunities, tenant-based assistance (and some project-based developments) may help families secure a better education for their children.[58]

The Gautreaux program and the Baltimore MTO site both provide evidence of the educational benefits of moving to lower-poverty neighborhoods. A study by researchers at Northwestern found that, compared with the children of city movers, the children of suburban Gautreaux movers were less likely to drop out of high school (5 percent versus 20 percent), more likely to be enrolled in a college-track curriculum (40 percent versus 24 percent), and more likely to go to college (54 percent versus 21 percent). Among the Gautreaux youth not attending college, "a significantly higher proportion of the suburban youth had full-time jobs than city youth (75 versus 41 percent)" (Rosenbaum 1995, 244).

---

[57] Among others, see Buerkle (1997); Hennepin County Office of Planning and Development (1998a, 1998b); Newman, Harkness, and Yeung (1999); Rothstein (2000); and Tenenbaum n.d.

[58] For a review of the literature on the influence of neighborhood on children's educational attainment, see Ellen and Turner (1997). See also Cuban (1999).

Similarly, five years after the intervention, Ludwig, Duncan, and Ladd (2001) found that elementary school children in the MTO experimental group (those restricted to moving to low-poverty neighborhoods) were 18 percentage points more likely to pass a Maryland standardized reading test than the control group children who remained in public housing; the passing rate was roughly double that of the control group. Elementary school students in the experimental group also scored more than 7 percentage points higher than control group children on the reading and math components of the national Comprehensive Test of Basic Skills.[59] Comparing test results solely for children who moved with housing vouchers, moving to low-poverty neighborhoods appears to have resulted in gains on the reading and math components of the test that were about twice as large as those of Section 8–only movers, in addition to a sixfold improvement in the pass rate on the Maryland reading test compared with the improvement shown by the Section 8–only movers (Ludwig, Duncan, and Ladd 2001).

On the basis of data from the Panel Study of Income Dynamics (PSID), Newman, Harkness, and Yeung (1999) found that children's exposure to high-poverty neighborhoods between the ages of 6 and 10 tends to reduce educational attainment. This suggests that there may be some educational benefits from moving to a low-poverty area. In a separate article, however, Newman and Harkness conclude that residence in public or assisted housing has *no* statistically significant effect on the educational attainment of children (2000). It should be noted that the data set analyzed by these authors does not include information on which households have Section 8 certificates and vouchers, the type of assistance provided to relocating households in the Gautreaux program.

Vartanian and Gleason (1999) suggest that the impact of neighborhood conditions on children's educational attainment may vary by race and income. Analyzing PSID data, they found that improved neighborhood quality had a significant positive impact on the high school graduation rates of disadvantaged African-American households, but no statistically significant impact on other African-American households. By contrast, improved neighborhood quality had no statistically significant impact on the high school graduation rates of white children, at any income level, but did have a positive impact on the college graduation rates of children of higher-income white households.

Child Health. The results of a series of studies by doctors in Boston suggest that housing subsidies may benefit children's health. One study found that children of families on a waiting list for housing assistance

---

[59] No statistically significant educational test results were found for teens (Ludwig, Duncan, and Ladd 2001).

were six to seven times more likely to suffer from stunted growth than children of families receiving housing subsidies (Meyers et al. 1995). As part of the Children's Sentinel Nutrition Assessment Project (C-SNAP), this study was recently replicated in six sites throughout the country, including Boston. Meyers et al. (2001) report that young children of families on waiting lists for public and subsidized housing were about four times more likely to experience somewhat stunted growth than children in similar families living in public or subsidized housing, probably because children on waiting lists had less adequate nutrition. Although the primary reason why subsidized housing improves children's health appears to be the increased ability of subsidized families to afford nutritious food, some of the benefits may also be related to improved housing quality.[60] Substandard housing has been linked to increased rates of asthma, respiratory disease, and lead poisoning.[61]

Also, some evidence suggests that moving to low-poverty neighborhoods may help reduce child health concerns and improve child safety. A study of MTO participants in Boston found that the children of families who received assistance in moving to low-poverty neighborhoods were less likely to experience serious asthma attacks or non-sport-related injuries and also less likely to be the victim of violent crime than the children of families in either of the two control groups (Katz, Kling, and Liebman 2001; Kling, Liebman, and Katz 2001). The study of the New York MTO site also found significant improvements in physical and mental health for children in the experimental group restricted to moving to low-poverty areas compared with children who remained in public housing (Leventhal and Brooks-Gunn 2001). (Improvements in mental health were also statistically significant for children in the regular Section 8 group.)[62]

---

[60] Sharfstein et al. (2001) compare housing hazards experienced by families near the top of the Boston Housing Authority's Section 8 waiting list in the summer of 1999 with data on housing problems experienced by families living in voucher-assisted units from the 1998 American Housing Survey's 1998 Boston-area sample. Significantly more families waiting for housing assistance experienced recent rat infestations, prolonged lack of heat and/or running water, broken toilets, and exposed wiring than families with housing vouchers.

[61] For more information on how children's health may be adversely affected by housing problems, see the related reports by the Doc4Kids Project of Boston Medical Center, Children's Hospital (1998) and Sandel, Sharfstein, and Shaw (1999).

[62] Parents in the Boston and New York MTO sites who received vouchers to move out of public housing also reported significant improvements in physical and mental health (Del Conte and Kling 2001). Over time, improved health may contribute to increased rates of employment and decline in public assistance (Sweeney 2000).

Teen Employment, Crime, and Pregnancy. Ellen and Turner (1997) provide a critical assessment of the literature examining whether the neighborhoods in which adolescents live affect their labor market success, the likelihood that they will be involved in criminal activity, and the likelihood of sexual activity and pregnancy. Although the evidence in each of these areas is mixed and it is sometimes difficult to identify which neighborhood characteristics are most important, the authors conclude that neighborhood does appear to matter in each of these areas. By helping families access better neighborhoods, tenant-based housing assistance (and some project-based assistance) may help increase adolescent employment and decrease juvenile crime,[63] sexual activity, and pregnancy.

As noted earlier, Newman and Harkness (1999b) found that residing in a public housing development as a youth may have a positive effect on adult employment rates. They also found a positive association between public housing residence as a youth and postsecondary education.[64] Since households in public housing (including households with and without welfare income) are more likely to be located in high-poverty census tracts than AFDC households generally (Khadduri, Shroder, and Steffen 2003; Newman and Schnare 1997), these results are unlikely to be due to the location of the public housing developments.[65]

Domestic Violence. Housing vouchers can help victims of domestic violence escape abusive living situations. Without access to housing subsidies, people may be forced to stay in an abusive living situation or to leave their homes and possibly become homeless.

---

[63] Early data from the MTO demonstration project suggest that providing families with housing assistance that enables them to relocate outside areas of high poverty concentration can help reduce the number of violent crimes that children in those families commit. See Ludwig, Duncan, and Hirschfield (2000). Data from the Boston and New York MTO sites showed reductions in children's behavior problems (significant only for boys in the Boston site) (Del Conte and Kling 2001). Over time, reduction in behavior problems could contribute to reduction in criminal activity, as well as to educational improvements.

[64] Newman and Harkness (1999b) did not find similarly significant results in their instrumental model, suggesting to them that "unobserved family background characteristics of youth who lived in public housing prompt them to acquire post-secondary education" (32).

[65] However, Newman, Harkness, and Yeung (1999) suggest that residing in a public housing development or privately owned HUD-assisted development between the ages of 6 and 10 could have a negative impact on the number of years of education a child achieves.

Recommendations for Local Admissions Preferences That Promote Welfare-to-Work Objectives

In our view, the families that stand to benefit the most from the work-promoting attributes of housing subsidies are those that are actively engaged in moving from welfare to work or are struggling in low-wage jobs. Such households are at a critical juncture: They may move ahead on the path to self-sufficiency, or they may fall back into the ranks of the unemployed. In light of the federal lifetime limits on welfare receipt and even shorter time limits in certain states, many households that fail to find and keep a job could find themselves destitute.

To reach households at this critical juncture, we recommend that PHAs and private owners adopt an admissions preference for households that are on welfare and enrolled in a welfare-to-work program or have extremely low incomes and some income from work. In addition, to the extent that PHAs choose to serve families with incomes between 31 and 50 percent of AMI, we recommend that such assistance be provided only to households with severe housing problems. Finally, we recommend that PHAs and private owners consider using some of their turnover subsidies as barter to obtain work-promoting services for their existing tenants.

Before discussing our proposals in greater depth, we note a few qualifications. First, we are not recommending that PHAs and private owners devote 100 percent of their turnover subsidies to households meeting our proposed admissions preference criteria. It is important to balance such preferences with others designed to meet local needs. A preference for homeless households, for example, has merit independent of whether it advances welfare-to-work objectives.

We do not recommend, however, that PHAs and private owners apply these or similar preferences only to the proportion of subsidies required by law to be provided to extremely low income households. Given the limited supply of deep federal rental subsidies, it is important to view QHWRA's income targeting requirements as a floor and not a ceiling. These requirements represent the minimum proportion of assistance that must be targeted by law for extremely low income households. With respect to public housing and project-based housing, in particular, the income targeting rules are quite lax, requiring that only 40 percent of newly available subsidies be targeted for extremely low income households. Given the prevalence of severe housing needs among extremely low income households, sound housing policy would suggest that such households should receive a greater share of available subsidies.

Finally, to comply with applicable civil rights requirements and HUD rules, it is important that elderly and disabled households receive the benefit of any preferences provided to households that are working or enrolled in welfare-to-work programs.

An Admissions Preference for Households in Welfare-to-Work Programs

Research suggests that households participating in welfare-to-work programs are well positioned to take advantage of the work-promoting aspects of housing subsidies. Accordingly, our first recommendation is that PHAs and private owners adopt preferences that favor households participating in welfare-to-work programs. This could be accomplished either by adding a new preference or by expanding an existing preference for working households to include such applicants.

It is important to note that such a preference would not cover everyone on welfare. Each state has discretion to determine who is subject to the state's work requirements. Only four states have no exemptions at all. The more common exemptions from state work requirements are for persons who are (a) caring for a young child (typically up to one year of age), (b) disabled or who have a temporary illness or incapacity, (c) caring for a disabled household member, (d) of advanced age, (e) a victim of domestic violence, (f) pregnant, or (g) unable to obtain child care for a young child.[66] Each of these exemptions has been adopted by one-third or more of the states.[67]

A number of PHAs already have adopted admissions preferences designed to cover people enrolled in welfare-to-work programs. These include a partnership between Utah's PHAs and the state government called "SUCCESS" (State of Utah's Community Collaboration for Economic Self-Sufficiency), in which eight PHAs adopted admissions preferences giving top priority to families that are enrolled in the state's welfare/job training program (the Family Employment Program) and that also promise to participate in such housing-based self-sufficiency programs as the Family Self-Sufficiency or Family Investment Center programs ("Public Housing: Utah Ties Housing" 1997; Sidor 1998).

---

[66] This information is based on a draft chart of 2000 data from the State Policy Documentation Project. Contact information for the project is available on the World Wide Web at <http://www.spdp.org>.

[67] To the extent that a housing agency wishes to limit the scope of the preference further, it should consult with the local welfare agency for an appropriate limitation. One possible arrangement would be to give preference to households certified by the welfare agency as demonstrating full compliance with applicable work requirements.

Within its admissions preference framework, the statewide tenant-based Section 8 program run by the New Jersey Department of Community Affairs gives first priority to households that are either disabled or participating in Work First New Jersey, the state's welfare-to-work program (New Jersey Department of Community Affairs 1999). The latter policy ensures that housing subsidies are directed to households attempting to make the transition from welfare to work. On a smaller scale, the Metropolitan Council Housing and Redevelopment Authority in Minneapolis makes a small number of subsidies available each year for households participating in "an acceptable city sponsored self-sufficiency program" (Metropolitan Council Housing and Redevelopment Authority 2000, 19).

An Admissions Preference for Extremely Low Income Households with Some Income from Work

Our second recommendation is that PHAs adopt an admissions preference for extremely low income households with some income from work. This preference would target households that have recently left welfare for work, as well as households that have not entered the welfare system but nevertheless have extremely low earnings. It also would target households likely to have severe housing problems. In our view, such a preference should cover households with a member who is working part-time or for part of the year, as well as households with a full-time worker, because it is fairly common for parents making the transition from welfare to work to move in and out of the labor market or to work only part-time.

The Incomes of Households Moving from Welfare to Work. As table 7.4 shows, most families that are in the process of (or who have recently succeeded in) moving from welfare to work have earnings that fall below the 30 percent of AMI threshold that HUD uses to determine who is extremely low income. The U.S. Department of Health and Human Services, Office of the Assistant Secretary for Planning and Evaluation (2000), funded a series of studies that employed a consistent methodology for measuring the earnings of welfare recipients who left the rolls in late 1996 or 1997 ("leavers"). The nine studies from that series that have reported median earnings are listed in table 7.4. The second column shows the median earnings for employed single-parent leavers in the fourth quarter following their exit from the welfare rolls.[68] The third

---

[68] The studies tracked specific cohorts of welfare "leavers," defined as households that left cash assistance for at least two months. The median earnings data in table 7.4 exclude leavers with no earnings in the fourth quarter. Missouri, Illinois, and Georgia included single persons who were not parents.

Table 7.4. **Earnings of Households That Left Welfare in Late 1996 or 1997**

	Median Earnings in the Fourth Quarter Following Their Exit	Estimated Percentage of Area Median Family Income for a Family of Three*
Missouri	$2,535	25.43% of FY 98 AMI
Georgia	$2,218	22.30% of FY 98 AMI
Illinois	$2,660	22.22% of FY 98 AMI
Arizona	$2,754	28.14% of FY 98 AMI
Wisconsin	$2,602	25.42% of FY 97 AMI
Washington	$2,923	26.51% of FY 98 AMI
Cuyahoga County, OH	$2,776	26.31% of FY 97 AMI
San Mateo County, CA	$3,572	23.16% of FY 98 AMI
Los Angeles	$3,290	28.48% of FY 97 AMI

Source: U.S. Department of Health and Human Services, Assistant Secretary for Planning and Evaluation 2000, HUD 2002, and state area median family income estimates.

*The following is an example of how these estimates were prepared: The Georgia evaluation tracked a cohort of welfare recipients who left the rolls during the first quarter of 1997. Since the fourth quarter following that exit fell during FY 1998, the earnings of leavers during that quarter were compared against HUD's FY 1998 AMI estimate for Georgia ($44,200). Because most welfare recipients live in three-person households, we adjusted this state-level AMI estimate by a factor of 0.9—the standard adjustment HUD uses to compute income limits for three-person households ($44,200 × 0.9 = $39,780). On a quarterly basis, this equals $9,945. Accordingly, the $2,218 in median quarterly earnings by employed welfare leavers in the fourth quarter following exit from the rolls in Georgia is estimated to represent 22.3 percent of AMI for FY 1998, as adjusted for a family of three.

column provides an estimate of the percentage of AMI (as adjusted for a family of three) that such earnings would have represented in the fiscal year for which they were reported.[69] In each of the evaluations, the typical employed leaver earned less than 30 percent of AMI.

Research also shows that families moving from welfare to work tend to move in and out of the workforce, often because their jobs are tenuous. For example, a 1998 Mathematica Policy Research study based on the National Longitudinal Survey of Youth showed that the substantial majority of welfare recipients who found jobs lost them relatively quickly (Rangarajan, Schochet, and Chu 1998).[70] According to a review by the Center on Budget and Policy Priorities of studies of the earnings of current and recent welfare recipients in recent years, "While recipients work a large number of hours when they are employed, quarterly

---

[69] A note to the table outlines how these estimates were computed.

[70] In their sample, nearly 45 percent of employment spells ended within four months, and more than 75 percent ended within a year. The median employment spell lasted only five months. Only about 16 percent of their sample had employment spells that lasted for at least two years. On average, sample members worked only one-half of the months during the two-year and five-year follow-up periods.

earnings data from these and other studies suggest that, over a three-month period, many recipients experience weeks in which they either do not work at all or work less than the number of hours they report as typical" (Parrott 1998, 8). This is consistent with the findings of Edin and Lein (1997) who determined, based on the work histories of single mothers leaving welfare, that such mothers generally depend on seasonal jobs and industries in which they are subject to frequent layoffs or reduction in weekly hours (Edin and Lein 1997).[71]

The fact that many households attempting to make the transition from welfare to work move in and out of the workforce during the year, or work part-time, has two implications for subsidized housing admissions policies. First, it reinforces the importance of broadening a "working" preference to cover households with a member who works part-time or for only part of the year. Second, it suggests that determining whether a family qualifies as extremely low income should be based on the past year's annual income, rather than on a projection from the current month's income. This practice will ensure that any variations in income experienced by the household during the year are taken into account. HUD has clarified that such a policy is permissible. (See 24 C.F.R. 5.609(d) and the preamble at 65 *Federal Register* 16,712 (March 29, 2000); National Housing Law Project 2000).

Minimum Wage Earnings. A preference for extremely low income households with some income from work would also reach households working full-time at very low wages. As shown in table 7.5, in 49 of the 50 largest U.S. metropolitan areas (San Juan, PR is the exception), persons working full-time at the minimum wage had incomes below 30 percent of the FY 1999 AMI, as adjusted for a family of three. In 1999, nationwide, nearly 90 percent of the U.S. population lived in areas where a person working full-time at the minimum wage would have an income of less than 30 percent of AMI, as adjusted for a family of three.[72]

---

[71] These data are also consistent with the experience of working poor households generally. Approximately 29 percent of working poor parents in recent years worked only part of the year for economic rather than personal reasons (FitzPatrick and Lazere 1999). This finding is based on tabulations of the U.S. Bureau of the Census March *Current Population Survey* data from 1996–98. "Working poor parents" are heads and spouses in families with children whose annual income in the previous calendar year was at or below the poverty threshold for that year for their family size. Parents were considered to have worked part-year for "economic reasons" if they worked for less than 52 weeks in the previous year and were laid off, unemployed and looking for work, or not looking for work because none was available.

[72] The areas where this is not the case tend to be nonmetropolitan. Some 56 percent of the nonmetropolitan population lives in areas where persons working full-time at the minimum wage would have incomes below 30 percent of AMI, as adjusted for a family of three. As noted earlier, however, many households moving from welfare to work do

Table 7.5. **Ratio of Full-Time Minimum Wage* to FY 1999 AMI (As Adjusted for a Family of Three) for the 50 Largest Metropolitan Areas**

Metropolitan Area	Ratio: Minimum Wage/Three-person AMI	Metropolitan Area	Ratio: Minimum Wage/Three-person AMI
Los Angeles–Long Beach, CA	22%	San Juan–Bayamon, PR	41%
New York, NY	21%	Denver, CO	20%
Chicago, IL	18%	San Francisco, CA	16%
Philadelphia, PA–NJ	21%	Kansas City, MO–KS	22%
Detroit, MI	19%	Portland–Vancouver, OR–WA	22%
Washington, DC–MD–VA	15%	San Jose, CA	14%
Houston, TX	21%	Cincinnati, OH–KY–IN	22%
Boston, MA–NH	18%	Norfolk–Virginia Beach, VA	24%
Atlanta, GA	19%	Milwaukee–Waukesha, WI	20%
Dallas, TX	20%	Indianapolis, IN	22%
Nassau–Suffolk, NY	16%	Fort Worth–Arlington, TX	21%
Riverside–San Bernardino, CA	24%	Columbus, OH	22%
Minneapolis–St. Paul, MN–WI	18%	Sacramento, CA	22%
San Diego, CA	22%	San Antonio, TX	27%
St. Louis, MO–IL	24%	Bergen–Passaic, NJ	16%
Orange County, CA	17%	New Orleans, LA	28%
Pittsburgh, PA	27%	Fort Lauderdale, FL	22%
Baltimore, MD	19%	Orlando, FL	24%
Phoenix–Mesa, AZ	23%	Buffalo–Niagara Falls, NY	25%
Cleveland–Lorain–Elyria, OH	22%	Charlotte–Gastonia, NC	24%
Oakland, CA	17%	Hartford, CT	19%
Tampa–St. Petersburg, FL	25%	Providence–Fall River, RI	24%
Seattle–Bellevue–Everett, WA	18%	Salt Lake City–Ogden, UT	23%
Miami, FL	26%	Rochester, NY	23%
Newark, NJ	17%	Greensboro–Winston-Salem, NC	23%

* 2,000 hours per year at $5.15/hour.

Housing Needs of Extremely Low Income Households. Limiting the preference to working households with extremely low incomes substantially increases the likelihood that subsidies are provided to households with severe housing problems. As table 7.6 shows, renters at the lowest end of the income spectrum are by far the most likely to have a severe need for rental assistance. In 1997, some 70 percent of unassisted

---

not in fact succeed in working full-time. (Moreover, housing costs tend to be lower in nonmetropolitan areas, so households with full-time minimum wage income there are less likely to have severe housing problems.) In any event, 99 percent of the nonmetropolitan-area population lives where full-time minimum wage-earners have incomes below 40 percent of AMI. As long as the results of their preference systems comply with minimum income targets and other requirements, agencies that have trouble locating enough welfare-to-work households with incomes below 30 percent of AMI could raise the threshold for this preference to 40 percent of AMI.

Table 7.6. **Housing Problems of Unassisted Renters by Income, 1997**

	0 to 30% of AMI	31 to 50% of AMI	51 to 80% of AMI
All households (thousands)	5,989	4,717	5,754
Affordability measures:			
(a) Rent and utilities exceed 50 percent of income	67%	23%	3%
(b) Shelter poor	80%	32%	1%
Quality measure: (c) severely inadequate housing	5%	3%	3%
Combined measures:			
Priority problems: a or c	70%	26%	6%
Shelter poor or severely inadequate: b or c	82%	34%	4%
Families with children (thousands)	2,350	2,105	2,324
Affordability measures:			
(a) Rent and utilities exceed 50 percent of income	70%	14%	1%
(b) Shelter poor	90%	45%	2%
Quality measure: (c) severely inadequate housing	5%	3%	3%
Combined measures:			
Priority problems: a or c	73%	17%	4%
Shelter poor or severely inadequate: b or c	92%	47%	5%
Other households (thousands)	3,639	2,612	3,697
Affordability measures:			
(a) Rent and utilities exceed 50 percent of income	66%	30%	5%
(b) Shelter poor	73%	21%	1%
Quality measure: (c) severely inadequate housing	6%	4%	3%
Combined measures:			
Priority problems: a or c	69%	32%	7%
Shelter poor or severely inadequate: b or c	76%	24%	4%

Source: 1997 American Housing Survey.
Note: Households are shelter poor if, after paying for housing costs, they are unable to afford other necessities.

renter households with incomes below 30 percent of AMI had one or more of the "priority" housing problems HUD measures for its periodic reports of worst-case housing needs.[73] By contrast, only one-fourth of unassisted renter households with incomes between 31 and 50 percent

---

[73] Under the methodology employed by HUD, a household has a "priority" housing problem if it pays more than 50 percent of its income for rent and utilities or lives in severely substandard housing but receives no government housing assistance. These are two of the categories used to determine qualification for preference under the former federal preference rules. The other main federal preference categories—homelessness and involuntary displacement—are not included in the definition of priority housing problems because the American Housing Survey does not measure them. Our analysis of 1999 American Housing Survey data suggests that the basic patterns have not changed significantly since 1997.

of AMI and less than 5 percent of households with incomes between 51
and 80 percent of AMI had priority problems in 1997.[74]

The substantial housing needs of households with incomes below
30 percent of AMI are confirmed by an alternative approach, developed
by Michael Stone (1993, 1994), in which a household is deemed to be
"shelter poor" if, after paying for housing and utilities, it is unable
to meet its nonhousing needs at a minimum level of adequacy.[75] As
table 7.6 shows, some four-fifths of all unassisted renters with incomes
at or below 30 percent of AMI (including both families with children
and other households) were shelter poor in 1997. By contrast, only
32 percent of unassisted renter households with incomes between 31
and 50 percent of AMI and only 1 percent of unassisted renter households with incomes between 51 and 80 percent of AMI were shelter
poor in 1997.

*Admissions Preference for Households with Incomes between
31 and 50 Percent of AMI and Severe Housing Problems*

The high incidence of priority housing problems among households
with incomes below 30 percent of AMI suggests that this cut-off is a
fairly good proxy for housing need. Because only one-quarter of households with incomes between 31 and 50 percent of AMI have priority
housing problems, however, this income level is not a good proxy for
housing need. Accordingly, to the extent that PHAs and private owners
choose to serve households with incomes between 31 and 50 percent of
AMI, we suggest limiting assistance to such households with severe
housing problems.[76]

Although collecting and verifying data on housing problems involves
additional administrative burdens, it is worthwhile in light of the
importance of directing the limited supply of housing subsidies to those
in need. Relative to the old federal preference rules, our proposal
involves substantially less administrative burden since there is no need

---

[74] As table 7.6 shows, only a small proportion of households with priority problems
lived in severely inadequate housing. This suggests that the dominant housing problem
is affordability.

[75] One advantage to this methodology over the conventional approach to determining
when housing is affordable is that it does not depend on changing federal policies or
definitions. Another benefit to the "shelter poverty" approach is that it rests on
assumptions that can be debated and tested.

[76] This could be defined as per the old federal preference rules, or in some other
manner.

to collect or verify data on the housing problems of extremely low income applicants.

We include this proposal within the scope of recommendations on helping families move from welfare to work for two reasons. First, when both parents succeed in finding work, two-parent welfare households are likely to have earnings in excess of 30 percent of AMI. (See Cancian et al. 1999, Loprest 1999, and Meyer and Cancian 1996.) Second, the data indicate that many families with children continue to struggle with shelter poverty at incomes between 31 and 50 percent of AMI. Such housing problems could undermine these families' ability to retain work and increase their incomes.

As table 7.6 shows, approximately 45 percent of unassisted families with children and incomes between 31 and 50 percent of AMI were shelter poor in 1997, compared with only 21 percent of other unassisted households in this income group. The most likely explanation for this divergence is that families with children are appreciably larger than other household types, averaging 3.8 persons per household, compared with 1.3 persons for elderly households and 1.6 persons for nonelderly households without children. Families with children thus have correspondingly greater income requirements for nonhousing necessities.[77]

We do not include renter households with incomes above 50 percent of AMI within the scope of our proposed preference for three reasons. First, the data in table 7.6 indicate that priority housing problems and shelter poverty are rare among these households.[78] Second, households with incomes above 50 percent of AMI are less likely to need deep federal rental subsidies to increase their work effort. Third, these

---

[77] At this income level, the shelter poverty approach yields outcomes that are different from the approach that defines housing as unaffordable when housing costs exceed half of a household's income. As shown in table 7.6, the latter approach suggests that among unassisted renter households with incomes between 31 and 50 percent of AMI, families with children are *less* likely than other households to live in unaffordable housing. One potential explanation is that families with children are more likely to include a second wage earner. But families with children also have higher expenses for nonhousing items, which are considered in the shelter poverty approach, but not in one that defines housing costs as unaffordable when they exceed a certain proportion of income.

[78] Although PHAs may derive financial benefits from admitting applicants with incomes above 50 percent of AMI into public housing (Sard 2003), the prospect of such additional income must be weighed against the core mission of housing programs, which is to serve those who need affordable housing. Since severe housing problems are rare among these households and income and wage diversity can be achieved by admitting working households with lower incomes, the balance clearly tilts away from providing scarce public housing units to households with incomes above 50 percent of AMI. Note that PHAs and private owners do not experience any net income gains from admitting higher-income tenants into the Section 8 programs (Sard 2003).

households are more likely than households with lower incomes to be able to secure affordable housing through shallow subsidy programs like the Low-Income Housing Tax Credit.

Using Admissions Policies to Leverage Services for Existing Residents

Since families with housing assistance are well positioned to benefit from welfare-to-work programs, PHAs and private owners interested in promoting employment among their tenants should consider ways of linking the tenants to welfare-reform programs and other work-promoting services. One way for PHAs and private owners to accomplish this is to use the housing subsidies generated through turnover or incremental voucher allocations as barter to obtain social services for their tenants.

Housing subsidies have value not just to applicants and recipients, but also to a wide range of organizations that wish to use them to help their clients. Agencies that provide work-promoting services, in particular, may be willing to provide their services to some number of a PHA's tenants in exchange for the PHA's agreeing to give priority to the agency's clients for turnover subsidies. A similar arrangement could be negotiated by a private owner of project-based Section 8 housing.

An arrangement along these lines appears to have been made in Utah's SUCCESS program. As part of a package in which eight PHAs agreed to give preference in admissions to SUCCESS participants, the state agreed to allow existing public housing tenants to participate (Public Housing: Utah Ties Housing" 1997). Similarly, the Tulare County (CA) Housing Authority has agreed to set aside 300 rental assistance slots for welfare recipients making the transition to work, in return for the welfare agency's agreeing to grant priority to housing authority tenants for services and training in the welfare-to-work program (Bryson 2000).

Conclusion

Recent research suggests that, under certain circumstances, housing subsidies may help families obtain or retain employment. Particularly when combined with welfare reform interventions that reward work effort and provide work-promoting services, housing subsidies appear to be helpful in promoting employment among welfare recipients. Further, because of the types of jobs that welfare recipients are likely to obtain, families that have moved from welfare to work but have not yet attained self-sufficiency need continued housing assistance.

Our analysis of this research leads us to question the popular view that the best way for PHAs and private owners to promote welfare reform is simply to adopt an admissions preference for households with a full-time worker. Such a preference fails to cover many of the households most likely to benefit from the work-promoting aspects of a housing subsidy, especially households attempting to make the transition from welfare to work, while including some households with relatively higher incomes that are less likely to need the work-promoting aspects of housing subsidies and less likely to have a severe housing problem.

In our view, to promote welfare reform, PHAs and private owners should adopt an admissions preference for households that either are on welfare and enrolled in a welfare-to-work program or have incomes below 30 percent of AMI and some income from work. In addition, to the extent that PHAs choose to serve families with incomes between 31 and 50 percent of AMI, we recommend that such assistance be provided only to households with severe housing problems. Finally, we recommend that PHAs and private owners consider using some of their turnover subsidies as barter to obtain work-promoting services for their tenants.

Authors

At the time of the writing of this chapter, Jeffrey M. Lubell was Director of the Policy Development Division of the Office of Policy Development and Research at the U.S. Department of Housing and Urban Development. Kathryn P. Nelson is an Economist in the Office of Policy Development and Research at the U.S. Department of Housing and Urban Development. Barbara Sard is Director of Housing Policy at the Center on Budget and Policy Priorities.

This chapter represents the opinions of the authors and does not reflect the policy or position of either the U.S. Department of Housing and Urban Development or the Center on Budget and Policy Priorities.

References

Auspos, Patricia, Cynthia Miller, and Jo Anna Hunter. 2000. *Final Report on the Implementation and Impacts of the Minnesota Family Investment Program in Ramsey County.* New York: Manpower Demonstration Research Corporation.

Berlin, Gordon L. 2000. *Encouraging Work and Reducing Poverty: The Impact of Work Incentive Programs.* New York: Manpower Development Research Corporation.

Bloom, Howard S., Larry L. Orr, George Cave, Stephen H. Bell, and Fred Doolittle. 1993. The National JTPA Study: Title II–A Impacts on Earnings and Employment at 18 Months. Research and Evaluation Report, Series 93–6. Washington, DC: U.S. Department of Labor, Employment and Training Administration.

Boushey, Heather, and Bai Ding. 2000. *Leaving Welfare: An Analysis of the Probability of Welfare Exits for New York City Public Housing Residents*. New York: New York City Housing Authority, Department of Research and Policy Development.

Bratt, Rachel G., and Langley C. Keyes. 1997. New Perspectives on Self-Sufficiency: Strategies of Nonprofit Housing Organizations. Unpublished paper. Tufts University, Department of Urban and Environmental Policy.

Bratt, Rachel G., and Langley C. Keyes. 1998. Challenges Confronting Nonprofit Housing Organizations' Self-Sufficiency Programs. *Housing Policy Debate* 9(4):795–824.

Briggs, Xavier de Souza. 1997a. Moving Up versus Moving Out: Neighborhood Effects in Housing Mobility Programs. *Housing Policy Debate* 8(1):195–234.

Briggs, Xavier de Souza, ed. 1997b. *Yonkers Revisited: The Early Impacts of Scattered-Site Public Housing on Families and Neighborhoods*. A Report to the Ford Foundation from the Yonkers Family and Community Project. Ann Arbor, MI: University of Michigan Press.

Bryson, David B. 2000. *Welfare and Housing: How Can the Housing Assistance Programs Help Welfare Recipients?* Oakland, CA: National Housing Law Project.

Buerkle, Karla. 1997. Mobile Children and Families: Qualitative and Quantitative Explorations of the Meaning and Impact of Residential Mobility and School Change. Ph.D. diss. University of Minnesota, Department of Psychology.

Cancian, Maria, Robert Haveman, Thomas Kaplan, Daniel Meyer, and Barbara Wolfe. 1999. Work, Earnings, and Well-Being after Welfare: What Do We Know? In *Economic Conditions and Welfare Reform*, ed. Sheldon H. Danziger, 161–86. Ann Arbor, MI: University of Michigan Press.

Coulton, Claudia, Cara J. Pasqualone, Toby Martin, Neil Bania, Nina Lalich, and Lisa Nelson. 2001. Issues of Housing Affordability and Hardship among Cuyahoga County Families Leaving Welfare, Quarter 4, 1998–Quarter 3, 1999. Special Topics in Welfare Reform Report No. 1. Unpublished paper. Center on Urban Poverty and Social Change.

Council of Economic Advisers. 1999. *Economic Expansion, Welfare Reform, and the Decline in Welfare Caseloads: An Update*. Technical Report. Washington, DC: Executive Office of the President of the United States.

Cuban, Larry. 1999. Housing, Not School, Vouchers Are Best Remedy for Failing Schools. *Los Angeles Times*, January 31, p. M2.

Currie, Janet, and Aaron S. Yelowitz. 1998. Public Housing and Labor Supply. Working paper (Draft). Joint Center for Poverty Research.

Del Conte, Alessandre, and Jeffrey Kling. 2001. A Synthesis of MTO Research on Self-Sufficiency, Safety and Health, and Behavior and Delinquency. *Poverty Research News* 5(1):3–6.

Doc4Kids Project of Boston Medical Center, Children's Hospital. 1998. *Not Safe at Home: How America's Housing Crisis Threatens the Health of Its Children*. World Wide Web page <http://www.bmc.org/program/doc4kids> (accessed July 21, 2002).

Edin, Kathryn, and Laura Lein. 1997. *Making Ends Meet: How Single Mothers Survive Welfare and Low-Wage Work*. New York: Russell Sage Foundation.

Ellen, Ingrid Gould, and Margery Austin Turner. 1997. Does Neighborhood Matter? Assessing Recent Evidence. *Housing Policy Debate* 8(4):833–66.

FitzPatrick, Christina Smith, and Ed Lazere. 1999. *The Poverty despite Work Handbook*. Washington, DC: Center on Budget and Policy Priorities.

Frees, J.W., Gretchen Locke, Ingrid Gould Ellen, and Christian Holm. 1994. *Operation Bootstrap: Volume 1: Program Administration*. Research and Evaluation Report Series 93–6. Report prepared by Abt Associates, Inc., for the U.S. Department of Housing and Urban Development, Office of Policy Development and Research. Washington, DC: U.S. Department of Labor.

Goering, John, Joan Kraft, Judith Feins, Debra McInnis, Mary Joel Holin, and Huda Elhassan. 1999. *Moving to Opportunity for Fair Housing Demonstration Program: Current Status and Initial Findings*. Washington, DC: U.S. Department of Housing and Urban Development, Office of Policy Development and Research.

Hanratty, Maria H., Sara A. McLanahan, and Becky Pettit. 1998. The Impact of the Los Angeles Moving to Opportunity Program on Residential Mobility, Neighborhood Characteristics, and Early Child and Parent Outcomes. Working Paper No. 98–18. Princeton University, Bendheim-Thoman Center for Research on Child Well-Being.

Hennepin County Office of Planning and Development. 1998a. Findings from the Minneapolis Student Mobility Research File. Unpublished paper.

Hennepin County Office of Planning and Development. 1998b. A Report from the Kids Mobility Project. Unpublished paper.

Houser, Scott, and Stacy Dickert-Conlin. 1998. The Effects of After-Tax Wages, Transfer Payments, and Child Care Expenses on Labor Market and Transfer Program Participation. Working paper. Joint Center for Poverty Research.

Johnson, Amy, and Alicia Meckstroth. 1998. *Ancillary Services to Support Welfare to Work*. Washington, DC: U.S. Department of Health and Human Services.

Katz, Lawrence F., Jeffrey R. Kling, and Jeffrey B. Liebman. 2001. Moving to Opportunity in Boston: Early Impacts of a Housing Mobility Program. *Quarterly Journal of Economics* 116(2):607–54.

Keane, Michael, and Robert Moffitt. 1998. A Structural Model of Multiple Welfare Program Participation and Labor Supply. *International Economic Review* 39(3):553–89.

Khadduri, Jill, Mark Shroder, and Barry Steffen. 2003. Can Housing Assistance Support Welfare Reform? In *A Place to Live, a Means to Work: How Housing Assistance Can Strengthen Welfare Policy*, ed. Barbara Sard and Amy S. Bogdon, 23–62. Washington, DC: Fannie Mae Foundation.

Kingsley, G. Thomas, and Peter Tatian. 1999. Housing and Welfare Reform: Geography Matters. In *The Home Front: Implications of Welfare Reform for Housing Policy*, ed. Sandra J. Newman, 81–122. Washington, DC: Urban Institute Press.

Kling, Jeffery R., Jeffrey B. Liebman, and Lawrence F. Katz. 2001. Bullets Don't Got No Name: Consequences of Fear in the Ghetto. Working paper. Joint Center for Poverty Research.

Knox, Virginia, Cynthia Miller, and Lisa A. Gennetian. 2000. *Reforming Welfare and Rewarding Work: Final Report on the Minnesota Family Investment Program*. New York: Manpower Demonstration Research Corporation.

Lazere, Ed, and Jennifer Daskal. 2003. Will Changing the Rent Formula Encourage Moves from Welfare to Work? In *A Place to Live, a Means to Work: How Housing Assistance Can Strengthen Welfare Policy*, ed. Barbara Sard and Amy S. Bogdon, 181–210. Washington, DC: Fannie Mae Foundation.

Leventhal, Tama, and Jeanne Brooks-Gunn. 2001. Moving to Opportunity: What about the Kids. Unpublished paper. Columbia University Teachers College.

Loprest, Pamela. 1999. *Families Who Left Welfare: Who Are They and How Are They Doing?* Washington, DC: Urban Institute.

Lubell, Jeffrey, and Barbara Sard. 1998. *Proposed Housing Legislation Would Divert Subsidies from the Working Poor and Weaken Welfare Reform Efforts*. Washington, DC: Center on Budget and Policy Priorities.

Ludwig, Jens, Greg J. Duncan, and Paul Hirschfield. 2000. Urban Poverty and Juvenile Crime: Evidence from a Randomized Housing-Mobility Experiment. Working paper. Joint Center for Poverty.

Ludwig, Jens, Greg J. Duncan, and Helen F. Ladd. 2001. The Effects of MTO on Baltimore Children's Educational Outcomes. *Poverty Research News* 5(1):13–15.

Ludwig, Jens, Greg J. Duncan, and Joshua C. Pinkston. 2000. Neighborhood Effects on Economic Self-Sufficiency: Evidence from a Randomized Housing-Mobility Experiment. Unpublished paper. Georgetown University.

Martinson, Karin. 2000. *The National Evaluation of Welfare-to-Work Strategies: The Experience of Welfare Recipients Who Find Jobs*. Washington, DC: U.S. Department of Health and Human Services, Administration for Children and Families, and U.S. Department of Education.

Metropolitan Council Housing and Redevelopment Authority in Minneapolis. 2000. Annual Plan for Fiscal Year 2000. March 1 unpublished draft.

Meyer, Daniel R., and Maria Cancian. 1996. Life after Welfare: The Economic Well-Being of Women and Children following an Exit from AFDC. Discussion Paper No. 1101–96. University of Wisconsin, Institute for Research on Poverty.

Meyers, Alan, Deborah Frank, Nicole Roos, Karen Peterson, Virginia Casey, Adrienne Cupples, and Suzette Levinson. 1995. Housing Subsidies and Pediatric Undernutrition. *Archives of Pediatric Adolescent Medicine* 149:1079–84.

Meyers, Alan, et al. 2001. Subsidized Housing, Food Security, and Growth among Families with Children: Data from a Multisite Surveillance Study. 2001. Presented at the annual meeting of the Pediatric Academic Societies in Baltimore, April 28.

Miller, Cynthia. 1998. Explaining MFIP's Impacts by Housing Status. Unpublished paper. Manpower Development Research Corporation.

Miller, Cynthia, Virginia Knox, Patricia Auspos, Jo Anna Hunter-Manns, and Alan Orenstein. 1997. *MFIP: Making Welfare Work and Work Pay: Implementation and 18-Month Impacts of the Minnesota Family Investment Program.* New York: Manpower Development Research Corporation.

Murray, Michael P. 1980. A Reinterpretation of the Traditional Income-Leisure Model, with Application to In-Kind Subsidy Programs. *Journal of Public Economics* 14:69–81.

Nagle, Gloria. 2001. *Comparing Housing-Assisted and Unassisted Welfare Leavers in Massachusetts.* Boston: Massachusetts Department of Transitional Assistance.

National Housing Law Project. 2000. Final Admission and Occupancy Regulations Issued. *Housing Law Bulletin* 30:33–42.

New Jersey Department of Community Affairs. 1999. Section 8 Tenant-Based Housing Program Administrative Plan. May draft.

Newman, Sandra J., and Joseph Harkness. 1999a. The Effects of Welfare Reform on Housing: A National Analysis. In *The Home Front: Implications of Welfare Reform for Housing Policy*, ed. Sandra J. Newman, 29–80. Washington, DC: Urban Institute Press.

Newman, Sandra J., and Joseph Harkness. 1999b. *The Long-Term Effects of Housing Assistance on Self-Sufficiency: Final Report.* Washington, DC: U.S. Department of Housing and Urban Development.

Newman, Sandra J., and Joseph Harkness. 2000. Assisted Housing and the Educational Attainment of Children. *Journal of Housing Economics* 9(1/2):40–63.

Newman, Sandra, Joseph Harkness, and Wei-Jun J. Yeung. 1999. Neighborhood Poverty, Assisted Housing, and the Educational Attainment of Children. Revised version of a paper prepared for the first annual research conference on the Moving to Opportunity Demonstration and Research Program, Washington, DC, November 21, 1997.

Newman, Sandra J., and Ann B. Schnare. 1989. Memorandum re Results of Site Visits to Maryland, Vermont, and Washington. In *A Report of the Joint Advisory Panel on the Housing Component of Welfare Reform*, Appendix F. Washington, DC: National Association of Housing and Redevelopment Officials and the American Public Welfare Association.

Newman, Sandra J., and Ann B. Schnare. 1993. Last in Line: Housing Assistance for Households with Children. *Housing Policy Debate* 4(3):417–55.

Newman, Sandra J., and Ann B. Schnare. 1997. "…And a Suitable Living Environment": The Failure of Housing Programs to Deliver on Neighborhood Quality. *Housing Policy Debate* 8(4):703–41.

Nudelman, Jodi. 2000. The Impact of Job Training Partnership Act Programs for Adult Welfare Recipients. In *Improving the Odds: Increasing the Effectiveness of Publicly Funded Training,* ed. Burt S. Barnow and Christopher T. King. Washington, DC: Urban Institute Press.

Ong, Paul. 1998. Subsidized Housing and Work among Welfare Recipients. *Housing Policy Debate* 9(4):775–94.

Painter, Gary. 2001. Low-Income Housing Assistance: Its Impact on Labor Force and Housing Program Participation. *Journal of Housing Research* 12(1):1–26.

Parrott, Sharon. 1998. *Welfare Recipients Who Find Jobs: What Do We Know about Their Employment and Earnings?* Washington DC: Center on Budget and Policy Priorities.

Primus, Wendell, Lynette Rawlings, Kathy Larin, and Kathryn Porter. 1999. *The Initial Impacts of Welfare Reform on the Incomes of Single-Mother Families.* Washington, DC: Center on Budget and Policy Priorities.

Public Housing: Utah Ties Housing to Welfare Reform Program. 1997. *Housing and Development Reporter,* July 28, p. 167.

Rangarajan, Anu. 1998. *Keeping Welfare Recipients Employed: A Guide for States Designing Job Retention Services.* Princeton, NJ: Mathematica Policy Research, Inc.

Rangarajan, Anu, Peter Schochet, and Dexter Chu. 1998. *Employment Experiences of Welfare Recipients Who Find Jobs: Is Targeting Possible?* Princeton, NJ: Mathematica Policy Research, Inc.

Rangarajan, Anu, and Robert G. Wood. 1999. *Work First New Jersey Evaluation: How WFNJ Clients Are Faring under Welfare Reform: An Early Look.* Princeton, NJ: Mathematica Policy Research, Inc.

Reingold, David A. 1997. Does Inner-City Public Housing Exacerbate the Employment Problems of Its Tenants? *Journal of Urban Affairs* 19(4):469–86.

Reingold, David A., Gregg G. Van Ryzin, Michelle Ronda. 2001. Does Urban Public Housing Diminish the Social Capital and Labor Force Activity of Its Tenants? *Journal of Policy Analysis and Management* 20(3):485–505.

Riccio, James. 1999. Lessons from Welfare-to-Work Experiments and Their Implications for Housing-Based Self-Sufficiency Programs. In *The Home Front: Implications of Welfare Reform for Housing Policy,* ed. Sandra J. Newman, 175–200. Washington, DC: Urban Institute Press.

Riccio, James A., and Alan Orenstein. 2003. Are Welfare Recipients in Public Housing Really Harder to Employ? In *A Place to Live, a Means to Work: How Housing Assistance Can Strengthen Welfare Policy,* ed. Barbara Sard and Amy S. Bogdon, 63–103. Washington, DC: Fannie Mae Foundation.

Rosenbaum, James E. 1995. Changing the Geography of Opportunity by Expanding Residential Choice: Lessons from the Gautreaux Program. *Housing Policy Debate* 6(1):231–69.

Rosenbaum, James E., and Stefanie DeLuca. 2000. *Is Housing Mobility the Key to Welfare Reform? Lessons from Chicago's Gautreaux Program*. Washington, DC: Brookings Institution Survey Series.

Rosenbaum, James E., and Susan J. Popkin. 1991. Employment and Earnings of Low-Income Blacks Who Move to Middle-Class Suburbs. In *The Urban Underclass*, ed. Christopher Jencks and Paul E. Peterson, 342–56. Washington, DC: The Brookings Institution.

Rothstein, Richard. 2000. Inner-City Nomad: Route to Low Grades. *New York Times*, January 19, p. B9.

Ryan, Elaine M. 1998. The Unfinished Agenda: Two Years after TANF. *Policy and Practice of Public Human Services*. 56(3):11.

Sandel, Megan, Joshua Sharfstein, and Randy Shaw. 1999. *There's No Place like Home: How America's Housing Crisis Threatens Our Children*. San Francisco: Housing America.

Sard, Barbara. 2003. The Role of Housing Providers in an Era of Welfare Reform. In *A Place to Live, a Means to Work: How Housing Assistance Can Strengthen Welfare Policy*, ed. Barbara Sard and Amy S. Bogdon, 107–65. Washington, DC: Fannie Mae Foundation.

Sard, Barbara, and Tim Harrison. 2001. *The Increasing Use of TANF and State Matching Funds to Provide Housing Assistance to Families Moving from Welfare to Work— 2001 Supplement*. Washington, DC: Center on Budget and Policy Priorities.

Sard, Barbara, and Jeffrey M. Lubell. 1998. *How the Statutory Changes Made by the Quality Housing and Work Responsibility Act of 1998 May Affect Welfare Reform Efforts*. Washington, DC: Center on Budget and Policy Priorities.

Sard, Barbara, and Jeffrey M. Lubell. 2000. *The Increasing Use of TANF and State Matching Funds to Provide Housing Assistance to Families Moving from Welfare to Work*. Washington, DC: Center on Budget and Policy Priorities.

Schoeni, Robert F., and Rebecca M. Blank. 2000. What Has Welfare Reform Accomplished? Impacts on Welfare Participation, Employment, Income, Poverty, and Family Structure. Working Paper No. W7627. National Bureau of Economic Research.

Schott, Elizabeth, Robert Greenstein, and Wendell Primus. 1999. *The Determinants of Welfare Caseload Decline: A Brief Rejoinder*. Washington, DC: Center on Budget and Policy Priorities.

Seattle Jobs Initiative. n.d. Human Services Integration. Seattle.

Sharfstein, Joshua, Meghan Sandel, Robert Kahn, and Howard Bauchover. 2001. Is Childhood Health at Risk While Families Wait for Housing Vouchers? *American Journal of Public Health* 91(8).

Shlay, Anne B. 1993. Family Self-Sufficiency and Housing. *Housing Policy Debate* 4(3):457–95.

Shroder, Mark, and Marge Martin. 1996. New Results from Administrative Data: Housing the Poor, or, What They Don't Know Might Hurt Somebody. Paper presented at the Midyear Meeting of the American Real Estate and Urban Economics Association, Washington, DC, May 29.

Sidor, John. 1998. *Implementing Collaborative Community Development: Interim Report*. Washington, DC: Council of State Community Development Agencies.

SRI International. 1983. *Final Report of the Seattle/Denver Income Maintenance Experiment. Vol. l: Design and Results*. Menlo Park, CA.

Stone, Michael E. 1993. *Shelter Poverty: New Ideas on Housing Affordability*. Philadelphia: Temple University Press.

Stone, Michael E. 1994. Comment on Kathryn P. Nelson's *"Whose* Shortage of Affordable Housing?" *Housing Policy Debate* 5(4):443–58.

Sweeney, Eileen P. 2000. *Recent Studies Indicate That Many Parents Who Are Current or Former Welfare Recipients Have Disabilities or Other Medical Conditions*. Washington, DC: Center on Budget and Policy Priorities.

Tenenbaum, Judith K. n.d. An Extended Review of the Literature: The Impact of Frequent Family Moves on School Achievement and Development for Low-Income Families. Unpublished paper. Hennepin County Office of Planning and Development.

Turner, Margery Austin, Susan Popkin, and Mary Cunningham. 2000. *Section 8 Mobility and Neighborhood Health: Emerging Issues and Policy Challenges*. Washington, DC: Urban Institute.

Turner, Margery Austin, and Kale Williams. 1998. *Housing Mobility: Realizing the Promise. Report from the Second National Conference on Assisted Housing Mobility*. Washington, DC: Urban Institute.

U.S. Bureau of the Census. 1997. *American Housing Survey*. Washington, DC.

U.S. Bureau of the Census. 1999. *American Housing Survey*. Washington, DC.

U.S. Department of Health and Human Services, Office of the Assistant Secretary for Planning and Evaluation (ASPE). 2000. *"Leavers" and Diversion Studies: Summary of Research on Welfare Outcomes Funded by ASPE*. Washington, DC.

U.S. Department of Health and Human Services. 2002. *U.S. Welfare Caseload Information*. World Wide Web page <http://www.acf.dhhs.gov/news/state/3697.htm> (accessed July 21).

U.S. Department of Housing and Urban Development. 1998. *A Picture of Subsidized Households in 1998: United States Summaries*. Washington, DC.

U.S. Department of Housing and Urban Development. 2000a. *Rental Housing Assistance—The Worsening Crisis. A Report to Congress on Worst-Case Housing Needs*. Washington, DC.

U.S. Department of Housing and Urban Development. 2000b. The Welfare-to-Work Program Evaluation. Conference materials (pp. 7–15) from the Welfare-to-Work Vouchers: Partnership to Success National Conference, Washington, DC, February 24.

U.S. Department of Housing and Urban Development. 2001. *A Report on Worst-Case Needs in 1999: New Opportunity amid Continuing Challenges*. Washington, DC.

U.S. Department of Housing and Urban Development. 2002. *Fiscal Year 2000 Income Limits and Section 8 Fair Market Rents*. World Wide Web page <http://www.huduser. org/datasets/:1/fmr00/index.html> (last updated July 23).

Vale, Lawrence J. 1993. Beyond the Problem Projects Paradigm: Defining and Revitalizing Severely Distressed Public Housing. *Housing Policy Debate* 4(2):147–74.

Vartanian, Thomas P., and Gleason, Philip M. 1999. Do Neighborhood Conditions Affect the High School Dropout and College Graduation Rates? *Journal of Socio-Economics* 28:21–41.